Cattle,
Capitalism,
and
Class

ILPARAKUYO MAASAI

TRANSFORMATIONS

Katau ole Koisenge, the author's younger brother. Photo by the author.

Cattle, Capitalism, and Class

ILPARAKUYO MAASAI TRANSFORMATIONS

Peter Rigby

 TEMPLE UNIVERSITY PRESS | PHILADELPHIA

Temple University Press, Philadelphia 19122
Copyright © 1992 by Temple University. All rights reserved
Published 1992
Printed in the United States of America

Library of Congress Cataloging-in-Publication Data
Rigby, Peter.
    Cattle, capitalism, and class : Ilparakuyo Maasai transformations
  / Peter Rigby.
      p.   cm.
    Includes bibliographical references and index.
    ISBN 0-87722-954-6 (alk. paper)
    1. Baraguyo (African people)—Social conditions.   2. Baraguyo
(African people)—Economic conditions.   3. Baraguyo (African
people)—Domestic animals.   4. Herders—Tanzania.   5. Herders—
Kenya.   6. Cattle—Economic aspects—Tanzania.   7. Cattle—Economic
aspects—Kenya.   8. Rural development—Tanzania.   9. Rural
development—Kenya.   I. Title.
DT443.3.B38R54   1992
306'.089965—dc20   91-38186

For the Maasai People,

and Ilparakuyo in particular

Enkoshoke naata osotua

Contents

Photographs

Figures and Sketch Maps

Preface

This book may be seen as a sequel to my *Persistent Pastoralists: Nomadic Societies in Transition* (1985); but it stands on its own as a distinct contribution toward understanding the political economy of development and transformation, as well as the anthropology, of pastoral societies, and, indeed, development problems in general. Although frequent references are made to the previous volume, the reader will not find it necessary to pursue them in order to become fully engaged in the present discussion. The wider context of this discourse is as follows.

◆ I   In most recently independent Third World countries, rural development is the first priority on national agendas. And "development" is usually defined as increased production in the rural sector of commodities for export (to bring in foreign exchange for other forms of development). Food products for internal consumption are often assigned a secondary status, with frequently disastrous consequences.

More recently, however, grandiose production goals have been seen as impossible to achieve as well as wasteful, since international price fluctuations for most commodities cannot be controlled, particularly by the producers. Instead, the trend in economic planning and aid has been from growth to basic needs, and the emphasis has shifted to the production of food crops for local consumption, including dairy and meat products from pastoral areas.

Development, however defined, is not only a goal of national government, particularly in the Third World; it is also a major factor in *their* survival or downfall. And since a primary characteristic of the political economy of developing countries is *uneven* development both internally and externally, support for governmental and international development policies varies from one local area to another within the nation.

Furthermore, most of these countries inherited governmental structures and international boundaries from their colonial past, affecting adversely and differentially all the pre-colonial societies within them in terms of economic, political, social, and cultural factors, as well as, more importantly, dividing ethnic groups among two or more nationally identified entities. Pastoral societies have been proportionately more often divided by international boundaries than predominantly agricultural or agro-pastoral societies, since colonial interest focused more upon the latter areas as susceptible to higher productivity and hence more profitable exploitation, making them the center of colonial and, now, independent states. Pastoralists, therefore, have been marginalized not only in the sense of their relevance for national development but also in their geographical location on or near "remote" international boundaries. Obvious cases of this are Somali, Boran, and Nilotic peoples of northern Kenya, Somaliland, Ethiopia, Uganda, and Sudan. Not so obviously, the Maasai peoples of Tanzania and Kenya, particularly in Kenya, had to be removed from their physical centrality to the colonial social formation by spurious treaties and agreements that the colonialists had no intention of honoring.

As a result of these and other factors, it is no longer (or should not be) feasible, in terms of optimum "strategies of development," to depend totally upon policies for socioeconomic change and transformation that address only the issues of uneven development "internal" to the nation states involved, particularly in the case of Maasai, but also elsewhere (for example, the pastoral communities of the Sahelian zone of Africa, from Senegal in the west to Ethiopia in the east; see Franke and Chasin 1980). The concept of "regional development" as it relates to numerous pastoralist societies must therefore include not only macro-level policies covering several independent countries in one region, but also more micro-level strategies of internationally integrated development in societies divided by these international boundaries.

In the case of Maasai pastoralists of Kenya and Tanzania, who have never considered themselves really divided by the international boundary in the past, even during the Anglo-German war of 1914–

1918 or when the border was "closed" by Tanzania between 1976 and 1983, the need for such an internationally integrated policy has become crucial. And it could be said without exaggeration that such a policy may also be extremely important for the continuation of amicable relations between Kenya and Tanzania, whose national governments have ostensibly chosen distinctive paths to national development, paths that are potentially productive of even more contradictory and hostile relations in the future.

But development and change are not categories exhausted by economic or even politico-economic factors, in the narrow sense. A political economy of development, especially if it is to encompass not only the often diverse peoples of *one* nation state but those of other neighboring nations as well, must incorporate historical, cultural, linguistic, and even (perhaps most particularly?) aesthetic dimensions. Very few studies, if any, have addressed these critical issues; I attempt in this book to initiate a discussion of them, both in particular relation to the Ilparakuyo and Maasai social formations of Tanzania and Kenya and in more general terms.

In order to do this, I address a number of empirical and theoretical problems introduced in my earlier book but not discussed in any detail there. I then raise a number of quite new and distinct theoretical issues that, I maintain, have considerable practical implications. I also bring up to date a discussion of several of the historical processes of transformation in these communities (e.g., class formation, ideological institutions, etc.) whose earlier phases and forms were examined in the previous book. Finally, I attempt to draw some epistemological conclusions from the nature of the work itself. The theoretical frameworks I deem necessary for these tasks are set out in the Introduction (Chapter 1). But first, a brief note on classification and terminology.

◆ **II**   As stated in *Persistent Pastoralists* (1985:7–8), Ilparakuyo (sing. Olparakuoni) constitute a historically distinct section (*olosho*) of pastoral Maasai within the overall cultural grouping of the Maa-speaking peoples of Tanzania and Kenya, whose common language, *Olmaa*, is also known descriptively as *enkutuk oo 'lMaasai*, "the mouth of the Maasai." The prefixes *ol-* and *il-* are masculine singular and plural respectively; their feminine counterparts are *en-* and *in-*. Thus one female member of the section is Emparakuoni, the plural of which is Imparakuyo. At the risk of inconsistency, I have used the correct prefixes when referring to Ilparakuyo and other sections of Maasai (e.g., Ilkisonko, sing. Olkisonkoi), but have retained the word "Maasai" throughout, since it is a term now generally accepted in the literature. The much more inaccurate term "Masai" was common until the last fifteen years or so, and is still in (mis-)use; in the German literature of an earlier period, "Massai" is also encountered.

Ilparakuyo are also known in the literature as "Baraguyu" (Beidelman 1960 *et passim*, who retains the term in a 1980 article) or "Parakuyu" (Berntsen 1979 *et passim*) and as "Wakwavi" by coastal and some other Bantu-speaking peoples, also rendered "Kuafi" (Krapf 1860). These last two terms, whatever their provenance, are totally rejected by Ilparakuyo. The Ilparakuyo have further been classified as "Iloikop" since the period of earliest missionary contact and colonial penetration (Krapf 1860; Johnston 1886; Baumann 1894), a term that is also derogatory since it means "murder," "cattle paid in compensation for murder," or "violent death," although people of the Isampur (Samburu) section may refer to themselves by this word while dissociating it from its general meaning (Rigby 1985:85–86 *et passim*; cf. Spencer 1973:109, n.7).

Some contemporary pastoral Maasai refer to Ilparakuyo as "Ilumbwa," a designation associated with peoples of "Kalenjin" origin, and with the terms "Wahumba" or "Wahumha," by which they are known by most central Tanzanian Bantu-speakers among whom many reside. Other Tanzanian and Kenyan Maasai accept the Ilparakuyo designation of themselves, but in the form "Ilparakuo," which literally means "people very well off in terms of livestock."

As with all such historical classifications of peoples by themselves and by others, these terms are relative to time and space and are not "fixed," historically stable categorizations. My usage is the result of consultations with my closest kinsmen and women, agemates, and friends; recent discussions and travels in other Maasai sections have not altered my opinion that it is the best currently available.

Acknowledgments

A book, like any other artifact of human endeavor, cannot be the product of one person. It is impossible for me to acknowledge personally all those in Tanzania, Kenya, and elsewhere who have made this book possible. I owe most to my brothers Toreto ole Koisenge and Katau ole Koisenge, and my parents, Olpayian Koisenge and Yieyio Ng'oto Toreto.

Without the help of Naomi Kipury, I would not have been able to live among the Iloodokilani Maasai of Kenya with such ease and friendship, especially that shown to me by her parents and Shark ole Kipury. In Tanzania, Daniel Ndagala was a source of constant help and encouragement. I am also indebted to my brother-in-law, Zakaria Kaheru, and Goran Hyden and their families for making it possible for my family to have a residential base in Nairobi in 1983. Abdul and Sara Ismail in Moshi also made us welcome before I travelled back to my Ilparakuyo homestead in 1987. In the village, my age-mate, Lapani ole Moreto, Mzee Mtumia, Deogratias Shayo, Stefano Schapiro, and Jonas Reuben Wanga were most helpful, as was Kemal Mustafa and other members of the Canadian Universities Service Overseas team in Dar es Salaam.

For penetrating comments upon earlier versions of the manuscript, I am deeply grateful to Valentin Mudimbe, Peter Biella, Thomas Patterson, Zebiya Rigby, Ron Berge, and Ananthakrishnan Aiyer. My editors at Temple University Press, Doris Braendel and Jennifer French, as well as freelancer Penelope Myers, have devoted enormous

xviii   *Acknowledgments*

energy and infectious enthusiasm at crucial moments when they were sorely needed by a jaded author.

Without the constant love and support of my wife, Zebiya Akiiki, and my daughter, Kimuli Abwooli, nothing of what follows would have been possible.

Peter Rigby,
Philadelphia

Cattle,
Capitalism,
and
Class

ILPARAKUYO MAASAI

TRANSFORMATIONS

1   Introduction

Memut elukunya nabo
eng' eno.
One head does not
encompass all
knowledge.

◆   The question of the future of pastoral peoples in
Africa and elsewhere is fraught with difficulties and contradictions
that are attributable not only to the historical specificities of these
particular social formations but also to the theoretical dispositions
of the researchers, planners, and implementers of development policies concerned with them. Over the past few years, massive amounts
of research in pastoral societies have produced a veritable mine (if
not a minefield) of facts and figures on herd size, variability, and composition, carrying capacities of grazing areas, marketing statistics,
inequalities in livestock holdings between families, and so on. Any
attempt at generalization from this bonanza of empirical detail seems
destined to result in auto-strangulation or, at the very least, severe
mental indigestion. While the detailed information provided by these
studies is enormously valuable, the basic questions concerning the
relationship between the aspirations of pastoralists themselves and
what is expected of—and for—them by national governments and
the development planners who work with them frequently become
obscured in a morass of often contradictory data.

    Despite this, there are a number of common connections that
may be discerned by a diligent excavation of the data, even if this
exercise lacks the theoretical sophistication of a cogent "archaeology
of knowledge." I make no claim to an exhaustive collation of data in
what follows. Instead, I extract what I consider to be the most persistent themes; I then approach them, not in terms of managerial or
"development" issues *per se*, but through a series of epistemological,

1

ideological, and philosophical investigations, in an attempt to understand what lies behind this mass of empirical material. Among these themes are that development strategies and plans for pastoralists are, in general, failures, whatever their form or content; that these failures are usually attributed to features intrinsic to, and characteristic of, pastoral societies; and that, as a result of the first two themes, we must conclude that the future of pastoral peoples is a dim and dismal one, leading to their inevitable demise.

✦ I   In a comprehensive and perceptive review of pastoral economic development programs in Africa, Walter Goldschmidt (1981:116) remarks, "Nothing seems to work, few pastoral people's lives have been improved, there is no evidence of increased production of meat and milk, the land continues to deteriorate, and millions of dollars have been spent." In answer to the question "what is wrong?" Goldschmidt rightly rejects the response given as in the second theme above: "The easy answer is to blame the pastoralists themselves; they are too ignorant, too traditional, too stubborn; they do not want to be helped." On the contrary, Goldschmidt correctly responds: "That the pastoralists are willing and able to change their ways is easily demonstrated. Those quintessential African pastoralists, the Maasai, repeatedly became fixed farmers or predominantly farmers, as exemplified by the Warush [the Ilarusa]."[1]

To the extent that Goldschmidt is still optimistic in concluding that pastoral peoples are not doomed to inevitable extinction, he lays the blame squarely upon "the planning process." This process is flawed because planners do not "learn from their own mistakes"; they "disregard pastoral peoples' own knowledge"; and, finally, "programs are initiated without coordination." All these observations are correct; Goldschmidt, however, singles out the final one for special corrective attention: "What is needed is a coordinated approach" (1981:117). While this partial "solution" necessarily entails, for Goldschmidt, that "the legitimate interests and aims of pastoralists, including their use of livestock as factors in their social relationships, are taken into account," he never asks the basic questions concerning the overall *aims* of development at the national level. In fact, the assumption that national development goals—and hence the strategies devised by the planners and managers of development—are not to be questioned underlies most of the recent literature on pastoralist social formations (but see Knowles and Collett 1989 for an interesting exception).

Thus, for example, in his important and wide-ranging study

of livestock development in Kenya Maasailand, Phylo Evangelou not only fails to question national development goals for pastoralists and their possible consequences (even at the national level), he also makes the achievement of such goals the general condition for avoiding the marginalization of Maasai pastoralists (Evangelou 1984:12–13):

> A common problem of livestock sectors of developing countries is said to be the continual struggle to balance supply and demand. Kenya's balancing of meat production and consumption can be translated into a single objective: expansion of the nation's meat supply in the hope of keeping pace with an inexorably rising demand. Unless conditions constraining livestock production levels in pastoral areas such as Maasailand are overcome, the required supply of livestock will not be forthcoming, and projected meat deficits for the nation will become a reality. Moreover, pastoral peoples like the Maasai will suffer general decline in welfare as population pressures invalidate traditional production regulating relationships. . . . Developing appropriate mechanisms [for implementing the country's livestock development projects] depends ultimately upon a clear understanding of the constraints.

And, lo and behold, Evangelou concludes (1984:125), "*traditional Maasai social structure and cultural institutions* fundamentally *constrain* development initiatives" (cf. Doherty 1979a, 1979b). *Ergo*, Maasai social structure and cultural institutions must be *dismantled*, if they are to survive, an oxymoron all too evident in the literature on pastoralists.

My intention in raising these questions, with a view to interrogating the impact of national policies upon Maasai social formations in both Kenya and Tanzania, is not inspired by a sentimental preoccupation with the preservation of anachronistic societies; rather, it is related to a realization of a number of clearly demonstrable historical processes. Among these are that Ilparakuyo and other Maasai social formations have undergone continual and often drastic transformations for a long time, that they continue to "adapt" to constantly changing conditions, that these changes are manifested in various kinds of contradictions that inhibit or modify tendencies toward class formation, and that class formation is now occurring in very specific ways in both Tanzania and Kenya Maasailand and among Ilparakuyo Maasai, despite these countries' ostensibly opposed development aims, methods, and strategies. These are the basic problems addressed in this book.

As a result of this focus, I must raise the question: If it is the intention of government policies for pastoralist development in Maasailand (and, by extension, in other areas as well) to create class differentiation in hitherto relatively egalitarian and classless social formations, together with the attendant structures of exploitation, marginalization, and conflict, then these "development" policies are succeeding, even if they fail to provide enough meat and other livestock products for national consumption. The processes of class formation are generated precisely by the long-term commoditization of herds, land, and labor (in that logical and chronological order), accompanied by the penetration of capital in its merchants', usurers', and, eventually, wage-labor forms. In order to understand the contemporary situation, we must examine the history of these processes; and this is also what I attempt to do in this book.

From the point of view adopted here, then, the destruction of pastoralist societies, and particularly Ilparakuyo and Maasai, is not a question of their failure to "adapt" to modern conditions; neither is it a failure of "development" policies. It is precisely that the modern conditions themselves are based upon false premises of what development *is*, a situation in which the road to the slavery of capitalist wage-labor is already mapped and constitutes its ultimate end. It is in the light of *this* perspective that the disappearance of pastoralist social formations becomes a historical tragedy, especially when the very characteristics that define their specificity could be the basis for true *socialist* development (Rigby 1969a, 1985). In doing this I am not recommending a relativist position; on the contrary, I am frankly evaluating Ilparakuyo and Maasai egalitarian, non-exploitative, and classless formations as good for socialism, and for very explicit reasons. I am advocating political *praxis* on the basis of them. Ndagala can, perhaps, properly lament for Ilparakuyo in Tanzania (1986:20):

> The pastoralists, persistent as they have been (Rigby 1985), cannot avoid the inevitable demise of their production system unless the status quo is changed. In spite of its overt advantages things are not likely to change in favor of pastoralism in the foreseeable future. The question of rationality seems to be irrelevant to the decision-makers unless it embraces their interests. In Tanzania, a country striving for self-reliance, should not those in power support the interests of the producers, including the pastoralists?

I am not, however, as pessimistic as my friend and comrade Ndagala. By outlining in some detail the historical roots and contemporary nature of the transformations in Ilparakuyo and Maasai society, the future of pastoral peoples may yet be re-defined *by themselves*. For I believe that those in power are not omnipotent, neither do they hold all the cards; and some of them are not unamenable to change, especially when they are confronted with revolutionary forms of knowledge. The heightening of historical self-awareness is an important part of intellectual *praxis* and the *empowerment* of those whose fate seems to lie exclusively in the hands of "others"; future political practice *can* be based upon a historically self-conscious understanding of the pastoralists' contemporary "predicament" (Parkipuny 1975, 1979, 1983, *et passim*). The lineaments of what this self-consciousness is among Ilparakuyo and Maasai, and the possibilities that lie in its subversive character is, also, a focus (perhaps *the* focus) of this book. But all of this must, as an initial task, be theorized; the rest of this introduction is devoted to laying the theoretical groundwork for the materials and discussions presented in subsequent chapters.

◆ **II**   The specificity of pastoralist social formations cannot be illuminated without considering the different disciplines and theoretical frameworks employed in "studying" them (Rigby 1985:1–24 *et passim*). Maasai of Kenya and Tanzania have been particularly prone to representation in a great variety of forms and media, and this ultimately not only affects subjective attitudes toward them and their society but also has an impact upon those who have the power to affect their future and, ultimately, to influence Maasai self-identity in the contemporary world.

If, as I have already indicated, the dominant idea of the planners and administrators who deal with Ilparakuyo and other Maasai pastoralists is their eventual demise (sooner for many than later) as a viable social formation, the "experts" involved are not in contradiction with popular attitudes, both within and outside East Africa. The "end of the Maasai" has long been foretold by foreigners; I devote a whole chapter (Chapter 2) to a discussion of some of these notions of "ethnocide," and what I have called a self-fulfilling prophecy of "ethnosuicide."

But an examination of the ways in which Ilparakuyo and Maasai are represented in relation to their future raises, in turn, the problem of the authenticity of anthropological knowledge purporting to deal with them. There is both an epistemological and a moral dilemma here. If anthropological knowledge (or any other kind of knowledge, for that matter), is predicated upon the assumption of the demise of its subject, by what authority is such a knowledge constituted? Surely not upon the authority of the people themselves, unless it can be demonstrated that they are consciously contemplating ethnosuicide?

In pastoralist studies, non-pastoralist observers have taken one of two paths to extricate themselves from this dilemma. The first proposes that, although Ilparakuyo and Maasai have a *moral* right to remain Ilparakuyo and Maasai (and hence involved in labor-intensive, transhumant pastoral *praxis*), they can be coaxed into integration with a "market-oriented," and therefore "capitalistic," national economy. To this, it is also frequently added that this transition to market orientation, although it may be rough on Maasai, should not be too difficult, because pastoralists are, after all, really incipient capitalists in disguise (Schneider 1979 *et passim*; Spencer 1984; but cf. Hart and Sperling 1988). All they need to effect this transition into being "proper" capitalists is managerial and technical assistance. This assistance, it is further argued, can be provided only by an "interdisciplinary team."

As a consequence of this approach, most heavily funded research among Maasai and other pastoralists is now concentrated in team efforts of an interdisciplinary nature.[2] For example, in 1982, the *East African Range Livestock Systems Study* (EARLS) under the direction of the International Livestock Centre for Africa (ILCA), focused largely on Ilkaputiei section of Kenya Maasai, was being conducted by a team of nineteen people. This team was led by a development economist, and included another economist, two anthropologists, three ecologists (one of whom was also an expert in animal nutrition), five people with varying degrees of professional expertise in "animal science," one person whose field was human nutrition, three in veterinary science, and one field assistant in social science.

This team, although changing in composition and size over time, produced large amounts of highly significant data. But the team leader in 1982 commented that, between 1977 (when the project began) and 1980, "the ILCA/Kenya programme lacked clear objectives and suffered from a lack of proper direction and coordination" (Bekure 1982:1). This led to a situation in which "a few isolated sociological studies were . . . carried out on the group ranches but there was no effort at integrating them with studies in ecology and livestock production." As a result, the ILCA Programme Committee "recommended a reorientation toward integrated systems research while reducing the funds for the programme by 25%. Following this recommendation, ILCA started to form an interdisciplinary team" (1982:1).[3]

More recently, an anthropologist concerned with the "future of the Maasai," an issue that seems to rest uneasily upon the "horns of a dilemma," also recommends an interdisciplinary approach, but for quite other reasons. Concurring with Neville and Rada Dyson-Hudson (1980), this anthropologist notes (Holland 1987:4):

The dynamics of each of the components of the pastoral production system are complex, which means that the production systems based on their interactions are even more complex. This is why the appeals for an interdisciplinary approach to development have been so important. . . . Minimally, lip-service is paid to the role of the social sciences, and anthropology in particular in the whole process of problem identification, implementation and evaluation, but there is a long way to go yet before there is a truly integrated and systemic approach to development among pastoralists. There is a danger that an "anthropological approach" alone may overemphasize the isolation of pastoral systems from the wider societies of which they are usually a part . . . but this difficulty has to be met and is probably better dealt with through an interdisciplinary and holistic approach to pastoralist development.

The second path taken by anthropologists, if not to circumvent the issue of "ethnocide-by-development," at least to find a refuge from it, is derived directly from the dangers evident in the isolationist tendencies of anthropology so clearly intimated by Killian Holland and the Dyson-Hudsons. But before I turn to this, let me point out a basic flaw in Holland's otherwise admirable argument. This is the *equation* that is implied between *interdisciplinarity* and *holism*. The truth of the matter is, in fact, quite the contrary. Apart from the fact that the individual followers of different disciplines can seldom act in concert, the disparate epistemological frameworks for the sciences as represented, say, in the ILCA/EARLS team noted above, militate against any possibility of achieving a "holistic" approach. Even fellow anthropologists seldom share a common epistemology. Holism cannot be attained by resting upon the assumption that the whole is merely the sum of its parts; but more of that later.

This second path taken by the anthropological refugee from the fields of conflict between ethnocide and ethnogenesis leads directly back to a relativist, isolationist, functionalist, and hence out-dated anthropology that is inauthentic for again very different reasons. Here the anthropologist, usually working alone or at the most as a member of a family, goes in search of the "pristine," "untouched" part of the society under scrutiny. That the resulting community described, bounded in space and frozen in time, is largely a figment of the observer's imagination seldom bothers these anthropologists; to them, the history of capitalist imperialism and penetration, the destructive forces of economic, political, and social violence upon dominated societies, remain irrelevant. Their quest is to "save," for their *own* (anthropological?) posterity, a picture of a discretely different culture or society, with which they have no relation other than that of a mythical "scientific" and "value free" observer. That studies predicated upon such proverbially ostrich-head-in-the-sand-like grounds are still carried out and their results published by reputable publishing houses is clear to anyone familiar with recent literature on East African pastoralists in general and Maasai in particular.

It is evident that neither of these all-too-common lines of anthropological resistance, that of self-immolation in the fires of untheorized interdisciplinarity or the alternative of temporal and theoretical retreat into functionalist innocence, can provide a discourse that is both holistic in the strongest sense of the term and capable of illuminating the enormous pressures of domination and change experienced by Ilparakuyo and Maasai pastoralists. They are both external to the discursive and political space occupied by the pastoralists and therefore relevant only in a negative sense for political *praxis*. For the interdisciplinarian, responsibility is diluted by its dissipation; to the isolationist, it does not even arise. Both positions are *dangerous* for the subjects of such discourses: in this case, Ilparakuyo and Maasai of Tanzania and Kenya.

◆ **III**   I have maintained elsewhere (Rigby 1985:*passim*) that Ilparakuyo and Maasai social formations were extremely egalitarian prior to the penetration of colonialism and merchant capital in the eastern African area. This egalitarianism, I also asserted, is not only manifested in the lack of class exploitation in these societies, but also in the complementarity (rather than exploitation) exhibited in the division of labor based upon gender and age (Kipury 1989; cf. Llewelyn-Davies 1978, 1981; Spencer 1988). In doing so, however, I have also intimated that institutionalized inequalities, incipient class formation, and disparities based upon gender occur in Ilparakuyo and Maasai society; but they arise in specific historical circumstances that must be established and not assumed. I also show later that the specificity of the Ilparakuyo and Maasai social formations inhibited the development of two antagonistic classes, at least until the end of the nineteenth century, and probably much later in certain sections.

But since then, and particularly in the last fifteen years or so, class differentiation has become more pronounced and easily identifiable (Chapter 7). In this analysis, therefore, class and gender exploitation, which now exist in these societies, is seen as generated by specific historical processes, and are not assumed to be part of an isolated pre-capitalist pastoralist system characterized by an assumed "patriarchy" and "gerontocracy" (*pace* Spencer 1965, 1988).

Similarly, the rise of the fetishism of commodities is also seen as a result of the process of commoditization and increasingly distorted forms of ideological representation.

A historical approach such as this, I maintain, dissolves the assumptions of universal "class functions" of exploitation in ostensibly "classless" societies (cf. Rey 1979 *et passim*); of the universal presence of "rudimentary capitalism" as characteristic of pastoralist societies (Spencer 1984, 1988; cf. Schneider 1979);[4] of universal "patriarchy" and gender exploitation in patrilineal societies (cf. Llewelyn-Davies 1978, 1981; Spencer 1988); and of the universality of "false consciousness" as the basis of all precapitalist ideological formation (cf. Bonte 1975, *passim*). In fact, as I have already touched upon, there is a curious and unacceptable convergence between the ahistorical bourgeois notion that all pastoralists are rudimentary capitalists, merely awaiting the chance to become "true" capitalists, and the equally ahistorical Marxist analysis of these societies as resting upon age/gender exploitation and an ideological false consciousness that disallows conscious political action by pastoralists in combating the forces of commoditization and consequent class formation in their societies.

Furthermore, we cannot understand these historical processes in Kenya and Tanzania Maasailand without looking at the role of the colonial and post-colonial state, at least insofar as its reproduction directly impinges upon the reproduction of Ilparakuyo and other pastoral Maasai. Chapter 5 is devoted to a consideration of some aspects of this problem. It is proposed that, as far as Ilparakuyo and Maasai are concerned, the state is largely authoritarian in structure and process, this authoritarianism being represented by nationally and internationally generated, and hence necessarily "top-down," development interventions. That these interventions, advertently or inadvertently, actively promote class formation has already been mentioned; but the processes through which this occurs differ markedly between Tanzania and Kenya (Chapter 7).

The negativity inherent in the rejection of the false assumptions outlined above, however, is of secondary importance in this book. I am primarily concerned with heightening an awareness of the possibilities of revolutionary *praxis*, in order to create the conditions under which pastoralists themselves can "make their own history" (as they had been prior to formal colonialism) before it is too late. In order to illuminate the subversive character of pastoral theory and *praxis*, at least two epistemological conditions must be established. First, I must develop a theory of "privileged knowledge," based upon a historical materialist problematic and leading to an understanding of political and counter-hegemonic struggle; and, second, I must devise a materialist theory of ideology, discourse, and language. At the risk of some repetition, I outline these epistemological issues here; their more particular characteristics are developed in the context of specific applications in the chapters that follow.

◆ **IV**   In my previous book (Rigby 1985:*passim*), I introduced the notion that, in Ilparakuyo and Maasai social formations, the relations of production and the production process itself are *transparent*, at least until penetrated by merchant capital and incipient class relations. In historical materialist theory, since *all* able-bodied Ilparakuyo and Maasai, male and female, are "primary producers," we can develop an analogy with the position of the proletariat in, at least, the early stages of mature capitalism (Lukács 1971:149–222 *et passim*).

Furthermore, the sources of alienation generated by separation of the producer from the major means of production and his or her consequent mis-apprehension of the use-value of the final product do not occur in these societies. The appropriation of surplus value is focused upon the reproduction of the social formation as a whole, not upon one class within it. While another source of alienation, that derived from the relatively simple development of the productive forces, does exist, the relations among knowledge, ideology, and what I have called pastoral *praxis* are immediate: hence the transparency of the relations of production. This relative transparency, I have argued, has played a significant role in Ilparakuyo and Maasai rejection, until recently, of all forms of wage-labor and alien religious systems, such as Christianity and Islam (Rigby 1985:*passim*). The positions I adopt in this book upon the issues of transparency and ideology in Ilparakuyo and Maasai society are brilliantly expanded and historically generalized in studies by Samir Amin and Goran Therborn; I must briefly discuss both of them.

In his attempt to globalize historical materialist theory and debunk "Eurocentricism" in all its forms (including some Marxist theorizing), Samir Amin develops a broad categorization of modes of production into the communal, the tributary, and the capitalist. The break between the tributary and capitalist formations is characterized by the inversion of "the order of the relationship between the realm of the economic and the political ideological superstructure" (Amin 1989:2). Communal and tributary societies, however, share a "transparency of production relations" and differ largely with respect to the necessary *coherence* of the ideological in the latter while the communal formations do not require this. Although Amin is not directly concerned with the transition from communal to tributary forms of society, it does provide an important condition for his overall argument. This is how he puts it (Amin 1989:22):

> Earlier communal relationships did not require . . . coherence from their ideological constructs; that is why the [communal] forms of ancient thought juxtapose empiricism, mythology of nature, and mythology of society without any problem. The passage to the tributary form demands a greater degree of coherence and the integration of the elements of abstract knowledge into a global metaphysicis. It is not until the modern age that the mystification of social relationships, peculiar to capitalism, can overthrow the domination of this sacred ideology and replace it with the rule of the economic.

In order to locate what Amin here calls "empiricism, mythology of nature, and mythology of society" in concrete ideological form, I adopt in this book a notion of ideology that cannot equate it with "false consciousness," which itself is based upon an unequivocal opposition between science and ideology, so pronounced in the work of Louis Althusser; rather I approach the issue from the more flexible interpretations of such theorists as Goran Therborn and L. N. Moskvichov (Rigby 1985:92–94, 186; cf. Moskvichov 1974). Ideology cannot be reduced to a mere reflection of "class interests," as some Marxist analysis implies (cf. the penetrating critique of this position by Hugh Collins 1984:35–74 *et passim*).[5] Therborn admirably sums up his position as follows (1980:5):

> The broad definition of ideology adopted here departs from the usual Marxist one, by not restricting it to forms of illusion and miscognition, and also from the usual liberal conception, which is not accepted mainly because I think we should refuse to take what it implies for granted—that forms of consciousness and meaning that are not set out in more or less coherent doctrines are either unimportant in the organization of, and struggles for, power, or are self-evident, pragmatic "common sense" (as in the notorious "end of ideology" thesis).

By adopting this broader view of ideology, we are able to explore the relation between a heightening awareness that leads to *ideological mobilization* (counter-hegemonic struggle), but only if it is a *path to political mobilization and practice* (cf. Therborn 1980:116–117). And the concept of ideological mobilization in turn demands a materialist theory of language.

◆ **V**   Ideological mobilization manifests itself at the levels of both groups of people, either discrete classes or communities within larger social formations, as well as in the constitution of the individual subjects in any social formation. Both levels are important for political mobilization and counter-hegemonic struggle; they cannot, in fact, be understood in isolation from each other. The dialectical interaction between the formation of groups and individual subjects on the one hand and the formation of *ideologies* at societal level on the other is accessible only if our theoretical framework is both materialist and existentialist, both phenomenological and simultaneously aware of objective historical conditions. Therborn states most succinctly the basic elements of this problematic (1980:117):

> Ideological mobilizations, even of an explicitly class character, always have a strong existential component and are never reducible to revolutionary class consciousness. An intense ideological commitment involves a transformation and mobilization of the individual subjectivity of those committed, a subordination of their own suffering and possible death to a meaning-of-life defined by the ideology. Indeed, in a revolutionary mobilization the meaning of life is itself set by the revolutionary agenda. Political-ideological mobilizations are not fixed in class and "popular-democratic" interpellations alone. Their success hinges largely upon their capacity to tap and harness the existential dimension of human subjectivity.

I have already noted the distinctive ideological transformations postulated by Amin for the transition from communal to tributary social formations, and from tributary to capitalist state structures. In the Ilparakuyo and Maasai case, one is faced with a direct, violent confrontation and transition from communal to (admittedly backward) capitalist forms. The hegemonic and ideological struggle is intense, involving as it does the insinuation of class relations into hitherto classless formations; I have described some aspects of this in my previous book (Rigby 1985). Here, I attempt to explore in more detail the way in which language materializes elements of this struggle. I make no claim to any deep insight here; in approaching this complex problem, and commencing with Marx and Engels, I have turned to the work of Mikhail Bakhtin, Antonio Gramsci, V. Y. Mudimbe, Jean-Paul Sartre, V. N. Voloshinov, Raymond Williams, and Charles Woolfson. All these theorists tackle the central question: what is the relation between language and ideology, and how can the use of specific forms of understanding language and meaning uncover the way in which ideology is both constituted by and itself constitutes the conditions for political practice? These ideas are not new in anthropology (cf. Parkin 1982, 1984); but the relevance of these authors for new forms of understanding in this area of discourse has only just begun to be explored (cf. Karp 1987).

The importance of grasping the real nature of ideology in the counter-hegemonic struggle being waged by Ilparakuyo and Maasai against capitalist penetration and bureaucratic/managerial forms of "development" interventions cannot be overemphasized; I deal with various aspects of this in Chapters 5–8 below. In approaching the question of ideology through a materialist theory of language, I began my theoretical investigations, as did Raymond Williams (1977:2,201–202), with the seminal work of Jean-Paul Sartre, particularly (but not solely) his later writings. I then proceeded to the contributions of Gramsci and Georg Lukács. More recently, I turned to the immensely fruitful, if sometimes contradictory, writings of Mikhail Bakhtin and, of course, Voloshinov (Bakhtin 1981,1984; Voloshinov 1973[1986], *et passim*; cf. Clark and Holquist 1984).[6] Just as Sartre's notion of the materiality of language represents both the "interiority" of the subject and the "exteriority" of history and the public domain (Sartre 1976a:98–99), so too, for Bakhtin: "A genre's conceptualization has both inward and outward focus; the artist does not merely represent reality; he or she must use existing means of representation in tension with the subject at hand. This process is analogous to the dual nature of the utterance, its orientation simultaneously toward its past contexts and and its present context (Stewart 1986:54)." This is also strictly analogous to Marx's notion of how people make their own history, but only within the limits set by the past.

While I take issue with Susan Stewart's characterization of *all* Marxist views of ideology as "reflectionist" (this is patently not true; and she herself qualifies this statement by saying that she is talking about "early" or "traditional" Marxist positions), it is important that she emphasizes Bakhtin's conception of ideological signs as not reflecting, but refracting historical and social reality (Stewart 1986:53)

> [Bakhtin] moves the materiality of language away from essence into the domain of practice. . . . What Bakhtin's theory of ideology offers is a model of ideological production. In this model, ideology is not assumed to be either a foggy lens or a mirroring cloud. It is, rather, assumed to be an ongoing product and producer of social practice. The semantic transition from reflection to refraction marks a movement from repetition to production.

Bakhtin is at pains to avoid both idealism and psychologism in his theory of ideology and language, stressing the material basis for the generation of both (Voloshinov 1973:12, 23; cf. Williams 1977). Bakhtin sums up his position as follows (Voloshinov 1973:22–23):

> In order for any item, from whatever domain of reality it may come, to enter the social purview of the group and to elicit ideological semiotic reaction, it must be associated with the vital socioeconomic prerequisites of the particular group's existence; it must somehow, if only obliquely, make contact with the group's material life. . . . An ideological theme is always socially accentuated. . . . The theme of an ideological sign and the form of an ideological sign are inextricably bound together and are separable only in the abstract. Indeed, the economic conditions that inaugurate a new element of reality into the social purview, that make it socially meaningful and "interesting," are exactly the same conditions that create the forms of ideological communication (the cognitive, the artistic, the religious, and so on), in turn, shape the forms of semiotic expression. . . . The process of incorporation into ideology—the birth of theme and birth of form—is best followed out in the material of the word. This process of ideological generation is reflected two ways in language: both in its large-scale, universal-historical dimensions . . . and in its small-scale dimensions as constituted within the framework of contemporaneity, since, as we know, the word sensitively reflects the slightest variations in social existence.

But for the sign to be socially accentuated, it is subject to what Voloshinov calls *multiaccentuality*, and it is this quality that allows it to represent and become the focus of political *praxis*. He goes on (1973:22–23):

> Existence reflected in sign is not merely reflected but *refracted*. How is this refraction of existence in the sign determined? By an intersecting of differently oriented social interests within one and the same sign community, i.e., *by the class struggle*. Class does not coincide with the sign community, i.e., the community which is the totality of users of the same set of signs for ideological communication. Thus various different classes will use one and the same language. As a result, differently oriented accents intersect in every ideological sign. Sign becomes an area of the class struggle.

In this book, however, I am not only concerned with the issues of class formation, commoditization, and the political and counterhegemonic struggle of Ilparakuyo and Maasai, in their historical and contemporary circumstances. I am also, as I have already stated, concerned with the epistemological claims made by anthropologists and other social scientists in order to qualify as being fit to represent social and historical reality. While many African anthropologists, sociologists, and historians have long since addressed the problem of the "authenticity" of representations of African social formations (e.g., Mafeje 1976, 1988; Okot p'Bitek 1970; Owusu 1978; Temu and Swai 1981; Barongo 1983; Nzongola-Ntalaja 1987; Onimode 1988), and have frequently and correctly criticized attempts at the mere "Africanization" of the bourgeois social sciences, much of the debate upon epistemological issues in "African studies" has occurred within the orbit of African philosophical discourse.

◆ **VI** It is not my intention, nor is it appropriate here, to enter into a discussion of the sometimes acerbic debate between the proponents of African ethnophilosophies as opposed to professional philosophy in Africa, save to note that this debate has been superseded. Neither am I concerned with the issues of whether historical materialism abolishes philosophy; it does not, since Marx was interested mainly in dissolving a "self-sufficient" philosophy of introspection, devoid and independent of history and social formation, and to reject idealism and vulgar materialism (e.g., Lenin 1961, 1972; Callinicos 1983; Gollobin 1986; Kitching 1988).

It is my contention that, if there is such a thing as African philosophy (or philosophies), it must stem from the *common historical experience* of Africa and African social formations. As such, at the level of the local community it must be open to the existence of distinctive "ethnophilosophies" and there may be some common structural features of pre-colonial African social formations at this level (e.g., Diop 1974, 1978, *et passim*). Second, an African philosophy must be capable of engaging discourse at the level of the struggle for national independence from colonial rule (a historical necessity); at this level, unfortunately, African philosophy is sometimes used as a mystifying smokescreen to hide the realities of power, interest, and control by comprador and petit bourgeoisies. And this leads directly to the third aspect: African philosophy must address the contemporary issues of international capitalism, imperialism, class formation, socialism, and the nature of the state. If African philosophical discourse fails to address *all* these three aspects of African historical reality, it may itself lack authenticity; the specific ontological and epistemological issues that are traditionally addressed by philosophy would then become superfluous.

If this position is accepted, the discourse about the authenticity of knowledge in and about Africa, and hence its epistemological groundings, are inseparable from the new discourse about

African historiography. I attempt to deal with this question for Ilparakuyo and Maasai social formations, specifically in Chapter 8, but
also more generally throughout the book. For the time being, I rest
with Mudimbe's admirable summation of the major points at issue
(1988:175–176):

> The history of knowledge in Africa and about Africa appears deformed
> and disjointed, and the explanation lies in its own origin and devel-
> opment. As in the case of other histories, we face what Veyne has
> called "the illusion of integral reconstitution [that] comes from the
> fact that the documents which provide us with the answers, also dic-
> tate the questions to us." Furthermore the body of knowledge itself,
> whose roots go as far back as the Greek and Roman periods, in its
> constitution, organization, and paradoxical richness, indicates an in-
> completeness and inherently biased perspective. The discourse which
> witnesses to Africa's knowledge has been for a long time either a geo-
> graphical or an anthropological one, at any rate a "a discourse of com-
> petence" about unknown societies without their own "texts." Only
> recently has this situation been gradually transformed by the concept
> of ethnohistory, which in the 1950s postulated the junction of anthro-
> pological *topoi* with those of history and other social sciences, and
> later on integrated oral tradition and its expressions (poetry, fixed for-
> mulas, anthroponymy, toponymy). In so doing, this discourse began
> contructing simulacra about the relations existing between present
> African social organizations and history.

There is now the possibility of a newly found, epistemologically authentic knowledge of (and *in*) Africa. Anthropology must
grapple with the foundations for such a knowledge. The need for this
is especially urgent for such communal social formations as that
of Ilparakuyo and Maasai, which, as I have noted, are historically
confronted by capitalist and hierarchical systems, whose unchecked
consequences destroy the very principles of communal organization,
not merely transforming them as they do in the case of already hierarchical tributary formations. The results of this confrontation for
Ilparakuyo and Maasai are manifested in two contradictory trends:
The first is the *increasing* mystification of relations of production
hitherto relatively transparent; the second is an awareness of the
intense need for a counter-hegemonic *and* political struggle, relevant at all three levels of social formation already outlined. Counter-
hegemonic struggle is useless unless it leads to heightened awareness
for revolutionary action; it must not be left at the level of constituting merely the "weapons of the weak" (*pace* Scott 1985). It is as a
tentative contribution to such an awareness, in all its specificity and
generality among Ilparakuyo and Maasai, that this book is offered.

2   The "Last of the Maasai": Self-Fulfilling Prophecy or Frustrated Death Wish?

Sipat ake eng'ari;
meng'ari mpukunot.
Only truths are
shared; characters
are not.

◆   Outsiders, both European colonialists and other Tanzanians and Kenyans, have always displayed a striking ambivalence in their conceptions of pastoralists in general and Maasai in particular. But the "romantic" component of this ambivalence, largely confined to European administrators, has been repeatedly overstressed by commentators on the topic. A contemporary expression of post-colonialist attitudes is somewhat amusingly illustrated by Elspeth Huxley in her foreword to the book of text and photographs entitled *The Last of the Maasai* (Amin *et al.* 1987:13–14):

> Ever since white men came to eastern Africa, they have been having an unhappy kind of love affair with the Maasai people. Unhappy, because admiration and exasperation have been almost equally blended in their feelings towards these handsome, arrogant and stubborn tribesmen. . . . In colonial days, there was a disease known as "Maasai-itis" to which district officers, especially young ones, sometimes succumbed. In its advanced stages the victim was said to shake, quiver and even froth at the mouth, as moran [*sic*] were wont to do when working themselves up to battle pitch. Before this stage was reached, it was considered advisable to post that officer to a non-Maasai district.

17

Less amusingly, the unhappiness attributed by Huxley to these white victims of the disease in their relations with Maasai has always been, for Maasai, overshadowed by the imperialists' theft of their lands, attempts at forced labor, high taxation, and a cynical disregard for the welfare and future of Maasai—in fact, a conscious effort to destroy their society and culture, a deliberate ethnocide. Such attitudes and activities still find (perhaps more subtle) expression in the contemporary plans of "development" agencies and "experts" in collaboration with post-colonial governmental institutions. Maasai have continually contested these disruptive forces in order to reproduce their system of pastoral *praxis*, a struggle which includes a counter-hegemonic confrontation with the power of the colonial and post-colonial state and its class interests (Rigby 1985).

One of the earliest and most hypocritical examples of British efforts to annihilate Maasai by theft of their best land, as well as by any other means available, is represented by a 1904 dispatch from Sir Charles Eliot (then Commissioner of the East African Protectorate) to Lord Landsdowne (the British Foreign Secretary). In it, Eliot admits (Sorrenson 1968:76):

> No doubt on platforms and in reports we declare we have no intention of depriving natives of their lands, but this has never preventd us from taking whatever land we want. . . . Your Lordship has opened this protectorate to white . . . colonization, and I think that it is well, in confidential correspondence at least, we should face the undoubted issue—viz., that white mates black in very few moves. . . . There can be no doubt that the Masai [*sic*] and many other tribes go under. It is a prospect that I view with equanimity and a clear conscience. . . . I have no desire to protect Masaidom. It is a beastly, bloody system, founded on raiding and immorality, disastrous to both the Masai and their neighbours. The sooner it disappears and is unknown, except in books of anthropology, the better.

Eliot's duplicity set the tone and content of later justifications for expropriating Maasai grazing land and other forms of exploitation, though under the guise of (a) protecting neighboring peoples from assumed Maasai depredations, as well as Maasai against themselves, and (b) expropriating land for settlers by claiming that Maasai had supposedly "stolen" it from their neighbors and, moreover, that they did not need it anyway. Before his resignation, Eliot had appointed Charles Hobley as district officer in Maasailand in 1905. Hobley's views and activities accurately represent the well-meaning hypocrisy which would characterize British colonial attitudes toward Maasai for a long period to come, despite the claim by G. H. Mungeam that Hobley was "very pro-African in his sympathies" (Mungeam 1967:xi).

In his memoirs, first published in 1929, Hobley set about creating the myth of the aggressive, predatory Maasai who indiscriminately attack and murder their neighbors (Hobley 1929:125): "Before our advent if Masai wanted to expand and another tribe was in the way, they simply drove them out, massacring as many as possible, the survivors taking refuge with neighbouring tribes."

Significantly, Hobley gives no examples; but, having set the scene, he moves surreptitiously from a supposed philanthropy (see *a* above) to the secure complacency of *b* (Hobley 1929:125): "The Masai are entirely pastoral in their habits, and are semi-nomads; that is to say, they follow the grazing, each group having a dry and wet season location." This is completely accurate; but see his conclusions:

> This means that they have pre-empted a vast area of highlands [absolutely essential for dry-season grazing and called isupuki—sing. osupuko—by Maasai]. Further, given a few years' freedom from epidemic disease among their stock or a few successful raids, they have been in the habit of seeking grazing further afield. Whether European settlement had come in to complicate the matter or not, this could not continue indefinitely once government control was established.

Hobley fails to explain how Maasai had pre-empted grazing lands that they had used for centuries, and which was theirs by mutual agreement with their neighbors; neither does he mention that the epidemic diseases among Maasai livestock had been introduced by colonial penetration, nor that their successful raids at that time had been encouraged by the British themselves! (see below).

In a final stroke of genius, Hobley incorporates Eliot's arrogance into his own more "benign" visions (1929:125–126):

> Eliot saw that the time would come when the Masai tribe would have to be confined to definite limits. He also held the belief that the land on each side of the stretch of seventy miles of the railway in or near the Rift Valley [i.e., in Maasailand] was of considerable productive value if properly farmed. His vision has come true, for the southern half of this section of the Rift Valley now holds many valuable stock farms, and the northern half is an area of maize. In addition, the Masai are no worse off than they were twenty years ago.

In the next paragraph, Hobley continues to maintain that all of this was in the best interests of Maasai, who otherwise would have perpetrated some "outrage" that, in turn, would have resulted in the "capture of the Masai stock and the partial destruction of the tribe" (1929:125–126). As I show later, contemporary interventions in Maasai society continue to be justified on the grounds that they are "in the best interests" of Maasai. But what is very clear from all this is that, beginning with Eliot, the British projected onto Maasai their own greed for territorial expansion, as a form of colonial primitive accumulation[1] on behalf of the white settlers. Maasai were then accused, tried, and convicted, *in absentia*, by the British for "stealing" these expropriated lands from others. This later became the justification for the Maasai-British so-called "treaties," and the Maasai "moves" of 1904 and 1911, through which Maasai lost vast areas of their best lands (Rigby 1985:109, 111, 114–116, *et passim*; cf. Sorrenson 1968:193–210 *et passim*).

The point of this brief historical excursion is to establish the continuity between a *real* history of colonialism and its myths and hypocrisies about the nature of Maasai society on the one hand, and current attempts to "re-present" Maasai today in relation to "development" ("for their own good") on the other. It is to a discussion of this that I proceed; but first, a digression upon the "crisis of representation" in anthropology and the postmodernist debate.

◆ **I**   If postmodernist discourses could initiate a substantial critique of ethnography and anthropology, as both text and practice, they would have of necessity to establish the *conditions* for the production of an authentic knowledge and, hence, the *recognition* of authenticity and its negation. In this enterprise, postmodernism fails utterly, for the notion of authenticity implies the resolution of an alienation generated by specific historical and structural processes; postmodernism recognizes none of these categories. As Terry Eagleton admirably phrases it (1985:61):

> The depthless, styleless, dehistoricized, decathected surfaces of postmodernist culture are not meant to signify an alienation, for the very concept of alienation must secretly posit a dream of authenticity which postmodernism finds unintelligible. . . . There is no longer any subject to be alienated and nothing to be alienated from, "authenticity" having been less rejected than merely forgotten. . . . Postmodernism is thus a grisly parody of socialist utopia, having abolished all alienation at a stroke.

Similarly, the bourgeois notion of an epistemology has reached its *reductio ad absurdum* as an "obsession" which represents an "accidental, but eventually sterile, turning in Western culture" (Rabinow 1986:234). Paradoxically, the latter development vitiates postmodernism's claim to be "post"-anything; for, as Rabinow (following Rorty 1979), argues, "epistemology as the study of mental representations arose in a particular historical epoch, the seventeenth century; it developed in a specific society, that of Europe; and triumphed in philosophy by being closely linked to the professional claims of one group, nineteenth-century German professors of philosophy." Whatever, we may ask, happened to Marx?

While I am sympathetic toward George Marcus and Michael Fischer's (1986) delineation of the current crisis as an "experimental moment in the human sciences," their project is seriously compromised when they note that it is carried out at a "time when confident metanarratives or paradigms are lacking," an era which is characterized by "post-conditions—postmodern, post-colonial, post-traditional" (1986:24). If this *is* the case, then how can we understand, or even *posit*, the "changing historical circumstances" in which the "cultures of world peoples need constantly to be *re*-discovered as these peoples reinvent them"?

Marcus and Fischer's "solutions" to this crisis in the social sciences include the notion of the "repatriation of anthropology" to the context in which anthropology was born, as a production of the societies (largely Western and capitalist) and classes (bourgeois) in which it arose as a distinct discipline. This is an admirable project. And at one point they acknowledge that the subjects of much "repatriated anthropology," which are the "traditional" anthropological topics of "kinship, migrants, ethnic minorities, public rituals, religious clubs, countercultural communities" (Marcus and Fischer 1986: 153), are not the really important issues for epistemological critique. Instead, they rightly turn our attention to the "most important subject for cultural criticism," which is "the study of mass-cultural forms, and, somewhat more tentatively, mainstream middle-class life":

> These pose the kinds of broader questions addressed by the cultural critics of the 1920s and 1930s about stratification, cultural hegemony, and changing modes of perception. The study of the mass-cultural industry, popular culture, and the formation of public consciousness has emerged as one of the most vigorous of new research directions. The 1950s elitist contempt for mass culture and fears that it would simply institutionalize a lowest-common-denominator conformity have been replaced by ethnographic elaborations of how working-class, ethnic, and regional communities and youth generations [*sic*] can appropriate the "rubbish" available within a preconstituted market—drugs, clothing, vehicles—as well as the means of communication, in order to

construct statements of their own sense of position and experience in society.

But this possibly exciting "re-direction," together with the mention of the work of such Marxist cultural critics as Raymond Williams, is immediately vitiated by these authors when they dismiss the need for understanding the political economy of these "cultural expressions," reducing them instead to "rich cultural texts through which may be read the larger society, society-wide struggles for defining authoritative and other possible meanings of events for a diverse public" (Marcus and Fischer 1983: 153). While promising that such studies would provide us with an epistemological critique by "identifying critiques developed 'out there' in various domains of the social structure," the dynamic constitution of these domains through the historical political economy is brushed aside and reduced to "raising questions about cultural hegemony and how meaning structures are formed and negotiated by competing segments in society" (Marcus and Fischer 1986: 153–154). They conclude: "For cultural analysis and criticism, the contesting of the meaning of things or events is what centrally constitutes politics." Whatever happened to oppression, exploitation, power; and bullets, blood, guns, and guts?

In such a context, epistemology becomes merely the "clarification and judgment of the subject's representations" if, indeed, there is any longer a subject (Jameson 1988:16–18; Rabinow 1986:235). Philosophy becomes restricted to a "theory of representations," lacking historical content and any reference to *praxis*. In postmodernist discourse, as in post-structuralism, the subject is dead; it is replaced by "text."

Postmodernism, then, denies the possibility of a historically grounded epistemology, rejects the need for a dialectical theory of knowledge, and returns us squarely to a displaced bourgeois ideological positivism while strenuously denying its own provenance. Postmodernism can be historically located; it cannot locate itself historically. While it mimics parody and satire, it is really pastiche, but a pastiche that has reactionary and dangerous political implications for any revolutionary project (Jameson 1981, 1984, 1988:15–126; Eagleton 1985). Critique itself becomes devoid of historical content and practical referent, except in terms of itself. The births and deaths of concrete social formations and real peoples and cultures disappear.

Fredric Jameson sees a parallel between postmodernist "textuality" and Lacanian concepts of schizophrenia as a "breakdown of the relationships between signifiers," let alone relationships between signifiers and signifieds; postmodernist texts have as their referents not historical reality but other (absent) texts (Jameson 1981:123; 1988). The consequences of this for anthropology, as Paul Rabinow admirably indicates (1986:250), is that the peoples whose cultures are represented in ethnography are reduced to "practitioners of textuality." A mere *recognition* of this reductionism is not, however, enough; anthropology cannot return to "earlier modes of unselfconscious representation," but neither does postmodernism offer a solution. The dilemma thus created, at this "experimental moment" in anthropology, is concisely expressed by Rabinow (1986:250–251): "We cannot solve [this problem] by ignoring the relations of representational forms and social practices either. If we attempt to eliminate social referentiality, other referents will occupy the voided space." One cannot help wondering who would go to all that trouble, and for what reasons?

It is my contention here that the problems of ethnocide and ethnogenesis can only be addressed through a critical historical materialism in which not only anthropology becomes concrete "social critique" (*pace* Marcus and Fischer 1986) but also the philosophical discourses of the societies which are the subjects of anthropological representations become a part of such critique. For Ilparakuyo and Maasai, these discourses are inextricably related to their unique form of pastoral *praxis*, and they assume a political significance for subversive action. This significance can only be discovered in the concrete historical relations between, in our case, Ilparakuyo and Maasai social formations and the colonial and post-colonial states of Kenya and Tanzania.

◆ **II**   Maasai social formations and, by extension, Ilparakuyo Maasai of Tanzania (Rigby 1985; Beidelman 1960; Ndagala 1986), are probably among the most variously "represented" of East African peoples. That this is something of an anomaly for popular audiences is illustrated in an article in the Nairobi *Sunday Standard* of June 12, 1981, by Paul Toulmin-Rothe, and entitled "Introducing the Masai [sic] to the 20th Century." Toulman-Rothe begins his article as follows:

> Of all the tribes of Africa, perhaps the most famous in Europe and America are the Masai. Why is this? They are not nearly so numerous as certain other tribes, nor are they more handsome or cleverer than

many other African peoples, and their arts and crafts are admittedly less notable than those of other ethnic groups. The answer must be hidden in their way of life. Like other nomadic groups . . . the Masai have inspired Western man with a longing for a life of freedom, wandering over the face of the earth with a herd of cattle, occasionally spearing the odd lion. . . . As different as possible, in fact, from the life of a city based wage-earner.

Then—"The truth, of course, is very different."

Such statements do not seem to present any apparent contradiction to Western audiences who, on other occasions, claim that "freedom" is inseparable from capitalism and bourgeois culture; but then, perhaps, we should not ask too much of such audiences? At any rate, in representations ranging from documentaries on Maasai culture and society as part of a "disappearing world," in films on wildlife in East Africa, in sculptures, batiks, paintings and photographs, to published scholarly articles and books, as well as memoirs by colonial settlers and administrators, to novels by "outsiders" and "insiders," Maasai have appeared in various guises. In fact, Isampur, because of their relatively more relaxed attitudes to wage labor and the humoring of tourists, are often persuaded to "stand in" for other sections of Maasai in visual representations.

Recently, Maasai have shown up in television commercials in the United States, and in block-buster movies. In the film *Out of Africa*, based on Isak Dinesen's (Karen Blixen's) texts, first published in 1927, Maasai make a mercifully brief entrance and exit as a group of "warriors" (*ilmurran*) jog into frame out of "nowhere," and into "elsewhere," though they are also the subject of a short philosophical discourse by one of the story's main protagonists. In Dinesen's original work, Maasai make frequent and generally sympathetic appearances; for her time, Dinesen was considered "liberal."

More importantly, in the last ten years or so, a substantial number of texts by Maasai authors, both scholarly and literary, have made a welcome debut. Perhaps the earliest examples of indigenous literary output by Maasai themselves are represented by the texts which appear in A. C. Hollis's *The Masai: their Language and Folklore* (1905) and in the much later *Inkuti Pukunot oo lMaasai*, by John Tompo ole Mpaayei (1954). Interestingly, Hollis's main informant was Sameni ole Kipasis, an Olparakuoni of Ilparakuyo section, who was converted to Christianity and came to be known as Justin Lemenye (Olomeni; see Hollis 1905:v; Fosbrooke 1956*b*: Rigby 1985:108–110, 114, 116, 121–122). Apart from academic dissertations and theses by Maasai scholars, popular and literary works are represented by, for example, Henry ole Kulet (1971, 1972), S. S. ole Sankan (1971), Tepilit ole Saitoti (1986), and by Naomi Kipury's superb collection of Maasai oral literature (1983a). Maasai have also been the focus of numerous novels by fellow Kenyans, both African and non-African (e.g., Watene 1974; Read 1982), as well as often very odd literary works such as Alan Dean Foster's (1986).[2]

The point at issue here is that, with so many competing genres in the field of representations of Maasai, any comprehensive critique is a book-length undertaking. Out of this plethora of materials, I select only a couple that have some significance, both positive and negative, for Maasai political *praxis*, in relation to the reproduction of their social formations and its embeddedness in the contemporary state—that is, in relation to the political economy of the processes of ethnocide and ethnogenesis. It is, as I have already noted, only in this context that one can pose the questions of authenticity and inauthenticity.

I have already considered the ambivalence of colonial approaches to Maasai social formations and culture. But Eliot's duplicity and Hobley's rationalization of it have even earlier historical roots. The British colonial administration, which took over government of what is now Kenya from the British Imperial East Africa Company in 1895, creating the British East African Protectorate, opened their formal dealings with Maasai through exploitation in the guise of a military alliance (cf. Waller 1976). The decimation of Maasai herds in the rinderpest epidemic, and the death of very large numbers of Maasai from famine and small-pox, in the early 1890s, had greatly weakened Maasai social formations by the late 1890s. A military alliance with the British offered them a chance to rebuild their herds and re-establish the conditions for viable pastoral *praxis*. The British administrator made responsible for these early contacts with Maasai and Ilparakuyo was Sidney Langford Hinde who, together with his wife Hildegarde, published in 1901 a book entitled *The Last of the Masai*. This is how Hinde describes the context of his relationship with Maasai in 1896 (Hinde and Hinde 1901:x–xi):

> On first taking up my duties at Machakos, I found the natives of that neighbourhood (Wakamba) hostile to the administration. Several parties of police had been attacked and cut up by them, and the enemy only stopped short of attacking the Fort itself. . . . It was, therefore, decided to invite the Masai under our protection to assist the Government police. To this they made immediate response, and with a thousand Masai to scout and guard the flanks, an expedition shortly reduced the surrounding country to submission. A few months later,

when a military company was stationed at Machakos, the rebels further afield were subdued by a combined military and police force, assisted by over a thousand Masai warriors.

As I have noted, Maasai acquiesced to this and other later alliances with the British for one reason only: they were permitted to keep confiscated cattle to rebuild their herds. I have indicated elsewhere (see Chapter 4; cf. 1985) that, as soon as the British had exploited Maasai *ilmurran* (so-called "warriors") in this fashion, they set about destroying the institution of *murrano* ("warriorhood") in the belief that this would destroy the Maasai social system (cf. Tignor 1972, 1976; cf. Waller 1976). The elimination of *ilmurran* age-grade is still the priority of the Kenya Government in its dealings with Maasai.

Hinde's initial experience with Maasai in a military context gave him an opportunity to develop *his* representation of them. His comments on these early colonial-Maasai relations are instructive for my later discussion; they also provide the basis for Hinde's view that, if Maasai culture and society were not going to be deliberately destroyed by the efforts of such later colonial agents as Eliot and Hobley, they would in any case "self-destruct." If later administrators had to find excuses for their ethnocidal intentions, Hinde's theory of inevitable self-destruction or Maasai "death-wish," provided a more acceptable hypothesis for Western morality of what we might call "ethnosuicide." But let me return to what Hinde has to say (1901:xi–xii):

> On these [two military] occasions I worked with and amongst the Masai, and was greatly impressed by their fine physique, manly bearing and response to discipline; and when later I was appointed Resident to the Maasai chief [sic] and Collector of Masailand, the opportunity of becoming acquainted with the life of this interesting people presented itself. Residence among Masai supplied the reasons why there has been practically no information on this subject since the publication in 1884 [1885] of Joseph Thomson's famous book, "Through Masailand," which almost exhausted the knowledge to be gleaned from the Swahilis and neighbouring peoples. The Masai are naturally reticent, and until the last two or three years no pure Masai adult had learnt Kiswahili, while the young boys and girls who were acquainted with the language, or had been taken into service, were not only disqualified from being admitted to the tribal councils, but might not return to their villages.

There is some truth in this rather exaggerated claim of the reticence of Maasai and their realization of the possibilities of self-alienation through education; but the form of its expression allowed the Hindes to establish another tenacious element in the mis-representation of Maasai, and to consolidate the myth of their own cultural demise. This was the claim of supposed "racial purity" and "racial distinctiveness" of Maasai from their neighbors. This myth, also subscribed to by other early commentators such as Joseph Thomson, is still a factor in current representations (especially in popular literatures), albeit clothed in cultural disguises of one kind or another. I return to this; for the present, let us note the Hindes' reasons for the title of their book (1901:xiii):

> Since the title of this book may lay itself open to criticism, some justification for its adoption is called for. By the "last of the Masai" I do not mean the last individuals of the race, but rather the last of the rapidly decreasing band of pure blood, whose tendencies, traditions, customs and beliefs remain uncontaminated by admixture with Bantu elements and contact with civilization.

In terms of Maasai philosophical notions of "identity," both physical and social, nothing could be further from the truth. The myth of racial superiority and inferiority are totally imposed European categories. In philosophical terms, the dialectical nature of knowledge and *praxis* in Maasai culture and social formation is not posited upon any notion of an "internal" state of "purity"; on the contrary, it is historically constituted upon dialectically conceived relations with non-Maasai, and the latter category includes not only their pre-colonial neighbors, but the agents of colonial intrusions as well as post-colonial interventions (Rigby 1985:*passim*; Galaty 1977, 1982, 1989, *et passim*). But what is one to make of the imputed "contamination" emanating from "civilization," coming from such a pillar of the British empire?

Unfortunately, the Hindes' attempt to "praise" Maasai at the expense of their "Bantu" neighbors not only violates the real openness of Maasai society but also came to characterize colonial views of Maasai throughout the history of Tanzania and Kenya until independence; it still characterizes many of the attitudes of outsiders, especially Europeans and Americans, toward Maasai in the post-colonial situation. In fact, the Hindes' own observations contradict their "purity" argument when they state quite explicitly that it is difficult to describe Maasai culture without describing Kikuyu society as well (Hinde and Hinde 1901:15).

Nevertheless, the position adopted by the Hindes enables them to conclude with a faint-hearted plea for avoiding what they conceive of as the otherwise inevitable destruction of the Maasai, even if their reasons for arriving at it are entirely erroneous (Hinde and Hinde 1901:109):

> The Masai are, unquestionably, of far greater interest than most African peoples, and the fast approaching extinction of the pure stock is a matter to be largely regretted. Although under the conditions of European government they would not be allowed to resume their lawless raids among the surrounding tribes, the destruction of so virile a race would, nevertheless, be a permanent loss to East Africa.

What we have again is the fundamentally racist and contradictory nature of colonialist conceptions of the history and culture of Africans in general and Maasai in particular. On the one hand, there is the nostalgic admiration for an invented past; on the other, an oft-repeated and therefore deeply desired end to the Maasai. This contradiction is still manifested, not only in popular representations of Maasai (where it might be expected on grounds of racist or ethnic prejudice) but also in professional commentaries on development problems in Maasailand.

Most disturbingly, however, it also surfaces in ethnographic and comparative anthropological accounts of Maasai, texts that may be used by those "experts" who design policies for Maasai development, as well as for nefarious political ends. *None* of these three kinds of texts, based on mis-representation of Maasai, can be authentic; none of them can be counteracted, or even understood, unless they are functionally located in the political economy of Maasai social reproduction. In other words, they are both cause and effect of the alienation engendered by unreflexive forms of knowledge, and they therefore have unfortunate political effects.

◆ **III**   In an important book on "livestock development" in Kenya Maasailand, Evangelou noted (1984:1–2): "The underexploited productive potential of range areas, regions mainly utilized by largely self-sufficient, non-market oriented pastoral peoples, is increasingly attracting the attention of national governments." At the same time, Evangelou continues, "Traditional Maasai social structure and cultural institutions fundamentally constrain development initiatives" (1984:125; cf. Doherty 1979a, 1979b).

Both these statements, including the notion of "livestock development" itself, and the research upon which they are based, occupy a discursive space totally displaced from Maasai society, culture, and politics. The first statement involves a notion that "national governments" somehow represent social categories distinct from "largely self-sufficient non-market oriented pastoralists" who, nevertheless, seem to live in areas over which these "national governments" apparently hold sway. It is implied, *ab initio*, that the interests of pastoral peoples are essentially different from those of the national governments; and, in fact, this is often true, but for reasons quite at odds with the ones adduced by Evangelou. The only manner in which these divergent interests will coincide, it is averred, is through a relation of inequality between the two parties concerned and, hence, the exercise of power by one over the other. The struggle is predetermined; the outcome is assumed.

The second statement by Evangelou embodies a judgment upon a number of things, the two most important of which are: *who* defines what "development initiatives" are and *who* decides that these initiatives are "constrained" by the "traditional" social structure and culture of Maasai pastoralists? The idea of (good) development occupies an external space in relation to the Maasai social formation; the "traditional" (bad) social structure and culture are internal to Maasai society; we arrive again at contradiction which can only be resolved by political confrontation and differential power.

It is claimed that anthropologists intervene in these two social fields, helping *both* sides resolve an otherwise unresolvable conflict. But in reality, researchers have already made up their minds as to who will (or even should) win; they set about *appropriating* knowledge from the already identified "loser" and supplying it to the "winner." At the very least, this implies hegemonic control by the state over not only the *place* occupied by Maasai but also their entire vision of the future. More than this, Maasai are presumed to adhere to what are called "traditional" culture and institutions, implying another form of *distancing* in both place and time, a state of affairs which seem to be accepted without contention by anthropologists (cf. Fabian 1983).

The very *language* of development is imposed upon a people, who are assumed to occupy a place, a time, separate from, and even antagonistic to, those of the planners of "progress." And the resulting gap is presumed to be caused by Maasai, not by the alienated knowledge of the "experts." Not since the fire-breathing missionaries of the 19th century has so much misplaced zeal been evident. I have discussed elsewhere (Rigby 1985:92–122) the relationship between the discourse of missionaries and Ilparakuyo Maasai *praxis*. Contemporary external hegemonic control, in the case of Ilparakuyo and Maasai, is purported to be exercised by the national governments of Kenya and Tanzania. Post-colonial states in contemporary Africa differ a great deal, at least ostensibly, from one another (as do Tanzania and Kenya) in the forms of development they pursue. They, in turn, are to a greater or lesser degree dependent upon external sources of power and accumulation for their own precarious reproduction (cf. Coulson 1979; Kitching 1980; Leys 1975; Shivji 1975; Saul 1979, 1985; cf. Thomas 1984). The reproduction of the state in the Third World, its power, and the *status quo* depend upon the achievement of certain *class* interests at the national level, even if the specific politico-economic and cultural conditions for the formation of these classes in Africa, and elsewhere in the Third World, are different from those in advanced capitalism.

To the extent that this is true, social formations such as Ilparakuyo and Maasai, other pastoralists (especially in Kenya), and the entire peasantry, occupy an exploited and marginal position analogous to, but very different from, the position of the proletariat in advanced capitalist social formations. It is here that an African discourse about class struggle and cultural resistance from within provides the juxtaposition of a knowledge diametrically opposed to the forms of "knowledge" espoused by commentators such as Evangelou, as well as many other theorists of "development interventions." They are committed to a capitalist path to a bourgeois revolution in the Third World, whatever comes later (e.g., Hyden 1980, 1983; Warren 1980; but cf. Hedlund 1979).

Yet even within the alienated (and hence inauthentic) problematic of development economics and sociology, in which "livestock development" replaces "people development," the capacities of Maasai to *incorporate* external elements into their pastoral *praxis* force themselves upon the observer's attention. Thus Evangelou expresses *his* version of the "Maasai contradiction" as follows (1984:269):

> The receptiveness of the Maasai to development change invariably has been inversely related to the social and economic adjustments thereby required. But the transition to a market oriented production system is necessary and inevitable. . . . The Maasai continue to be described as resisting change. But throughout the history of interventions in Maasailand, producers have welcomed technological development, including veterinary services [cf. Rigby 1985:24, 160, 166–167], and have shown an admirable fund-raising record to pay for these services. Sullivan (1979), for example, found the Maasai pastoralists included in his study of livestock systems in Tanzania to be highly receptive to interventions for improving their livestock. It is when interventions make demands upon social structure, and threaten existing political and economic relationships, that reluctance to change is encountered, and

rational decision-making at the household level is mistakenly aggregated by outside observers into a system-wide irrationality.

Is Evangelou really surprised that Maasai should be reluctant to participate in the dissolution of their own society; or is this another plea for ethnosuicide?

Then there is the argument that Maasai and other pastoralists have managed to resist societal breakdown and collapse only *because* they are essentially "capitalistic" in their economic practices. While Harold Schneider used this interpretation to suggest a positive form of pastoral ethnogenesis (Schneider 1979 *et passim*), others have used it to reinforce the myth of pastoral conservatism, and hence the inevitable disappearance of this mode of life. For example, while Paul Spencer, in his book on Ilmatapato section of Kenya Maasai, is aware of the problems of defining a "pastoralist mode of production" (there is no such thing), he defends his omission of dealing with Ilmatapato "involvement" in the "modern economy" on the grounds of the similarity between pastoral production and capitalist enterprise (Spencer 1988:20, 23):

> There is, I suggest, a more fundamental reason why Maasai generally have not extended their *opportunism* as pastoralists to the opportunities of the market economy in Kenya. This is the importance of time as a utility in a truly capitalist system. Such a concept is quite incompatible with Maasai perception of time and career progression created by their age system. This system provides an unfolding life experience for the individual male with its own fascination and rewards, both in youth and in middle age. *It is not that the Maasai lack a desire for independent acquisition. On the contrary, their economy might usefully be described as one of rudimentary capitalism*, just as their pastoralism is *essentially* a family *enterprise*. . . . A model of family enterprise and (arguably) of rudimentary capitalism provides the economic backcloth against which to assess the dynamics of what has proved to be a highly resilient alternative to the market economy.

How can one assess many of the disastrous consequences of capitalist penetration and commoditization with which Maasai have had to contend for at least one hundred years, such as famines and land loss, if they are really closet capitalists, waiting to "come out"? And, by implication, waiting for the colonialists to provide the conditions for their coming out? If the author of a major publication on Maasai which appears in 1988 ignores almost entirely the history of their social formations for the past three hundred years or more, where are we?

Finally, and at a more popular level of representation, John Eames's sympathetic and valuable narrative accompaniment to Mohamed Amin's brilliant photographs (Amin *et al.*, 1987) again raises the ugly head of contradictory representation.[3] What is most important in this text for our present purposes is how Eames attempts to resolve the contradiction. While Elspeth Huxley, in her foreword to the book, maintains that Eames does not answer the question "How much longer can [the Maasai] way of life survive?" he does end on a "note of hope" (1987:14–15). And his note of hope specifically depends upon the regeneration of a relative autonomy for the Maasai social formation, which involves the passing of control over all wildlife as well as "livestock development" in Maasailand to Maasai themselves.[4] This revolutionary proposal involves a restructuring of relations between Maasai and the state: the two national entities of Tanzania and Kenya. This is how Eames phrases his suggestion for Kenya Maasai (Amin *et al.*:182–183): "[Maasai suggest that] all wild and domestic stock [should be] assigned to the management of the Maasai. If this just and enlightened policy were to be adopted, they could guarantee positive self-development. As a designated State Conservation Area, Maasailand would cease to be a national liability and finally become half-way independent in the nation-state of Kenya."

This returns us to the major issue at hand: that ethnocide and ethnogenesis cannot be illuminated without a theory of the incorporation of previously autonomous social formations into the state, a specifically *political* and *historical* process, as well as its corollary in the contemporary world: the penetration of capitalism and commodity relations into these societies.

The relation between ethnogenesis and cultural authenticity has been admirably dealt with for precapitalist class and state structures in a number of recent publications (e.g., Gailey 1985*a*, 1985*b*, 1987*a*, 1987*b*; Gailey and Patterson 1987*a*; Diamond 1955, 1974; cf. Kapferer 1988). Building on Edward Sapir's (1961) notion of "genuine culture," Christine Gailey says (1985*a*:12):

> The success of attempts to forge authentic or "genuine" culture, that is, meanings that are autonomously created out of shared circumstances, rests upon the elimination of political subordination. Shared history provides one basis for movements aimed at political autonomy, the rejection of an ethnicity useful to the state in favour of identities developed in the subordination and resistance process.

It is crucial to note, with Gailey and others, that ethnogenesis as a concrete reponse to historical conditions of incorporation, subordination, and exploitation is distinct from ethnicity: the former is liberating and authentic, the latter is a reification of the *status quo ante*; the former is revolutionary project, the latter is to divide and rule (Gailey 1985a:11–12).

A similar and equally convincing argument about the relations between ethnocide and the capitalist state is advanced by Gerald Sider for the Lumbee (1976). Sider also discusses the dangers of a superficial ethnicity and cultural nationalism that can widen class divisions for no strategic purposes. These dangers are especially pronounced in the case of incorporation into the capitalist state (Sider 1976:171), with its much more sophisticated forms of domination, hegemony, and exploitation than those of the precapitalist state. In the case of Maasai, especially in Kenya, the vulnerability of the reproduction of pastoralist social formation and *praxis* is increased by the crudeness of specific forms of domination, often disguised as "development initiatives."

♦ **IV**   In Chapters 3, 4, and 5 (cf. Rigby 1985), I elaborate the complex forms of contradiction engendered by historical forces impinging upon Ilparakuyo and Maasai social formations. In these statements, I have emphasized that the *dialectical* nature of Ilparakuyo Maasai social thought and *praxis* allows for the relatively controlled incorporation of "external" events and forces, despite their unavoidable impact upon the processes of Maasai social reproduction. These dialectics are not "new"; that is, they existed in Maasai relations with non-Maasai long before even the pre-colonial penetration of merchant capital and later colonial domination. But what, it may be asked, has all this to do with the efforts of Maasai to deal with the reality of nationally and internationally supported development interventions, for it is the latter that present the most immediate threat of ethnocide to them?

It is my contention that, if there is to be any diminishing of the gap between what I have called the alienated discourse of development planning and Maasai philosophy, theory, and practical aspirations, a Marxist phenomenology must be employed. Without such an understanding, an authentic form of "ethno-regeneration" coupled with "people development" cannot take place among Maasai, since pastoral *praxis* would be subverted into mere ethnicity. The problem of this gap has been addressed in a seminal paper by Aidan Foster-Carter. In it, he presents the major issues as follows (Foster-Carter 1987:203):

Why *should* there be interactionism (or phenomenology, or hermeneutics, or whatever) in development sociology? . . . And yet the question would not go away. After all, the various sociologies which in their different ways stress the centrality (and, usually, the neglectedness) of human experience, subjectivity, everyday life or whatever are avowedly generalising in their scope, and universalistic in their claims. If sociology in general has suffered from an over-socialised concept of "man," and needs to bring "men" back in, then why not the sociology of development? If everyday life is a skilled accomplishment, as ethnomethodology insists that it is, can it be any less so in the Third World? If positivism is scientistic, structuralism is at best incomplete, and the sociological enterprise is necessarily (at least in part) interpretive and hermeneutic, then must not such considerations apply with equal force in development theory? In my own case, initial reluctance even to entertain such questions has given way to a conviction that they are central.

If we are to pursue such a project, then certain strategic issues become inescapable. I suggest we must turn to a historical materialist theory which is capable of combining a theory of everyday life with a Marxist approach to language. Elements of such a problematic are to be found in the work of such theorists as Michel de Certeau, Mikhail Bakhtin, V. N. Voloshinov, Gramsci, and Raymond Williams; but that is the subject of this book.

3　Class Formation in Historical Perspective

*Menya Enkai ananya
tung'ani.*
God doesn't eat what a
man eats.

◆　　　　　　There is a bewildering profusion of theoretical
formulations that claim to explain, once and for all, the transition
from classless to class society and, hence, the rise of the state through
processes of internal contradictions (usually historical), or intrinsic
factors (usually physical or biological in the sense of, for example,
population increase) in the development of human societies. It is one
of the intentions of this chapter to sort out some of the issues that
arise from this prolix and continuing debate in the context of the
particular East African social formations that are the subject of this
book. This debate may, after all, be considered as perhaps the central one in most elaborations of the political economy of historical
transformations, other than the (perhaps equally intransigent) issue
of the post-revolutionary transition to socialism and communism,
although my argument may suggest that the latter is more crucial
than the former. But in this sense, Marc Abélès is quite correct when
he locates the debate of the transitory cases of "non-state/state" and
"state/non-state" in essentially the same context of "two symmetri-
cal processes" (1981:12–13,n.1).

I attempt to establish some of the conditions under which
classes may arise in a particular social formation or formations—the
egalitarian or "non-stratified" pastoral formations in eastern Africa
(Bonte 1978). More specifically, I try to deal with the question of the
historical contradictions characteristic of Ilparakuyo and Maasai pre-
capitalist societies, with a view to providing a historical perspective
upon the way in which classes could possibly have arisen in these

"classless" formations prior to capitalist penetration (but did not), and the form these are taking after the latter event in contemporary Kenya and Tanzania. I deal with the historical period up to the time of formal colonization in the 1890s; the contemporary formation of classes among Maasai in Kenya and Tanzania is examined in detail in Chapter 7.

While a fuller exposition of this intractable debate would require an examination and evaluation of theories of class and state formation ranging from evolutionary problematics, through biological, ecological, and functionalist ones, to the historical materialist problematic (itself divided upon several lines), I prefer for the moment to commence with a critique of certain core concepts and their implications for an understanding of specific historical transformations. But two preliminary points must be made. First, some of the enormous range of these theories already mentioned have usefully, if somewhat superficially, been classified into two basic categories, "conflict theories" and "integrative theories" (Service 1978:21). Jonathan Haas (1982) attempts to go beyond these two theoretical categories by suggesting that they are not mutually exclusive and that a more synthetic (if not syncretic) approach may yield further insights.[1]

Second, although Elman Service's classification and its development by Haas and others is useful, it suffers from the effects of all such typologies: they fail to address the grounds for making any classification in the first place (see Johannes Fabian's discussion of taxonomic time and "the temporal wolf in taxonomic sheep's clothing," 1983:23–25, 53, 97–104, *et passim*). The voluminous recent literature in anthropology and archaeology on "types of states" is generally indistinguishable from expositions of different theories of how states are formed; it is not of immediate concern here except in relation to inferences about how classes are formed, and in any case is brilliantly contextualized and critically examined by Gailey (1985; cf. Patterson 1983). Perhaps more significant for our present purposes would be a discussion of the various theories of class and state from the point of view of whether they establish an explicitly evolutionary model on the one hand or focus instead upon the problem of the origin and transformation of political power as the dynamic historical element on the other, or both. I return to these issues at various points in what follows, but some preliminary discussion is necessary.

Although I have suggested that evolutionary models of class and state formation are different from those that focus upon the dynamic of political power, a closer examination of evolutionary theories shows that, in order to avoid a notion of the metaphysical *necessity* of evolutionary change, these theories fall back upon other reasons for evolutionary movement. In his discussion of the "evolution of political societies," for example, Morton Fried postulates a transformation through "ranked" and "stratified" systems, to the emergence of the state. The "mechanisms" for this transformation, however, are not intrinsic to the model but rely instead upon other factors, such as the "availability of food" or the "complex of inventions that we know as the 'neolithic revolution'" (Fried 1967:111–112) in the "pristine emergence of ranking." He also relies upon a basically voluntaristic Weberian notion of "power" and "authority" when he notes (Fried 1967:13–14): "'Authority' is taken here to refer to the ability to channel the behavior of others in the absence of the threat or use of sanctions. Power is the ability to channel the behavior of others by the threat of the use of sanctions."[2]

Evolutionary models of social transformation are, therefore, based either upon *other* transformations (such as changes in technology or upon the "harnessing of energy," e.g., in White, 1959:144–145), or are reduced to dynamics of a completely different order (e.g., population growth; see Fried 1967:112–113). In fact, as Paul Hirst has convincingly shown (1976:16), "There is no such thing as a general 'evolutionary perspective' nor are there common principles of evolutionary classification," particularly where theories of social evolution are concerned. Any *general* theory of social evolution, in fact, would have to be ahistorical and hence metaphysical.

In default of a historically constituted theory of evolutionary transformation from "non-class," egalitarian societies to class and state, then, the notion of political power emerges as the dynamic underlying directional historical change. The concept of political power, however, is inextricably linked in a historical sense with the ideas of of "law," "order," and the "state," and in particular the bourgeois state (see Passerin d'Entrèves 1967). As with Fried's problematic, the wielding of political power (or its "legitimate," "noncoercive" form as authority) in this contemporary bourgeois sense is essentially a voluntaristic concept in that it is only power when it is "legitimate" (and therefore indistinguishable from authority); otherwise it is not power, it is coercion (see Parsons 1963:240).

Georges Balandier, on the other hand, sees power as universal and essential to the maintenance and reproduction of the social order; it is immanent in social structure and is inseparable from the notion of coercion (Balandier 1970:35–36):

> Political power is inherent in every society: it arouses respect for the rules on which it is based; it defends the society against its own im-

perfections; it limits, within itself, the effects of competition between individuals and groups. It is these conservatory functions that get most consideration. Making use of a synthetic formula, power may be defined, for every society, as resulting from the need to struggle against the entropy that threatens it with disorder—as it threatens any system. But it must not be concluded that this defence has at its disposal only a single means—coercion—and can be ensured only by a clearly differentiated government. All the mechanisms that help to maintain or recreate internal cooperation must be considered. Rituals, ceremonies or procedures that ensure a periodical or occasional renewal of society, are instruments of political action in this sense just as much as rulers and their bureaucracy.

For both Talcott Parsons and Balandier, then, the notion of political power is not generated by historical circumstances, but can be universally defined in terms of its necessary functions in society. These functions are essentially integrative, given whatever structural framework is there to be reproduced, and they are both "internal" and "external" to the social system, an issue to which I return. For the moment, I may conclude that, when it comes to the problem of historical transformation from egalitarian social formations to stratified or class societies and those with the state, both the social evolution and universal political power theories tend to be reductionist or metaphysical, or both. Neither are compatible with the historical materialist problematic, and I must reiterate with Althusser and Stephan Feuchtwang that "Marxist analysis neither starts from nor seeks to discover some universal object, like Human Nature, or Society, or Power, or Ideology, or Religion which is a non-historical 'fact'" (Althusser 1971; Feuchtwang 1975). For Marx, power arises with the formation of classes and the state, since, "strictly speaking, political power is the organized use of force by one class in order to bring another into subjection" (Marx 1962). It is therefore an essentially historical phenomenon and hence cannot be the basis of any general theory of transformation. These are the issues upon which I focus in the following analysis, within the general context of the ongoing debates on the relations between class formation and the state as reflected in the works already cited, as well as others (e.g., Bonte 1975, 1978, 1979, 1981; Claessen and Skalnik 1978, 1981; Asad 1979; Godelier 1975, 1978; Abélès 1981; Coquery-Vidrovitch 1978; Bailey and Llobera 1981).

My opening and critical perusal of selected concepts derives from these debates, but is meant primarily to clear some of the confusions that may arise from the untheorized use of them, mainly but not exclusively in the context of the historical materialist problematic. In this, my debt to a number of exceptional contributors to the discourse in relation to African pastoral formations, particularly Pierre Bonte, is obvious in what follows, even if, on occasion, I may have cause to disagree with them. I begin, however, with a notion derived from a non-Marxist source, but that is not, as I shall show, unrelated to certain tendencies in historical materialist discourse. It involves the idea of the inherent capitalist character or movement of pastoral social formations.

◆ I   The point of commencing with a critical if brief look at this view is that it implies either an easy, if not automatic, transition to "capitalist society" on the one hand (Schneider 1979) or a mechanism for blocking the development of "indigenous form of class" on the other (Galaty 1981). But perhaps more importantly, it overlaps with arguments in the historical materialist problematic revolving around the shift from an analysis of *production* to *exchange* as the basis for precapitalist class formation (see Coquery-Vidrovitch 1978; Meillassoux 1978, 1981).

In the first case, "capitalism" is not seen as a mode of production generated in particular historical circumstances, but as having specific economic characteristics and associations that can be extracted and applied *mutatis mutandis* to other modes of production and social formations, particularly pastoral ones. This is because, it is argued by its protagonists, cattle and other livestock have all the attributes of "capital" (as attested to by the very etymology of the word itself) in that they may be accumulated as "pastoral capital," allowing for "management decisions that are lacking in agricultural regimes" (Schneider 1979:221). It is this characteristic of livestock, Schneider maintains, that defines the specificity of pastoral societies as opposed to others in which land and labor are essential to the production of "wealth." Labor as the source of value becomes irrelevant in this "economic analysis" of pastoral systems, which then becomes amenable to the application of such capitalist notions as "saving and investment," "credit and indebtedness," and "financial management" (Schneider 1979:221–222; Barth 1973)—in other words, to the whole paraphenalia of bourgeois economic concepts and theory. This inevitably leads Schneider to a "formalist" position within bourgeois economic anthropology (LeClair and Schneider 1968; Schneider 1974). Cattle are even "hard currency," subject to such things as "inflationary conditions" (Schneider 1979:226). For Schneider, therefore, there is a confusion in the debates on capitalism in general that results "from the unquestioned association of capitalism with the exploitation of labor" (1979:226). As a result, there are both "pastoral capitalism" and "modern capitalism," each associated with a form of "egalitarianism and freedom."

It is not necessary here to go further into this curious argument about the specific economic correspondence of pastoralist and capitalist societies, and hence the assumed transformability of the former into the latter, save to note that in it certain historically produced categories are taken to be universal elements, such as the postulated relation between capitalism and freedom, as well as the yearning for both among all men and women, the achievement of which culminates in the end of history. But more pertinently, as Schneider himself points out, an increasing number of anthropological students of pastoral societies (I. M. Lewis, Spencer, Barth, Goldschmidt, among others) are beginning to view them as explicitly capitalist, or at least potentially capitalist, as these anthropologists search for a broader historical meaning in, and application of, their studies in bourgeois economic theory. While not assuming an "identity" or direct parallel between pastoralism and capitalism, John Galaty cautiously sums up this theoretical trend, while at the same time defending pastoralists against the charge of "irrationality" (Galaty 1981:18):

> It would appear that various concepts derived from the contemporary market domain and the study of change may be usefully applied to a "traditional" epoch and a subsistence oriented sector, previously considered to be marked by an essential "irrationality." The argument is made more powerful because it does not imply that pastoralists are simply one more case of "economic man," but that a specific production rationality characterizes the pastoral system, which combines dynamic maximal production and accumulation with societal control and regulation, and—as Bonte points out—avoids the development of indigenous forms of class by transforming individual maximization into societal accumulation through the mechanisms of exchange and redistribution.

The significance of Galaty's reference to Bonte will emerge in my later discussion of accumulation in pastoral societies, in the context of a review of Bonte's analysis of potential class formation in these societies. But in the meantime it should be noted that there are, among others, two central implications of the bourgeois position under discussion: that inequality and stratification occur independently of the exploitation of labor, by whatever means, such as capitalist relations of production, and that there must inevitably be some inherent "affinity" between these two capitalisms in terms of their other characteristics, presumably allowing a smooth transition from one to the other, disturbed only by the misguided efforts of

modern development strategists to convert pastoralists into cultivators. As Schneider himself notes (1979:227), "A surprising result
of this view of pastoral capitalism is that it seems to fit with what
Milton Friedman has been saying about capitalism and freedom for
some time."

♦ **II**   While oversimplifying a complex argument, it
might be said with some accuracy that the search for the bases of
power, control, and (sometimes) the identification of classes in pre-
capitalist societies hitherto described as "segmentary," "communal,"
or "classless" has led to a shift in emphasis from relations of production to relations of reproduction, or circulation and exchange.
There are obviously identifiable, if not entirely sound, reasons for
this. Claude Meillassoux elaborates (1978:136–137):

> The fact that the *means of production* observed in these societies are
> simple and accessible means that they cannot be used as a means of
> controlling the producers. In this way these societies differ fundamen-
> tally from societies with more complex technology where the material
> importance of the means of production provides its possessors with
> the most efficient means of exercising control over the producers. . . .
> The fact that at this stage it is impossible to control the means of pro-
> duction effectively and therefore impossible to control the producer
> through them, makes control over the producer himself essential, by
> the development of prior relations of a personal rather than a material
> nature.

I cannot help asking *why* there must be an "efficient means of
exercising control over the producers," and *to whom* control over the
producer is "essential," in a social formation without classes? At any
rate, since control over the producer is effected, according to Meillassoux, through the process of reproduction, it is argued that we
must concentrate upon the latter in order to see how the former is
achieved. In a later work, Meillassoux argues (1981:50) that in the
"domestic community . . . production and reproduction are achieved
through circulation which, as Marx has taught us, is only analytically
separable from the process of production."

Despite the allusion to Marx, there is an evident shift from the
relations of production to the relations of circulation and exchange
in the analysis of such communities with the purpose of searching
for the sources of power and control. This shift occurs precisely because some Marxist authors, such as Meillassoux and Pierre-Philippe
Rey, do not ask "what the real nature of economic determinism is"
(Bonte 1981:32). And Bonte concludes, "If the question is left unan-

swered, there is the ever-present temptation to postulate an external determination by the production forces, considered as autonomous and periodically entering into contradiction with the relations of production." None of these authors has escaped this temptation.[3]

Furthermore, if I may repeat, neither do Meillassoux and Rey ask the question of what the nature of control and power *is*, and *why* they should appear as immanent in a particular form in all social formations, unless one adopts a position similar to that of Balandier or Parsons? It should be noted here that Rey has developed his position from an earlier conclusion (with Georges Dupré, 1978) that, in precapitalist formations, the exploitative powers of seniors over juniors are a "class function," even if they are not indicators of classes *per se*, toward an analysis of lineage societies in which they represent a clear case of class formation (Rey 1979:41). Rey's position here is, of course, one resolution to the problem posed by Bonte, but not the question we are currently addessing, namely, how can the transformation from classless to class society be explained in terms of Marxist concepts? We should add for good measure that social formations in which the ideology of descent and kinship is dominant are different in certain crucial ways from those in which age-organization prevails over them, an issue with which I have dealt in some detail elsewhere (Rigby 1985) and to which I return.

Now, although we could in all this be said to occupy a position opposite to that expressed by Schneider, Barth, Lewis, *et al.*, and we are at the other pole in the sense that capitalism is here not seen as an immanent quality of all egalitarian human societies, we are nevertheless in the presence of a historical imminence, the universal rise of exploitative relations and hence the inevitability of class (and, eventually, the state) out of precapitalist formations of all kinds, irrespective of their relations with capitalism itself, feudalism, or other forms of class society. While not for a moment suggesting that historical processes go "backward" (although sometimes they presumably do, if one has a "backward" and a "forward"), I am somewhat worried by the lurking notions of the inherent, universal, and necessarily impending rise of exploitative relations, class formations, and the state, especially when these notions are not theorized or couched in explicitly evolutionary terms and, most particularly, when we are positing their eventual dissolution.

It is here that the very notions of "classless," "stateless," "acephalous," and even "precapitalist," societies (as opposed to states, class and capitalist societies, and those with heads) take on the obfuscating and mystifying functions of other, now largely discarded, dichotomous terms such as "primitive" (as opposed to "civilized"). I am not suggesting we abandon the former terms, but rather than illuminating the possible forms of politico-economic transformation, they make opaque the conditions under which such transformations may occur, and have historically occurred, *unless* the terms themselves are given the historical context and hence relativity that Marx gave to such basic ideas as "production," "circulation," and "commoditization" in order to de-mythologize them (Marx 1973). Let me pursue this line of thought a little before I turn to the main topic of class formation among Maasai pastoralists.

While risking the censure of Marxist purists such as Tom Brass (1984) who aspire to stand in judgment upon what is and what is not Marxist theory, I find Pierre Clastres's comment on some of these issues cogent, and I quote him at some length (Clastres 1977:159–169):[4]

> Primitive societies are societies without a State. This factual judgement, accurate in itself, actually hides an opinion, a value judgement that immediately throws doubt on the possibility of constituting political anthropology as a strict science. What the statement says, in fact, is that primitive societies are missing something—the state—that is essential to them, as it is to any other society: our own, for instance. Consequently, those societies are *incomplete*; they are not quite true societies—they are not *civilized*—their existence continues to suffer the painful experience of a lack—the lack of a State—which, try as they may, they will never make up. Whether clearly stated or not, that is what comes through in the explorers' chronicles and the work of researchers alike: society is inconceivable without the State; the State is the destiny of every society. . . . How, then, can one conceive of the very existence of primitive societies if not as the rejects of universal history, anachronistic relics of a remote age that everywhere else has been transcended? Here one recognizes ethnocentrism's other face, the conviction that history is a one-way progression, that every society is condemned to enter into that history and pass through the stages that lead from savagery to civilization. . . . One may ask what has kept the last of the primitive peoples as they are. . . . In reality, the same old evolutionism remains intact beneath the modern formulations.

The *history* of the rise of capitalism and imperialism and their impact upon the world is totally lacking in the formulations attacked by Clastres (cf. Wolf, 1982).

More important than the ethnocentrism (whose "closest accomplice is evolutionism") identifed by Clastres, however, are the epistemological consequences of such a position, foremost among which is the assumption of an untheorized evolutionism or a reductive essentialism, both unfortunately present also in some historical materialist writing. Among the latter, the essentialist notion of power raises its familiar head (Clastres 1977:10–11):

> At this level, the approach is twofold: first make an inventory of societies according to the greater or lesser proximity their type of power has to ours; then assert explicitly (as in the past) or implicitly (as at present) a *continuity* between these various forms of power. Because anthropology, following Lowie's example, has rejected the tenets of Morgan and Engels as simplistic, it is no longer able (at least where the political question is at issue) to express itself in sociological terms. But since, on the other hand, the temptation to continue thinking along the same lines is too strong, *biological* metaphors are invoked. Whence the vocabulary: embryonic, nascent, poorly developed, etc. . . . For what is an embryonic power, if not that which could and should *develop* to the adult state? And what is this adult state whose embryonic beginnings are discovered here and there? It is none other than the type of power to which the ethnologist is accustomed—that belonging to the culture which produces ethnologists, the West.

But more specifically in relation to pastoral formations and the capacity of the historical materialist problematic to explain their specificity, Bonte (1979) outlines a brilliant critique of both the environmental and functionalist determinations of ecological anthropology as well as the "evolutionist biases" in Marshall Sahlins's (1961) and P. J. Newcomer's (1972) re-analyses of Nuer social organization. On the former, Bonte concludes (1979:228), "In the last analysis, Sahlins does properly identify expansion as the circumstance under which segmentary lineage organization has a tendency to develop, but he makes the error of identifying this expansion as a feature of the organization itself. This error results from his unacceptable evolutionist approach."

But what *are* the conditions for the transformation of such societies according to Bonte? He proceeds from his critique of Sahlins (Bonte 1979:228):

> I have tried to show, in fact, that the development of this mode of social organization is the result of a process of *economic growth* in these societies where the community structure is based on "kinship fetishism," the role of kinship in production, etc. Far from being its cause, segmentary lineage organization is rather the form which the expansion takes: it transforms economic growth into a process of peripheral expansion which then blocks the development of the contradictions internal to the society. . . . The social changes produced by an eco-

nomic cause consequently take the form of structural changes within the kinship system itself.

It is not my intention here to examine Bonte's persuasive analysis of "kinship fetishism" among Nuer and Dinka and his parallel concept of "cattle fetishism" among Maasai and other East African pastoralists. But for the moment, unless we demonstrate the conditions under which "economic growth" (unequal accumulation of livestock) takes place, *or* justify some notion of a universal and directional evolution, how can such an analysis demonstrate the transition to class society from a previously classless condition without confusion, purely on grounds of a condition "internal" to the semi-pastoral or pastoral *praxis* of such social formations?

It could, of course, be argued that this "accumulation model" is valid as a consequence of pastoralism viewed as a "special pre-capitalist case," as I have already noted, in which over-production of livestock involves a surplus and leads to a "motive of production [that] resembles that of early capitalism, by aiming at production maximization through the most efficient use of labor and material resources" (Galaty 1981:17; cf. Spencer 1984, 1988). But we are now back in the bourgeois domain of Schneider *et al.*

The *theoretical* problem with such formulations, addressed elsewhere by Bonte (1981), is that the "overproduction" of livestock cannot occur, since livestock are the means of production and are not "produced" in the precapitalist context; they begin to be produced when they attain surplus value as *commodities* through the penetration of merchant capital in the context of pre-colonial and colonial trade. On this issue, both Galaty (1981:17) and Schneider (1979) and, surprisingly, Gavin Kitching's Marxist analysis (1980:203) confuse totally the notions of "exchange" and the appearance of "exchange value," which are theoretically quite distinct phenomena. André Bourgeot (1981) is therefore quite correct in assigning the rise of exchange value among Sahelian pastoralists to articulation of pastoral formations with mercantile capital ("commercial relations") and, eventually, capitalist relations of production.

The answers to these diverse and numerous problems, terminological and theoretical, are, or course, to be found in Marx and the critical nature of the historical materialist problematic itself, with particular reference to the need for placing all such concepts historically, and not as the offspring of some grand transformational schema that could lead us back to the eventual imminence, if not the immanence, of capitalism in *all* transformations, without the historical analysis of imperialism, primitive accumulation, and world domination of the capitalist system.

◆ III   I now deal with the term "precapitalist," since the types of historical transition we may discern in the Maasai social formation can clearly (if not in any easy chronological sense) be divided into "precapitalist" and "capitalist." The latter arises not only in the late nineteenth century (where the analysis in this chapter stops; see Chapters 4 and 7 for the recent past and the contemporary situation), with the imposition of colonial rule in Kenya and Tanganyika, but much earlier in the form of the peripheral (though not negligible) impact of merchant and usurers' capital. Merchant and usurers' capital are not merely stages in the avatar of the capitalist mode of production, but are also the necessary concomitants of the latter's reproduction, both "internally" at the center and "externally" at the periphery in advanced capitalism's articulation with precapitalist modes of production (Marx 1967, vol.2:111, vol.3:310).

Since Ilparakuyo and Maasai generally refused to become involved in wage labor during the periods discussed here, and decline to do so as far as they can even today (Rigby 1985), merchant capital plays a crucial role in the penetration of commodity relations in the Maasai social formation. In its historical form, "Merchants' capital is originally merely the intervening movements between extremes which it does not control, and between premises which it does not create" (Marx 1967, vol.3:330). But as commoditization increases, merchant capital makes certain forms of production dependent upon it, when "commercial profit not only appears as outbargaining and cheating, but also largely originates from them. Merchants' capital, when it holds a position of dominance, stands everywhere for a system of robbery" (Marx 1967, vol.3:331). Some elements of merchants' capital thence are transformed into usurers' capital "as the characteristic form of interest-bearing capital [corresponding] to the predominance of small-scale production of self-employed peasant and small master craftsman" (Marx 1967, vol.3:594), represented frequently in the contemporary Maasai case not only by petty traders but also by internationally financed "development schemes" and local ruling classes (see Hedlund 1979; Mandel 1962:84n).

By the precapitalist mode of production of Maasai and other pastoralists in East Africa, therefore, I mean precisely that mode of production that existed before the introduction of capitalist relations of production, the latter preceded by, and still embedded in, merchant and usurers' capital, elements of which still exist and operate in the articulation of the Maasai social formation with its contemporary national and global political economies. All of these elements form the essential conditions for the historical and contemporary articulation of this mode of production with modern peripheral capitalism, which still includes the on-going process of primitive accumulation (Marx 1967, vol.1; compare Freund 1984:112).

Thus "precapitalist," as far as the Maasai are concerned, implies both that historical articulations have occurred and still occur with other precapitalist social formations, as well as that the penetration of various "capitals" is an inescapable element in its continued reproduction and politico-economic transformation. Hence, when I speak of precapitalist Maasai society as "classless," I mean it only in the historical sense, in which it is demonstrable (and this is the central point) that the contradictions that existed in this social formation were not class contradictions and did not have "class functions." It also implies that these contradictions do not necessarily arise out of the ideological "inversion" of the real relations of production represented by the alleged fetishization of either cattle or kinship, as suggested by Bonte, *unless* commoditization (a crucial factor in the development of capitalism) has already appeared; and the latter must be historically demonstrated.

Furthermore, there are few if any historical indications for assuming that there were in precapitalist Maasai society any contradictions "inherent" to the dominant mode of production that would have led automatically to the formation of classes and the rise of the state, independent of *some* external or exogenous factors. I have argued elsewhere (Rigby 1985:22) that any such transformational model is either "over-structuralist," in which case the imminence of transformation lies in the immanence of structure, or "under-historized," in that the analysis projects back onto the history of the precapitalist formation the contradictions apparent in an already partially transformed Maasai social formation, as in the work of Hans Hedlund (1979). Both approaches result in an inability to periodize phases of historical change for pastoral societies, a task I begin in this chapter. In fact, one of the few points upon which I can agree totally with Barry Hindess's and Hirst's study of precapitalist modes of production is their contention that there can be no *general theory* of the transformation of modes of production unless some overall evolutionary schema is added (Hindess and Hirst 1975:320 *et passim*; see also Hirst 1967). If this is so, there cannot be a *general theory* of class formation and the advent of the state as historical processes.

This brings me to my next and final conceptual critique: the notion of the "internal" and "external" (or "endogenous" and "exogenous") sources of historical transformation.[5] It is my contention that not only are these notions of the sources of change generated by the functionalist problematic and systems theory, but also that they are non-viable as operational tools of analysis and specifically anti-historical (and historical materialist) in their thrust. They assume that social formations can be isolated from one another for specific and lengthy periods of time, which is historically impossible to demonstrate in most cases, particularly in areas like eastern Africa, and/or that certain forms of historical influence and articulation are less crucial for change (or "development" and "progress") than others, which must be historically demonstrated and not assumed. I develop these points in relation to Ilparakuyo and Maasai history and the rise of the great prophets.

◆ IV   In grappling with the contradictions and conditions of transformation in the Maasai social formation, I make two basic theoretical assumptions derived from a certain interpretation of the historical materialist problematic, assumptions that I cannot defend in detail here (see Rigby 1985). The first is that, beginning with the *Formen*, Marx established a theoretical domain in which there are several paths of transformation of communal forms of production with the consequently various types of class formation (Marx 1973:472–485 *et passim*). One of these is the appearance of classical slave society; another is labelled the Asiatic mode of production. As Bonte notes concisely (1978:175), "Marx also considered a third way in which the communal structure could be transformed, setting out certain characteristics of this transformation in his study of *Germanic society*," based upon what may be termed the Germanic mode of production.

Secondly, for reasons I have elaborated in considerable detail elsewhere (Rigby 1985:15–19, 97–98, 100–101, 139, *et passim*) and to which I return below, the Germanic mode of production is characterized by the dominance of ideological structures (descent, kinship, age-organization, religion, and ritual), this dominance being a condition of its reproduction and transformation by whatever means (Marx 1967, vol.1:81–82; Althusser and Balibar 1970; Lefébure 1979).

I have also stated elsewhere, again in agreement with Bonte (Rigby 1985:16), that in its application to this social formation "the core concept in the utility of the Germanic mode of production is its categorization of the *domestic* and *community* levels of the relations of production and their articulation, and it is here that both its strength and weakness lie." In this articulation, Bonte has seen both the locus and the resolution of contradictions generated by un-equal accumulation at the level of real appropriation (the "domes-tic" level), as well as the basis for change in these societies (Bonte 1979:231–232, 1981:37, 41, 42). In the case of segmentary lineage societies, already mentioned, the community level of the relations of production is distorted or inverted by the fetishism of kinship, leading either to aggressive expansion or change into class relations; in the case of East African pastoralists, where lineage organization is subordinated to age-set organization, the community level of pro-duction relations is inverted and mystified by the fetishism of cattle (Bonte 1975, 1981).

According to Bonte, then, although politico-economic change occurs at the communal level, the process is generated at the level of real appropriation, where unequal accumulation occurs. Either this unequal accumulation is resolved at the domestic level by re-distribution or the resulting contradictions are "exported" to the periphery, where it results in expansion or transformation and the possible formation of classes. The dynamic is, therefore, located in pastoral *praxis* itself, while the reproduction of the community as a whole is effected through the distortions of alienated labor and the fetishism of kinship and cattle and hence the dominance of "reli-gion," represented in East Africa by the prophets, who sometimes assume political power and constitute an incipient class.

This is an excellent analysis, insofar as it places the conditions of transformation squarely in the production process and therefore differs from the approach of Meillassoux and Rey, already outlined. But it leaves out of the explanation a number of other possible contra-dictions and historical dimensions of the Maasai social formation: In particular, the changing role of the prophets, kinship, descent, and age-set organization remain relatively unexplained and subsumed under the dichotomy between household (domestic) appropriation and community appropriation of the means of production, the former "real" and the latter "fictitious." This is a "structural dichotomy," and Bonte himself puts it this way (1978:196):

> We can now conclude this study of the structural properties of the social and economic systems of the Nilo-Hamites [*sic*]. The analysis has gradually expanded to the point where it reaches out to beyond the confines of nomadic pastoral societies and calls for the study of neighboring societies. This digression has allowed me to present some ideas on the possible transformations of these structures over time and the emergence of class relations. . . . *The laws of structural transfor-mations and the conditions which they determine appear as the very laws of historical development.*

Bonte's call for the "study of neighboring societies" is congruent with my argument for the study of the history of Ilparakuyo and Maasai relations with their neighbors as a necessary element in any understanding of the transformation of these societies, and I deal with some aspects of this for Ilparakuyo elsewhere (Rigby 1985:48–66 *et passim*).

I now proceed to an outline of an alternative conceptualization for Ilparakuyo Maasai that, while not in disagreement with Bonte's, identifies a number of contradictions and tensions that are historically generated and that his analysis does not address, and that also attempts to dissolve the theoretical dichotomy noted above.

✦ **V**   Given the fact that pastoralism, closely allied or alternating with cultivation and gathering and hunting (as Bonte rightly indicated in 1978), has existed in the areas of East Africa now occupied by Ilparakuyo and Maasai, and other pastoralists, for at least four thousand years, and possibly as early as 7,000 B.P. (Robertshaw and Collett 1983a:284–295, 1983b; Marshall and Robertshaw 1982), the presently established historiography of Maasai social formations is relatively short. We can, however, arrive at a number of reasonable propositions.

Oral history, written records, and evidence from linguistic sources and archaeological materials suggest that a "Maasai" historiography can be roughly classified into four major phases: up to circa 1640; 1640–1890; 1890–1960; and 1960 to the present. The reasons for, characteristics of, and utility embodied in these phases are only briefly outlined here, in an attempt to hypothesize the historical processes giving rise to the various contradictions manifested in these social formations.

For the first period, up to about 1640, linguistic and archaeological evidence suggests that *Maa-speaking* peoples, whose economic practices ranged from mixed farming to almost total dependence upon pastoralism, have existed in at least some of the areas occupied by them in the late nineteenth century for roughly the past one thousand years. "Proto-Maasaian" precursors of the contemporary Maasai language were influencing, and being influenced by, other southern Nilotic and Bantu languages during the first millenium A.D.; and there may have been two initial expansions of Maasaian peoples into the areas they now occupy during this period (Ehret 1971:52–54, 76 *et passim*). Chinese sources of the ninth century indicate that "Maasai-like" peoples inhabited the present-day interior of eastern Africa, practicing pastoralism associated with certain customs characteristic of contemporary Maasai pastoralists (Duyven-dak 1949:15; Chittick 1975:21; Wheatley 1975:94; Jacobs 1968:22–23). These include living entirely on milk, meat, and blood drawn from living cattle. The Chinese text from Tuan Ch'eng-shih, who died in A.D. 863, reads as follows (Duyvendak 1949:13–14; Freeman-Grenville 1962:8; Jacobs 1968:22–23):

> The land of Po-pa-li is in the south-western Ocean. The people do not eat any of the five grains [cereals] but only meat: more frequently even they prick a vein of one of their own oxen, mix the blood with milk and eat it raw. Their women are clean and well-behaved. The [neighboring] inhabitants kidnap them, and if they sell them to foreign merchants, they fetch several times their price which they would fetch at home. The products of the country are ivory and ambergris. When Persian traders wish to enter this country, they form a caravan of several thousand men and present them with strips of cloth. All, whether old or young, draw blood and swear an oath, and then only do they trade their goods. From of old, this country has not been subject to any foreign power. . . . They have twenty myriads of foot-soldiers. The Arabs are continually making raids on them.

The identification of these "blood-drinking" pastoralists is not easy (Wheatley 1975:101–102) and although Paul Wheatley suggests that the best candidates may be Galla, he admits that the drinking of fresh blood among the Galla is "by no means universal"; he adds correctly that they were almost certainly not Somali (compare Lewis 1955). The possibility of their being Maasai or a related group remains strong, even if these written records and other early references are admittedly circumstantial. Taken with the linguistic evidence, how-ever, the existence of a Maasai social formation in eastern Africa for approximately a thousand years appears to be a reasonable assump-tion; that it has existed for the past three hundred to three hundred and fifty years as evidenced by oral sources is beyond doubt.

As important as this is for establishing a relatively early Maa-sai presence (a point to which I return), there is also strong evidence for the penetration of Chinese trade relations with the East African coast from the seventh century A.D. (Wheatley 1975:104). And much earlier, trading between Egypt and Rhapta on the East African coast (a "metropolis," probably on the Pangani River, south of contempo-rary Tanga on the northern Tanzanian coast [Strandes 1961:357]) is noted in the *Periplus of the Erythrean Sea*, written in Alexandria between A.D. 76 and 100.[6] The *Periplus* also mentions a great "snow mountain" inland from Rhapta, almost certainly Kilimanjaro, which lies in the heart of contemporary Maasailand (Mathew 1975:155; Freeman-Grenville 1962:1–2).

But apart from the strong linguistic and circumstantial documentary evidence already adduced, a further source for confirmation of an established Maasai pastoral formation, or formations, prior to 1640 is to be found not only in Maasai oral history, but also in the histories of neighboring peoples who had regular or intermittent contact with them. Among numerous recent reports of these histories, one or two examples must suffice.

Bethwell Ogot places early contact between southern Luo migrations and an already established Maasai people prior to the later sixteenth century (1571–1598 +/– 46: Ogot 1967:28, 73 *et passim*). And although suggesting Maasai movements in conflict with the linguistic evidence, S. C. ole Lang'at (1969:78, 81) presents strong evidence for Kipsigis contact with various sections of pastoral Maasai from the first quarter of the seventeenth century.

These and numerous other citations leave little doubt about the major point I wish to make here: that Maasai social formations committed to a relatively unique form of pastoral *praxis* were well established in various parts of eastern Africa by the middle of the seventeenth century at the very latest. Maasai traditional history definitely states (in a number of mutually consistent narratives) that the social institutions and structures characteristic of their contemporary mode of production and social formation were in place *before* the advent of the prophetic lineage, the Inkidong'i of the Ilaiser clan. The first great prophet (*oloiboni kitok*) is said to have been "found" by members of this clan in about 1640, earlier than the earliest *remembered* age-set (*olporror*), but not before the establishment of the age-set system itself (Fosbrooke 1948:3).[7] In fact, given the integration of pastoral *praxis*, descent, and the system of age-sets (Rigby 1985), it is an eminently reasonable assumption that age-set organization existed prior to the mid-seventeenth century, when the institution of the great prophets arose.

For present purposes, however, the rise of the great prophets, or *iloibonok kituaak*, in the mid-seventeenth century is associated with extensive movement and contact of peoples in the East African interior, dating from at least the fifteenth century and undoubtedly associated with the penetration of merchants and traders from the coast. Roland Oliver states (1963:171): "The first fact which becomes plain from an examination of the traditional evidence is that East Africa has seen within the last 500 years population movements on a scale which have not [*sic*] occurred in Europe since the Dark ages, in the Middle East since the coming of the Turks, in South Asia since the Mogul invasions."

These vast population movements, conflicts, and disruptions

characterizing the East African interior from the late fifteenth century are associated with other significant events, events that led to a peak of external intrusions into the area from the coast as well from other parts of the interior in the first half of the seventeenth century. I have already noted that Persian and Arab trade links with the East African coast extend over a very long period; these links undoubtedly had a major impact upon the peoples of the interior. By the time the Portuguese arrived in force in East Africa in the early sixteenth century, the penetration of merchant capital already influenced not only the production of commodities on the coast but also the extensive intrusions for trade commodities in the interior of the whole area (Swai 1985; cf. Strandes 1961:95). Conflict between Portuguese and Arabs, complicated by Turkish imperialist aspirations from the middle of the sixteenth century, exacerbated the situation on the coast, and almost certainly increased efforts to exploit the interior through sheer plunder as well as trade in commodities, including slaves.[8]

Virtually the whole of the seventeenth century on the East African coast was a period of struggle for control between local peoples, Arabs, and Portuguese, resulting in the eventual expulsion of the latter. They did not give up their efforts at domination, however, until the late eighteenth century, when their influence contracted toward their eventual colonial possession, Mozambique.

It seems inconceivable that Ilparakuyo and other Maasai sections could have remained isolated from these sometimes massive intrusions of violence and mercantile capital and their impact upon the processes and relations of production in eastern Africa generally (see Kjekshus 1977 for the latter part of this period). An already established pastoral social formation, with extensive ties with other peoples in the area, must have been seriously "engaged" one way or another in these disruptions. As Alan Jacobs notes, it is probable that, because Arab traders had been plundering Maasai for slaves and other goods from the first millennium A.D., the coastal Arab rulers subsequently invented the "myth" of the ferocious Maasai to keep later European intruders (British, American, German, French) of the nineteenth century out of the areas of their lucrative exploitation of the interior (Jacobs 1968:22, 28; 1979).[9]

Furthermore, drastic movements "within" Maasai social formations can be attributed to the period between A.D. 1600 and 1700, perhaps generating the need for transforming the minor prophets and diviners into politically significant great prophets, with their own sub-clan and lineage and heightened ideology of unilineal descent, commencing during this period. This interpretation and periodiza-

tion is strongly supported by Maasai oral history and further linguistic evidence concerning, for example, the formation of the Ilparakuyo section of pastoral Maasai from Iloogolala elements at this
time (Vossen 1977:10–11; Rigby 1985:83–85).

◆ **VI**   It would appear reasonable, then, to postulate
that during the "second phase" of suggested Maasai historiography,
from about 1640 to 1890, the increasing intrusion of merchant capital
(Arab, Portuguese, and later British, French, German, and American)
would have influenced production relations among most East African peoples in the direct path of these trading and raiding routes, as
well as having a considerable impact upon their relationships with
each other.[10] That Maasai (and other East Africans) retained their
"integrity" as a social formation, or series of social formations, during this period, let alone during the third phase of direct imperialist
control (1890–1960), is remarkable and needs more explanation than
is possible here. But it is precisely at this point that more detailed
Maasai oral history, as well as the rise of a new and important source
of contradiction and conflict within their social formation, became
apparent.

Given the later "politicization" of the prophets and their rise
to distinctiveness of descent as well as "greatness" (*enkitoo*) when
they *became* the "great prophets," it is also reasonable to surmise
that, even if they had existed before 1640, their political importance
arose at that time and resulted in an unusually elaborate (for Maasai)
genealogy (Fosbrooke 1948:12; Berntsen 1979; Rigby 1985). Their incipient "class functions," if this be the case, would also have become
apparent at this stage as a consequence of the new contradictions
that arose in the conditions necessary for reproducing the Maasai
social formation as a whole. But these contradictions can hardly be
ascribed to any one fact, either internal or external to the social
formation, such as the unequal accumulation of livestock at the domestic level, or the penetration of merchant capital and consequent
partial commoditization; all are present and historically variable.

The increasingly significant functions of the great prophets
from the seventeenth to the late nineteenth centuries can be seen as
a *partial* response to changes and disruptions caused by these multiple historical factors, and the intermittent necessity to co-ordinate
military power; but they also transform, emphasize, or weaken existing structures of reproduction of the social formation itself, such as
descent ties and age-set organization, introducing yet further new
forms of contradiction. Classes, however, do not really begin to ap-

pear in the Maasai social formations until the late colonial period (phase 3) and are not consolidated until post-independence policies of rural development intervene in both Kenya and Tanzania, but most particularly in the former (phase 4).[11]

With this complicating arrival of influential prophets upon the scene in the middle of the seventeenth century, the balance established in pastoral society between descent, kinship, and age-set organization is disturbed, and the Ilparakuyo and other Maasai social formations can be conceived as reproducing themselves upon at least three "levels," which require more elaboration than is possible here. Some further comment, however, is essential.

The first level is that of homesteads, or domestic groups, where "real appropriation" takes place in terms of control of the major means of production, the herd, and the process of production (or milk, meat, butter-fat, etc.)—that is, the immediate reproduction of the units of production through pastoral *praxis*. Domestic groups, however, are not isolated from each other, correct pastoral *praxis* being dependent upon several types of linkages (descent, kinship, age-set ties) among cooperating households. Ideological control is expressed in patrilineal descent (father/son-daughter) relations, inheritance, and ties of matrifiliation (mother/child). The appropriation of the labor of juniors by seniors and the conditions of cooperation are generated through descent as well as affinal and other kinship links.

The crucial (but not final) ritual for the transformation of young men and women through circumcision and partial clitoridectomy is performed at this level, and the descent-derived authority of a father over his children is replicated as well as contradicted in the age-set system by two factors: the placement of children in the alternate (or subsequent) age-set below the father, and the linking of alternate age-sets by the ritual firestick bond (*olpiron*, pl. *ilpironito*; see Rigby 1985).[12] The replication here is that, within the local community, and to some extent outside it, all fathers can control and appropriate the labor of their circumcised and initiated sons as well as their sons' age-mates. The contradiction lies in the fact that sons can appeal to the age-set organizational structure of spokesmen (*ilaiguenak*) and meetings or conclaves (*inkiguenaritin*) within and between local age-sets in case of conflicts or unreasonable demands placed upon their labor or loyalty by their fathers or other older kinsmen, taking the matter outside the purview of kinship and the ideology of descent.

Unilineal descent ties, however, classically emphasize the identification of alternate generations, linking grandparents and grandchildren; and Ilparakuyo and Maasai are no exception to this universal rule. Age-set alliances split generations in half, being roughly fifteen years rather than thirty years in span (Rigby 1985; Jacobs 1965a). While age-set organization thus enhances father/son ties through the *olpiron* sponsor, it weakens lineal descent allegiances of longer span. This facilitates the rapid segmentation of patri-central domestic groups, allowing a mobility of production units so crucial to good pastoral *praxis* (Jacobs 1965a, 1965b; see Chapter 7 below). These contradictory elements are, however, a primary source of tension in these social formations, a contradiction that is not internal merely to this level of production relations, since it is exploited at other levels, and now increasingly by those involved in the contemporary importation of commodity relations.

The second level upon which the relations of production are reproduced is that of local territorial sections (*iloshon*, sing. *olosho*) comprising various "localities" of frequently mobile domestic groups, in which the units of production at the first level have communal rights of appropriation of pasture, water, and salt. Maasai oral history points to the relative instability of these territorial sections, the increasing rate of conflict among them from the seventeenth century onward (culminating in severe violence in the nineteenth century), and the demise or absorption of some others during this phase (Fosbrooke 1948; Jacobs 1965a; Ehret 1971; Vossen 1977; Rigby 1985). Throughout Maasai history it has also been recognized that some sections are more "important" than others, demographically, politically, ritually, and militarily (Jacobs 1965a; Galaty 1981, 1983). Sections sometimes provide the local base for particular age-set rituals, but they have no particular relation to Maasai descent groups, which are dispersed. Although the appropriation of the labor of junior warriors (*ilmurran*) by elders usually occurs in small localities, their collective labor in terms of the defense of the sections' resources (wells, grazing, and so on) may occasionally be appropriated at this level.

Territorial sections thus cut across both descent and age-set ties, providing another locus for possible contradiction. As we have seen, according to Bonte it is basically the contradiction that arises between these two levels, the domestic and the community relations of production, that either allows in the best case the resolution of conflicts over discrepancies in accumulation of livestock at the domestic level or is the locus of unresolvable conflicts resulting in territorial expansion, or, in the worst case, the generation of class functions and the possible formation of classes (Bonte 1978, 1979, 1981). The very instability of territorial sections supports this conclusion; but if class functions take the form of the appropriation of labor of juniors by seniors, then another historical element needs to be added.

This leads to the third level of the productive relations, in which commoditization (and hence fetishization) may occur, and probably has occurred historically: the extra-territorial dimensions of age organization in both ritual and military contexts, in which a close relationship arose historically between the great prophets, the junior warriors, and their mothers (who play a crucial role in the *eunoto* ceremony that transforms junior warriors into seniors). The point that must be emphasized here is that this level becomes more prominent at a particular historical conjuncture, dating from the mid-seventeenth century, a time that coincides with the increasing penetration of merchant capital and early commodity relations.

This level of productive relations also varies over time, rising and declining in significance, with the political functions of the great prophets reaching a peak in the late nineteenth century with the penetration of German and British imperialist forces into Maasailand. The "inversion" of the social relations of production through religion (dominated at the communal level by the great prophets) and the fetishism of livestock postulated by Bonte is therefore not "inherent" to the system of pastoral *praxis*, but occurs for specific and identifiable reasons at a particular historical conjuncture: the entry of merchant capital and some specific forms of commodity relations into a specific type of social formation.

But for present purposes, it is important to note that the rise of the great prophets has a contradictory impact upon the relations of production and appropriation of labor at the first two levels. On the one hand, the ideology of descent is re-emphasized by the exclusive control and inheritance of major religious power and ritual authority exercised by the Inkidong'i lineage of the Ilaiser clan (Ilwarakishu among Ilparakuyo) (see Berntsen 1979). On the other hand, the great prophets establish their control by directly and increasingly appropriating the labor of junior warriors through frequent and large gifts of livestock by the latter to them, or indirectly through the appropriation of wives without the transfer of bridewealth or other gifts and services entailed by marriage. The basis of the power and authority that allows this approration by the great prophets lies in their historically necessitated control over the major age-set rituals, as well as their ritual blessings which must be conferred upon military activities or livestock raids by the junior *ilmurran*, without which their success is thrown into serious jeopardy.[13]

Thus the "control" of the elders at levels one and two over the labor of their sons and coeval junior warriors through descent ties and the local age-set structure may be ideologically strengthened by the resurgence of descent ideology, weak at the best of times; yet these very "sons" and their age-mates are committed to extra-territorial activities through which their labor and surplus value are appropriated, activities that are historically essential for the reproduction of the social formation as a whole, given the prevailing politico-economic environment. This is the locus of at least one of the major historically determined contradictions in Maasai social formations, leading to competition over control of labor and the appropriation of surplus value, rather than any postulated ahistorical (because "cyclical") process of unequal accumulation between production units and the unhistoricized fetishization of cattle.

To conclude, then, at all these levels, and varying over time, the two basic ideological principles of descent and age-set organization operate as relations of production, dominant and competing, but jointly ensuring the continuity of pastoral *praxis* and the reproduction of the relations of production at all levels, especially in times of crisis generated by the total politico-economic context of imperialism, colonialism, the post-colonial state, and neo-colonialism and their local entities, in historical sequence. There are contradictory and competing demands upon the labor of juniors by seniors at local and extra-local levels, as well as within and between the real production units (households) and the local community. The labor of *ilmurran*, uncircumcised youths and girls, but particularly the former, is not appropriated solely for the reproduction of the herd, but for the reproduction of the community at large.

These are the many-faceted contradictions encountered by the penetration of merchant capital from the seventeenth to the nineteenth centuries, and colonial control and capitalist production relations in the twentieth century. If class and class function relations had been of the simple dichotomous kind sought by some historical materialist theorists, the collapse of Maasai social formations into commoditization and wage labor would have been much quicker and easier. It is the very complexity of the contradictions that existed, became modified, and were born in the past five hundred or so years, becoming even more complex since the seventeenth century, that has enabled the Maasai social formations to resist, until very recently, the descent into, rather than the development of, class relations. And it is this recent history that must be the subject of further elaboration in what follows.

4   Ideology, Religion, and Capitalist Penetration

Erisio olporror o enkai.
Equal are the age-set
and God.

◆   I base my argument in this chapter about Ilparakuyo and Maasai ideology and, if you will, religion (although the
need for this concept as a distinct entity becomes increasingly slight)
upon the assumption that there can be no general theory of ideology
(and hence no general theory of religion), but only a general theory of
the conditions for the production of particular ideologies, in specific
social formations with particular modes of production. In a stimu-
lating critique of the sociological theories of Durkheim, Weber, Parsons, and phenomenology, Mark Harvey (1972:110) comments that
"the abstract character of the knowledge [produced by these theo-
ries] varies, while remaining equally abstract. Durkheim abstracts
common features from objective facts. The result is the supposed
universality of the lowest common denominator, the distinction between the sacred and the profane, which has no real existence outside
Durkheim's head." We have, it seems, returned to Marx's critical
comment upon moving from "the imagined concrete towards ever
thinner abstractions." But Harvey's critique, then, is not about the
ideological content of bourgeois social theorizing. It is rather "a critique of the conditions of production of that ideology" (1972:111). It
is from such a position that I wish to proceed.

Because I contend that religion is a specific form of ideology,
produced in definite historical conditions, I must commence with
a further brief discussion of the notion of ideologies in historical
materialism. This, of course, is an enormous question in relation to
which a great many recent contributions have been made and contro-

versies prosecuted. But it is possible here to make a few preliminary
points. Any simplistic view that ideology is a mere superstructural
"reflection" of economic relations belongs not to historical materialism but to bourgeois economic theory, or a vulgar materialist reading
of Marx. Gramsci put the point succinctly (1971:407):

> The claim presented as an essential postulate of historical material-
> ism, that every fluctuation of politics and ideology can be presented
> and expounded as an immediate expression of the [economic] struc-
> ture, must be contested in theory as primitive infantilism, and com-
> bated in practice with the authoritative testimony of Marx, the author
> of concrete political and historical works.[1]

Williams (1977) outlines three "common versions" of the concept of ideology in Marxist theory:

> (i) a system of beliefs characteristic of a particular class or *group*;
> (ii) a system of illusory beliefs—false ideas or false consciousness—
> which can be contrasted with true or scientific knowledge;
> (iii) the general process of the production of meanings and ideas.

The second of these notions, of ideology as false consciousness,
is the one usually attributed by bourgeois commentators to Marx and
Engels; and in superficial reading, it is undoubtedly true of some of
their earlier writings (as in *The German Ideology* of 1846). Williams
brilliantly shows (1977:56 *et seq.*), however, that this derogatory and
ultimately reductionist view of the nature of ideological production
has its roots not in Marx and Engels, but, rather, in the reactionary
and distorted visions of eighteenth- or nineteenth-century "men of
action" (such as Napoleon) who wished to identify ideology (a term
coined by Destutt de Tracy in the late eighteenth century) with "im-
practical theory" or "abstract illusion." Marx and Engels's position
in *The German Ideology* can be seen, in historical perspective, as a
"temporary surrender to the cynicism of 'practical men' and, even
more, to the abstract empiricism of a version of 'natural science'"
(Williams 1977:60).

It is in *Capital* that a broader idea of ideology, as represented
in Williams's versions (i) and (iii) above, appears. Here, Marx sees
ideology as "consciousness and its products," which

> are always, though in variable forms, parts of the material social pro-
> cess itself: whether as what Marx called the necessary element of
> "imagination" in the labor process; or as the necessary conditions of
> associated labor, in language and in practical ideas of relationship; or,
> which is so often and significantly forgotten, in the real processes—
> all of them physical and material, most of them manifestly so—which

are masked or idealized as "consciousness and its products" but which, when seen without illusions, are themselves necessarily social material activities (Williams 1977:61–62).

More recent formulations (in what Williams calls the "other tendencies in twentieth-century concepts of ideology"), based on this later Marx and Engels, are common to contemporary Marxist theory as well as revolutionary *praxis*. For example, Moskvichov (1974:65–66) notes that "it would be wrong to think that Marx and Engels put ideology on a par with false consciousness (this is precisely the interpretation of ideology that bourgeois sociologists ascribe to Marx and Engels . . .)," and he adds that Lenin "terms scientific socialism a proletarian ideology" (cf. Williams 1977:69).

Again, Althusser, who has had an enormous impact upon theorizing within what may be called "structuralist Marxism" and "Marxist anthropology" (Kahn and Llobera 1981:274 *et passim*), rejects any simplistic concept of "consciousness" and develops a materialist conception of ideology from his and Etienne Balibar's reading of *Capital* (Althusser 1971:162–186; see also Feuchtwang 1975:67–72). Significant and cogently argued as it is, however, Althusser's contribution to the theorization of ideologies has two implications that reduce its value for my present purposes. The first is his contention that "ideology has no history" (1971:159–162); and the second is the equally contentious issue of whether or not ideologies are confined only to a theory of hierarchical social systems (Althusser 1971:152; Feuchtwang 1975:70). In *The German Ideology*, Marx and Engels do suggest that "ideologists" as a class (that is, priests) appear only when "the division of material and spiritual labor takes place" (Marx and Engels 1976:44–45). But they do not claim that ideologies themselves are confined to class systems, and such an assumption would return us to the reductionist position we have abandoned—that all ideology is false consciousness.[2]

Nevertheless, Althusser realizes that "Marx's materialism precisely is not a fundamental categorical separation of thought from material human being" (Feuchtwang 1975:67). But before we proceed to the historical case of Maasai resistance to capitalist penetration, I must, as I have noted, strengthen the dimension of *praxis* and its relation to ideology.

In relation to practical activity, the practice of "transforming the world" that is the basis of all production, theoretical or ideological consciousness is dialectically linked to the form of the social relations through which *praxis* is achieved. This link, itself dependent upon mode of production and social formation, may be contradictory or complementary, politically and morally active or passive. The crucial importance of this point leads me to quote somewhat extensively from Gramsci's commentary upon one aspect of his notion of hegemony (Gramsci 1971:333):

> [Man's] theoretical consciousness can indeed be historically in opposition to his activity. One might almost say that he has two theoretical consciousnesses (or one contradictory consciousness): one which is implicit in his activity and which in reality unites him with all his fellow workers in the practical transformation of the real world; and one, superficially explicit or verbal, which he has inherited from the past and uncritically absorbed. But this verbal conception is not without consequences. It holds together a specific group, it influences moral conduct and direction of will, with varying efficacity but often powerfully enough to produce a situation in which the contradictory state of consciousness does not permit of any action, any decision or any choice, and produces a condition of moral and political passivity. Critical understanding of self takes place therefore through a struggle of political "hegemonies" and of opposing direction, first in the ethical field and then in that of politics proper, in order to arrive at a higher level of one's own conception of reality.

This "critical understanding of self" and "one's own conception of reality" are parallel to Althusser's claim that "ideology interpellates individuals as subjects" (1971:170). But more than this, ideologies allow subjects to *act upon* the "social conditions of existence," and thereby forge the necessary link between ideology and *praxis*. In this link, the role of language and "popular culture" (as represented in folk-tales, myths, etc.: see Davidson 1984), as well as that of ritual and ceremonial, is crucial for our present purposes of understanding the conditions necessary for the production and reproduction of the Ilparakuyo and Maasai social formations, especially in the context of the violent intrusion of colonialism and peripheral capitalism.

I have elsewhere demonstrated the unity of theory and practice, the historical emergence of a "practical ideology," among Ilparakuyo and Maasai (Rigby 1985:4, 92–122), which created the conditions for a "struggle of hegemonies" to arise during imperialist and missionary penetration. Although a fuller and more detailed examination of language, ritual, ceremonial, and the wider "popular culture" must await another time and place (see also Chapter 6 below), my earlier discussion of practical ideology and hegemonic struggle must be taken in a slightly different direction here, in which I must return to Gramsci and some of the theoretical issues already mentioned.

◆ I   In most of the discussions of pastoralist "resistance to change," and by a curious tautology, "change" is first
delineated in terms of the penetration of capitalist relations of production, such as the reputed benefits of wage labor and commodity
consumption, and their associated ideologies such as Christianity or
Islam (although they are obviously not identified in this manner).
Then, if Ilparakuyo and Maasai (or others) refuse to engage in these
"benefits of civilization" by going to school or working for whites
or other Africans, they are said to be resistant to change *per se*, and
are called "conservative" (Rigby 1985:92–122). "Factors inhibiting
change" must therefore be sought, and examples of this approach
abound (Schneider 1959; Dyson-Hudson 1962; Gulliver 1969; cf.
Rigby 1969b). A well-stated recent example is R. L. Tignor (1976:73):

> Among Maasai, the warrior class [*sic*] played an instrumental role in
> inhibiting change. In other societies, especially among Kikuyu, young
> men of warrior age were often the first school-goers and the first wage-
> laborers. . . . Young Kikuyu were recruited by chiefs and formed a para-
> administrative and military organization essential to early colonial
> change. But in Maasailand warriors were disinclined to go to school.
> They engaged only in a few highly specialized and well paid types of
> wage laboring, and they did not become coercive agents for colonial
> chiefs. On the contrary, they inhibited the development of a collabo-
> rating spirit in their society. By retaining a strong sense of their own
> identity and *esprit de corps*, the Maasai warriors were a significant
> element in blocking colonial change.[3]

While the overall thrust of this statement is correct, there is
considerable evidence to indicate that a few Maasai young men in
both German and British areas of colonization were open to experi-
menting with Christianity and its associated "educational" activities
(Rigby 1985; Sena 1986); some of Tignor's other excellent insights
are developed later, perhaps in directions with which he would not
agree. All I wish to point out here is: how "change" and "colonial
change" are equated by Tignor, and both are deemed to be identical
with "modernization"; and how we are left in the dark as to *how* and
why Maasai warriors retained a "strong sense of their own identity
and *esprit de corps*." If, on the other hand, we contend as I do that
resistance to the penetration of capitalist production relations and
alien ideologies by a precapitalist social formation is also, and necessarily, a form of change and transformation (including a "struggle of
hegemonies"), if not a more important one, then we are much more
effectively enjoined to look for the forms of *praxis* and ideology characteristic of Ilparakuyo and Maasai, which generate historical con-

frontation rather than collaboration, as Tignor rightly calls it. And this confrontation may be not only or even primarily a military one but a continuous struggle for identity and social reproduction that began prior to real domination of colonialism and continues after formal release from it.

Among Ilparakuyo and Maasai, these elements or factors that both resist penetration as well as effect the necessary internal transformations are definitely (as Tignor saw) the age-set organization and (which he did not see) their associated rituals, ceremonies, and "religious" ideas, as well as the embedding of these in the overall system of pastoral *praxis*, itself historically changing. Before we look at further historical evidence of Ilparakuyo and Maasai rejection of capitalist relations of production and the commoditization of labor, livestock, and land, therefore, we must examine very briefly some relevant features of age-set organization.

It has usually been assumed in studies of societies with formalized age-set and age-grade systems that these structures have important political functions; Ilparakuyo and Maasai are no exception (Jacobs 1965a, 1965b; Fosbrooke 1948; Rigby 1969a, 1985). It has also been recognized, however, that the most important ritual or religious occasions and ceremonies, particularly those of a more "public" nature, are inseparable from age organizations, if not completely bound up with them. This led P. H. Gulliver (1953), for example, to assert correctly that the "functions" of at least some age-set systems are largely ritual. More recently, one of the frequent noncontroversies so common in anthropology has arisen over this issue. Because "the political" and "the ritual" are assumed to be separable from each other as self-evident ontological categories, such statements as the following can be made in a comparative study of age-set systems (Baxter and Almagor 1978:19):

> A residual ethnocentricity still makes it difficult, even for professional observers, to recognize that a society may rub along happily without institutions which are obviously political. Yet, everyone has got used to not finding obvious economic institutions. Even Evans-Pritchard felt bound to stress that Nuer age-sets did not have political tasks however hard you looked at them as if that were a bit odd. We labor this point because, it seems to us, that the primary institutions on which the maintenance of social order depends, has been a barrier to our understanding of them.

Yet the "ethnocentricity" here lies precisely in the epistemological assumption that the "obviously political" or "political tasks" can be identified as objects of discourse in the first place.

Perhaps more cogently, P. T. W. Baxter and Uri Almagor argue
(1978:9) that age-sets cannot exercise major political functions since,
"though they influence the use of resources and flow of labor, they
neither own nor control stock nor any other means of material production. They do not even have the vestigial rights sometimes said
to reside ultimately in clans or lineages."

While this might appear to be something like an historical materialist argument for the lack of political functions attributable to
most age-set systems, I presently show that it is not. First, I want to
note that Galaty's response to the argument is an excellent starting
point for my subsequent discussion, when he notes in reference to
pastoral Maasai (1983:362) that, "while particular age-sets may not
represent corporate bodies, the *system* of age-organization constitutes the basis for local political assembly." Further, he continues:

> My essential point of difference with Almagor and Baxter lies in their
> narrowing of the notion of politics to the local and every-day exer-
> cise of influence and force based on individuals and neighborhood net-
> works, to the exclusion of the institutional framework and meaningful
> context in which these processes occur, and to the denial of a broader
> concept of politics as the long-term process of integrating local groups
> into larger totalities.

And he proceeds to address the question of ritual functions, which
"ultimately will raise again the question of politics."

Baxter and Almagor's apparently materialist claim that age-sets
cannot have major political functions because they are not corporate property-holding or controlling groups is, therefore, based upon
the spurious distinction between what "practical societal functions"
they may fulfil on the one hand, and "what ritual benefits they are
perceived as endowing individuals, and groups and society," with
on the other (1978:25; cf. Galaty 1983:361–362). If we begin with
the understanding of ideological production (and hence "ritual benefits") as *relating* individuals and groups in societal *praxis* ("practical societal functions") as I have done here, the proposed opposition
or dichotomy between these categories disappears. But Baxter and
Almagor's epistemological position leads them into all sorts of unfortunate statements, among which is the extraordinary idea that the
members of junior age-sets are associated with "martial activities"
and stock-raiding "because the members of junior sets have little to
contribute but their lives and little to lose but those very lives which
are not of much social value" (1978:16). At least for Ilparakuyo and
Maasai, as I have indicated elsewhere, the fact that age-sets are not
corporate property-holding groups in no way detracts from their func-

tioning as relations of production at the community as well as the section level, both beyond that of the primary units of real appropriation, the homestead or domestic groups. In fact, without the appropriation of surplus labor from the junior age-sets by the community as a whole through the mediation of the elders, the reproduction of the community and social formation would be completely impossible; and this applies as strongly in the present, when their "martial functions" are limited, as in the past, when this function was more prominent (Rigby 1985:123–167, and Chapter 3 above).

◆ **II**   From the beginning of European penetration in East Africa, soon to be followed by white settler occupation of "desirable lands"—many of which were in nineteenth-century Maasailand in both British East Africa (Kenya) and German East Africa (Tanganyika)—it became well-known that Maasai and Ilparakuyo would not work for whites, for wages. Although "junior warriors" (*ilmurran*) had been involved in military expeditions with the British (Waller 1976), frequently in order to regain livestock lost in the disastrous bovine pleuropneumonia and rinderpest epidemics of 1883 and 1889–1891 respectively,[4] they refused to be conscripted into either side's armies during the Anglo-German war in East Africa of 1914–1918 (Leys 1926:131–132; Huxley 1935:39–49). By 1919, as Norman Leys notes, "everyone of influence and authority in Kenya has . . . assumed that every tribe must find useful occupations in industries controlled by Europeans. This is the only kind of destiny for Africans which, in 1919, provision was made."

Maasai and Ilparakuyo completely refused to have anything to do with this "destiny" (Rigby 1985:92–122). Leys continues (1926: 132), "And the only reason the Masai in 1919 presented a problem while the Kikuyu, for instance, in the official view did not, was that by a variety of means the Kikuyu had been persuaded to become wage-earners *en masse* while the Masai had refused."

This refusal, in fact, was not merely "passive resistance." The *ilmurran*, or junior warrior age-set, in 1918, had *violently* rejected conscription into the armed forces, as already mentioned, when the British used coercion under the Native Followers Recruitment Ordinance in Kenya, leading to several deaths. These events prompted the British officer in charge of the Maasai "reserve" to attempt to destroy the "*moran* system," as it was called, by manipulating the crucial ceremony called *eunoto*. I return to this in greater detail; but we may begin by quoting Tignor on the aftermath of this "outburst" by *ilmurran* (1976:80):

For the next two decades, under Hemsted, and various successors, the administration tried to suppress those aspects of the warrior organization which they felt were inimical to social change and orderly government. This policy was carried out with great intensity as a result of large-scale raids made by Purko warriors into occupied portions of former German East Africa in 1918 and 1919—raids that brought loss of life and stock to both sides. The goal of Hemsted's program was to limit the military capabilities of the junior warriors; this was to be done by disarming them, hastening the *E-Unoto* ceremony, at which time they settled down and became senior warriors, and disbanding warrior *manyattas* where, according to Hemsted, young men lived *free of the control of elders* and conceived their plans of raiding and *opposing government policies*.

I have added emphases to the final sentence of this statement for reasons that will appear later. For the time being we must note that, in this policy, the colonial government was aided and abetted by the elders (*ilpayiani, ilmoruak*), who wished at the time to establish themselves in control of the situation in order to benefit from the penetration of commodity relations.

This is a controversial assertion that should normally be made after the presentation of considerable historical evidence and sociological analysis. The more common pattern for the intrusion of commodity relations into precapitalist social formations is that the younger members of these societies are the first to succumb to conversion, missionary education, and foreign ideologies. Following again Marx's tenet that "the concrete is concrete because it is the concentration of many determinations," I must now demonstrate the historical circumstances that gave rise to the peculiar situation implied by this assertion. This in turn entails a considerable elaboration of the Ilparakuyo and Maasai age-set systems and a further discussion of the forms taken by commodity relations, which are somewhat peculiar in pastoral social formations, as opposed to agro-pastoral or more purely agricultural societies. These processes cannot be elaborated outside of a discussion of specific historical conjunctures that follow rapidly upon one another over a period of about three or four generations.

The conditions necessary for the reproduction of Ilparakuyo and Maasai relations of production, which have been changing for at least the past three hundred years or more, manifest themselves upon at least three intersecting and interdependent "levels." The dynamics of transformation of these various levels prior to formal colonial penetration in the late nineteenth century have been elaborated in some detail in Chapter 3; however, a brief recapitulation is necessary here.

The first level is that of the domestic groups (*inkang'itie*, sing. *enkang'*), at which "real appropriation" of the means of production (the herd and the products of grazing lands, water, and salt) takes place, as well as the processes of production (of milk, butter fat, meat, blood, and hides) and hence the reproduction of the basic units of production through pastoral *praxis*. The second level upon which the relations of production are reproduced is that of local territorial sections (*iloshon*, sing. *olosho*) comprising in turn a number of "localities" of cooperating and frequently mobile domestic groups in which the units of production at the first level have communal but shifting rights of appropriation of pasture, water, and salt. Territorial sections and local communities cut across both descent and age-set relationships, which comprise the third level (*olaji*, pl. *ilajijik*).

Age-set organization is extra-territorial in its pan-Maasai orientation and ideology, and is also the context in which, as we have noted, local political action occurs. The dynamics of age-set organization since the mid-seventeenth century, until interfered with in the late nineteenth century, were linked increasingly to the influence and power of the great prophets (*iloibonok kituaak*), who played a major role in relations among Ilparakuyo and Maasai sections, as well as between these sections and external trade and imperialist forces during the early colonial period.

Just as kinship and descent systems emanate from the ideological instance of the mode of production, so too does the formalization of age relationships. All Ilparakuyo and pastoral Maasai, both men and women (but upon differing principles), are involved in the system of age-sets and age-grades; men and boys, however, are predominant in its formal manifestations. Every uninitiated youth (*olayioni*, pl. *ilayiok*) is circumcised (girls undergo partial clitoridectomy) as the initial rite of entry into the formal structure of age-sets and, after various other formalities, becomes a young man who has been circumcised and has provided a beast at his first meat-feast ceremony (*olpul*), commonly called a "junior warrior" (*olmurrani*, pl. *ilmurran*).

At the time of circumcision (*emurata*) and entry into a named age-set, these young men acquire "sponsors" who are ritually linked with them through the re-lighting of the homestead fires, which are extinguished during the circumcision ceremony. These sponsors must be at least of an alternate age-set above the youths; members of immediate age-sets cannot be linked by the ritual firestick bond (*olpiron*, pl. *ilpironito*). Therefore, the sons of a junior or senior elder must be of the alternate (or later) age-set below his. This alternate linkage is represented by the prohibition of marriage or sexual relations between any person and the child of an age-mate, a prohibition that is as strong as any rule of exogamy or incest. Boys and young men are junior warriors for varying periods of some five to ten years or more, during which time they should not get married and are subject to all the prohibitions and positive injunctions of *enturuj*, which is attained upon becoming an *olmurrani* (Rigby 1985:48–66).

As a new age-set is constituted as occupying the junior warrior age-grade, the age-set that previously occupied this grade moves up, through the *eunoto* ceremony, to senior warriorhood, at which time they begin to get married and settle down to domestic life, with most of the prohibitions of *enturuj* being relaxed while the positive injunctions fade away more gradually. Similarly, members of the age-set who were senior warriors become junior elders through a ceremony called *olng'esher*, and junior elders become senior elders; the latter then move gracefully into the elevated position of wise "retired elders" (*iltasat, oltasati*: masc. sing. and pl.; *entasat, intasati*: fem. sing. and pl.). These elderly people are the keepers and teachers of history, law, and cultural unity, which they pass on to *ilmurran* at meat-feast ceremonies and, among pastoral Maasai, warrior camps (*imanyat*, sing. *emanyata*; which no longer occur among Ilparakuyo). The cultural unity of "Maasai-ness" is embedded in the correct performance of age-set rituals, particularly those involving *ilmurran*.

It is evident that, at any historical period, each named age-set (and they get new names at crucial points in their movement through the age-grade system) occupies a position in the formal hierarchy of age-grades (junior warriors, senior warriors, junior elders, senior elders, retired elders), each age-grade with its specific tasks and functions and hierarchically ordered authority and influence. Long historical periods are remembered primarily by the age-set that happened to be *ilmurran* at that time; but elders nevertheless hold secular power and authority over all juniors, together with limited ritual powers (such as the power to curse and at least attempt to disinherit). Specific historical events, therefore, impinge upon the age-set structure in different ways, depending upon each set's position in the age-grade hierarchy at the time.

The recent past of Ilparakuyo and Maasai, therefore, from about 1890 to the present, has been characterized by varying responses by different age-sets to the penetration of colonial and post-colonial power and influence, as well as the forms of commodity relations associated with the colonial and contemporary state formations of Kenya and Tanzania and the position of these states in the political economy of world capitalism and socialism. These "external" relations of the recent past can be heuristically separated into: the commoditization of livestock; the commoditization of land and labor; the penetration of Christianity and formal education, both by missionaries and by later governmental institutions; and the associated processes of political integration through "development" interventions and exploitation by colonial and post-colonial states and international agencies (Sena 1981, 1986; Tignor 1972, 1976).

An understanding of these processes and their impact upon the Ilparakuyo and Maasai social formations is only possible through a rough periodization of this recent past into particular phases generated not only by events within these social formations themselves but also by exogenous forces that result in the "struggle of political hegemonies" posited by Gramsci as the arena of contradiction and conflict between classes in capitalist societies. The events that characterize these processes can, for our purposes, be grouped roughly into four periods: the late 1890s to about 1913, after the "Maasai moves" in Kenya resulted in considerable loss of land; the period from the first world war (1914–1918) to the end of the second in 1945; the period from about 1946 to immediately before the national independence of Tanzania and Kenya in 1961 and 1963 respectively; and the post-independence period of national development and integration.[5] All these four periods are distinguished by different kinds of interventions that impinged differentially upon age-sets occupying their hierarchical positions at each historical conjuncture. Although we cannot consider them all in detail in such a short compass, their distinctive features as far as Ilparakuyo and Maasai are concerned can be outlined.

The first period, from about 1890 to 1913, was both a culmination of processes of change, in most sections of Maasai and Ilparakuyo, that had begun at a much earlier time and a series of natural, economic, and political disasters experienced at the time. The former processes engendered the increasing secular influence and, later, power of the great prophets (*iloibonok kituaak*), particularly Mbatiany and his two sons, Olonana and Senteu. This growing power was manifested in close control of the *ilmurran* age-grade, their economic and political activities, and the rituals necessary for the functioning of the age-set system as a whole, and in the role of these great prophets toward the end of the period in "external" relations with the colonial powers, Britain in the case of present day Kenya and Germany in present-day Tanzania. Internally, these transformations weakened the secular power of the local elders, the representatives of influence and authority over the *ilmurran*, making this relationship even more ambiguous and contradictory than it already was (Chapter 3), especially in the elders' capacity to appropriate the labor of *ilmurran* for the reproduction of the local community as a whole.

The natural and economic disasters, as already noted, included an outbreak of bovine pleuropneumonia and rinderpest, which killed about 80 percent of Maasai and Ilparakuyo cattle and almost 50 percent of the people, and led many younger men to situations and activities they might not have considered under more normal circumstances. This period of disasters, caused largely by colonial penetration and mercantile capitalist trade, is known by Maasai as the time when people "sold" their children to other peoples (e.g., Kikuyu) in order that the children might survive and their parents eat, and the time when people ate donkeys, wild animals (which Maasai do not normally eat), and hides (Sankan 1979:105; Waller 1976:534; Sena 1986:20–31; Rigby 1985:108–110). But by 1893, herds were being reconstituted, and some Maasai allied themselves with the British in Kenya in order to raid for livestock "legally" by becoming associated with "punitive expeditions" against other peoples (Waller 1976). By the end of the period, however, Maasai relations with both Germans and British colonial powers had deteriorated. Richard Waller sums this up succinctly for Kenya (1976:529): "The treaties [and "moves"] of 1904 and 1911, while appearing to emphasize the special status which Maasai had enjoyed since 1895, in fact marked the beginning of a long retreat from involvement with the colonial power and the replacement of a highly flexible and innovatory response to the advent of colonial rule by a determination to preserve their society intact."

Despite this withdrawal, however, I have maintained that this re-discovered pan-Maasai identity and cohesion was of a social formation already drastically different from what it was in pre-colonial times, in which the political roles of the great prophets and the relative independence of *ilmurran* from local age-grade controls had been consolidated for at least a short time. But the increasing difficulties in relations between *ilmurran* and their local elders were further exacerbated by direct intrusions of the colonialists into age-set affairs, deeply affecting the functioning of the age-set system but not destroying it.

The intruders wanted, as we have seen, to use *ilmurran* to gain control over other East African peoples; later, they attempted to destroy the age-grade category of junior warriors in order to establish their control over Ilparakuyo and Maasai themselves. The former strategy enabled Ilparakuyo and Maasai to rebuild their herds in record time, but simultaneously altered relations between *ilmurran* and local elders on the one hand and their ties to the great prophets on the other. In Kenya Maasailand, "levies" of *ilmurran* were used by the British from 1893 to 1905 in expeditions against Kikuyu, Kamba, Kipsigis, and Nandi (Waller 1976:552). In tapping the military strength of Maasai, the colonialists first worked through the great prophet Olonana (whom they elevated to the entirely foreign position of "paramount chief") to gain the collaboration of the spokespersons (*ilaiguenak*) of the age-set who were *ilmurran* at the time, by by-passing the local elders and *their* spokespersons (Waller 1976:536).

By 1906, however, the British administrator of Kenya Maasailand, C. W. Hobley, became "concerned about the raiding propensities of the *moran* and proposed that the state cease to use *moran* in punitive expeditions." Maasai were to be encouraged instead to "trade, cultivate, use money, and work outside the reserve for wages" (Tignor 1976:75). This total reversal of colonial policy was consolidated by the enactment of a stock theft ordinance in 1913. This moves us essentially into the second phase of colonial intervention and its impact upon elder-*ilmurran* relationships.

The "legalized" raiding in which *ilmurran* had participated had made them relatively independent economically from the elders in power, their "fathers," particularly during the time when the herds had to be rebuilt. At first, the elders objected to the stock theft ordinance, seeing in the raiding activities of their *ilmurran* a way in which they could retain relative control of their domestic herds while still satisfying the young men who would come to them for cattle and small stock to establish their own future marriages and economic independence. However, when the colonial government began to impose huge fines for cattle raiding on the community, the elders in power at the time (of the Ilaimer and Iltalala age-sets in Kenya) rapidly began to revise their position on the matter.[6] Elders, as we have noted, are the major controllers (though not necessarily the "owners": cf. Rigby 1985:142, 146, 166) of the herd, and not only were they held responsible for the actions of *ilmurran*, but they also bore the brunt of the "communal fines" under the collective punishment ordinances in both Kenya and Tanganyika. Tignor (1976:77) sums up the differential effects of *ilmurran* cattle raiding in Kenya Maasailand:

> As soon as the new stock theft ordinance was put into effect, it had a severe impact on Maasai. As [retroactive] penalties for various raids carried out in 1910, the state assessed heavy fines on the population— fines which had to be paid by elders as well as moran and had the effect of driving these segments of Maasai society apart. These penal-

ties began to persuade elders that their interests lay in co-operating with the state in an effort to regulate the warriors and to channel their energies in other avenues.

It was also at about this time, from 1915 on, that the colonial government began to create government ("state") schools in Kenya Maasailand. The drive to "educate" Maasai youth was part of a comprehensive plan, devised largely by R. W. Hemsted, who had become administrator of the Maasai "reserve" in 1911. It attempted also to recruit Maasai into the King's African Rifles during the Anglo-German war in East Africa, and force them into agricultural production through "sedentarization" and "destocking" their herds by enforced sale of cattle to merchants, so that the people might become more enmeshed in commodity relations, referred to as becoming "more money and consumer orientated." None of these aims in the plan were effectively realized at any time during the colonial period; but, much more important, Hemsted's program was designed to eliminate *murrano*, or "warrior-hood," as an institution through the manipulation of the *eunoto* ceremony, which, as we have seen, transforms junior *ilmurran* into seniors. As Tignor accurately notes (1976:80), this plan for "directed change" was now designed to "strengthen the authority of the elders, who, unlike the warriors, showed a willingness to assist the government in transforming Maasai society." Almost overnight the relations between elders and *ilmurran* and the colonial government were reversed. The latter soon realized that the great prophets were not good "paramount chiefs" and that they would have to create a mission-educated category of men who would become administrative chiefs.

At this crucial point at the beginning of the second stage of colonial penetration and control over the Ilparakuyo and Maasai age-set systems, therefore, and despite the fact that the institution of *murrano* and the basic structure of the overall system survived, the relations between elders in power and active *ilmurran* were irrevocably upset for the first time, and each age-set and its subsequent reactions must now be identified. It was the young men of the Ilmeiruturut sub-set, the "right-hand circumcision," of Iltareto age-set among Kenya Ilpurko section (Iltareto among Ilkisonko section in Tanzania and Ilkijaro/Ilmetimpot among Ilparakuyo), who, in defiance of their controlling elders, refused to serve in either German or British territorial armies and rebelled against sending their younger brothers (uncircumcised youths, *ilayiok*) to school. In Kenya, as I have noted, this resulted in a battle between Ilpurko section and a company of the Kenya African Rifles at Ololunga in the Narok area, in which, according to official count, two Maasai women and fourteen *ilmurran* were murdered, over a period of two days (Sena 1986:39).

In a perceptive comment on the real motives underlying the Kenya colonial administration's drive to force *ilmurran* into the military, Leys (1926:132,n.1) notes: "A correspondent who was on the spot at the time says that the military did not want the men, that the reasons for trying to get them was that it was thought that conscription would do the Masai good, that at least several scores of Masai men, women, and children were killed by rifles and machine guns before the attempt at compulsion was abandoned." This interpretation, and the correction in the official count of the numbers of Maasai killed, is strengthened by the fact that these confrontations took place on 9 and 11 September 1918, when the Anglo-German war was nearly over. It should, however, be borne in mind that several members of the age-set who were junior *ilmurran* at this time (Iltareto/Ilkijaro) had been converted to Christianity (King 1971a; Rigby 1985:92–122), and this had an enormous impact upon the role their "sons," of the Ilnyankusi/Ilkidotu age-set, had to play in the late colonial period (see below).

Coming so soon after the late nineteenth century, during which, as we have noted, local elders' control over their *ilmurran* "sons" had been weakened by the latter's strengthened ties with the great prophets, these "rebellions" of the *ilmurran* (there was another one in Kenya Maasailand in 1922) expressed their growing opposition to what they considered to be the collaboration of the elders with the colonial authorities. Tignor sums up this period succinctly (1976: 81–82):

> The elders' support for government programs was not hard to understand. Collaborationist elders could benefit from government support, as was happening in Kikuyu society. More significantly, the military organization of the *moran* had become a serious liability to the elders. Not only were the defensive and military aspects of the system growing unnecessary in the new colonial era, but the illegal *moran* raids were [again] bringing onerous government fines. . . . Since the elders were obviously the wealthier [sic] element, they shouldered the heaviest burden of repayment. Their economic interest dictated cooperation with the government.

During the early "pacification" of Maasai and Ilparakuyo and the consolidation of colonial rule, therefore, elders were repeatedly recorded as "being emphatic in their support for the government policy for disbanding *manyatta* [*imanyat*, or warrior villages] and forcing *moran* to settle" (Kenya National Archives, District Commissioner Kajiado 5/1/2). The seriousness of this confrontation between *ilmurran* and colonialist intervention is indicated by the fact that, after the 1922 action by *ilmurran* against colonial policy, 210 *ilmurran* were arrested, 167 were sent to prison, and 7 were executed. But we must pass on quickly to the third and fourth phases.

The inter-war period and that of the second world war were marked by the political ascendancy of white settler interests and power, particularly in Kenya but also in British-mandated Tanganyika, coupled with a rapidly increasing nationalist political consciousness among East Africans as a whole. Maasai in Kenya and Tanzania were involved in these anti-colonial political movements, despite their reputation for "conservative backwardness" and relatively intact social and cultural organization. Once again, livestock diseases, drought, and colonial livestock quarantine and marketing regulations favored the settlers economically and created great hardship among Maasai in both Kenya and Tanzania.

At the same time, small groups of mission-educated Maasai of the Iltareto/Ilkijaro age-set who had been *ilmurran* from about 1907 to 1929, formed the Maasai Political Association in 1930, when they would have just become junior elders. Among the office holders were Maitei ole Mootian, Matanta ole Masikonte, and Mulunkit ole Sempele, who had been involved in nationalist politics since 1921 (King 1971*a*:18 *et passim*; Rigby 1985:110–112; Sena 1986:49). But it was the Western-educated "sons" of the Iltareto age-set, who were named Ilnyankusi (II, and Ilkidotu among Ilparakuyo) and were *ilmurran* from about 1942 to 1959, who became prominent, first as junior elders and then as senior elders (that is, "elders in power") during the third phase of colonial intrusion, in post-1946 national politics; they were the first Maasai members of parliament in Kenya and Tanzania (Sena 1986:65; Rigby 1985:84).

Most critically for our purposes, therefore, it was this age-set (Ilnyankusi/Ilkidotu) who were in authority when post–World War II "development policies" were forcefully introduced in the later 1950s and early 1960s by the waning colonial governments, in preparation for national independence in both countries. Their immediate juniors, of the Iseuri (Kenya) or Ilmedoti (Tanzania), were junior warriors between about 1955 and 1972, becoming senior warriors and junior elders too late in most cases to enhance their positions in the new order of commoditization under independence. They had little or no authority to accept or reject governmental and international aid policies, which were moving rapidly toward the commoditization of herds, land, and even labor. In Kenya, as a result, most of the members of this age-set ("fathers" of the newly forming set in the 1980s) were left out of access to grazing now owned "privately" by individuals or group ranches, had difficulties in establishing viable herds, and hence were involved in wage labor in significant numbers for the first time.

In Tanzania, however, Ilmedoti as current junior elders do have access to communal grazing, and many have built up viable herds despite the powerful role of their immediately senior age-set, the Ilnyankusi/Ilkidotu, and play a prominent role in contemporary class formation (Chapter 7).[7] In both countries, significant numbers of the sons of Iseuri/Ilmedoti have been sent to school (Sena 1986:65).

What I am arguing through this somewhat detailed discussion of the experiences of specific age-sets is that each age-set, or groups of sets, were "elders in authority" or junior *ilmurran* "in power," the latter struggling to become senior warriors or junior elders while retaining their roles in the age-grade system, the real and symbolic "re-creators" of pastoral society and its time-honored practical ideology and pastoral *praxis*. These specific historical conjunctures or crises temporarily polarized the elders, who stood to benefit at particular times and for distinct reasons by going along with external colonial and post-colonial interventions, at least in the short run, and junior *ilmurran*, who felt they were being seriously threatened, as they are now. These contradictions and temporary alliances fitted uneasily into the "ideal" structures of age-sets and grades, as well as descent relationships, as previously outlined.

The complexity of the way in which age-set organization is affected by rapidly changing external factors is dependent both upon the equally rapidly changing institutional and ideological conditions for the reproduction of the Ilparakuyo and Maasai social formations, as well as the specific historical events generated by the overall process of colonial and post-colonial penetration, with its concomitant pressures toward commoditization and ideological conversion. In this process, the role of the ritual bond between alternate age-sets cannot be over-emphasized (Jacobs 1981).

A more specific question, however, arises at this point. I have stated at the beginning of this chapter that the rituals and symbolic actions and meanings of Ilparakuyo and Maasai "religion," embedded in, and inseparable from, the dynamic structure of age-set organization and its ceremonial, *comment* upon changes, both "internal" and "external," generated by specific historical events, enabling these social formations to reproduce themselves while blocking some elements of the penetration of peripheral capitalism and its accompanying commodity relationships. This inhibiting function, which is neither conservative nor backward-looking, is integral to the struggle of hegemonies previously discussed, and is manifested in both kinship and age-set rituals and the symbolic power of such ritual relationships as the *olpiron* firestick bonds (see Arens and Karp 1989 for a comparative discussion). In an extremely perceptive paper, Jacobs (1981:6), in commenting upon the symbolic significance of fire-making, sexuality, and political authority among pastoral Maasai, demonstrates "how the syntax of fire-making is used consciously by pastoral Maasai as a clear expression of political authority." He concludes: "Although the age-set system of the pastoral Maasai continues to flourish even today . . . , subtle socio-political changes between men and women and within the age-set system *are* in fact ocurring. One aim of this paper . . . is to suggest that evidence of such changes are likely to be reflected in who continues to make fires in Masailand—when, where and how?"

I would go even further than Jacobs by stating that ritual activities and their associated verbal performances do not merely "reflect" changes; they control and channel them. In Chapters 5 and 6, a beginning is made in a discussion of this complex question, which involves an account of symbolic meanings and speech acts in all their referential, poetic, and conative power; here I merely conclude by opening up the basic questions in the light of what has already been said.

♦ III   In order to approach the problem of which questions to ask, we must attempt a brief theoretical reconciliation between Galaty's already mentioned semiotic analysis of the "poetics of Maasai ritual" (1983) and the historical materialist analysis of the conditions necessary for the production of the symbolic and religious ideas involved in them; a "practical ideology" that entails the historically changing patterns of pastoral *praxis* as a whole, and the role, ideology, and meanings underlying the age-set and kinship rituals of the Ilparakuyo and Maasai social formations. It is suggested that such a reconciliation enhances both levels of discourse. But since Galaty does not address the problem of the historical context and transformations faced by Maasai for the past three hundred years or more, particularly since the turn of the century and during more recent confrontations between pastoralists and the colonial and post-colonial states as outlined in this book, we must extend our theoretical framework to encompass the struggle of hegemonies that are entailed by these confrontations.

I have shown elswhere how *ilmurran*, the junior warriors, not only provide the conditions for both the real and symbolic reproduction of these social formations at the community level of the relations of production (Rigby 1985: 48–66, 123–167) but also how the age-set system as a whole provides for the historical movement or transformation of these societies in time, encompassing the myriad changes these processes entail (Rigby 1985:67–91).

The most important age-set "religious" rite is the *eunoto*, already mentioned, which transforms junior warriors into seniors; and this is the subject of Galaty's excellent essay (1983). The wealth of ethnographic detail as well as the penetrating interpretive insights provided by Galaty cannot be appropriately considered here; a comparison of similarities and differences between Ilparakuyo and pastoral Maasai *eunoto* ceremonies must await another time. For the moment, I wish to focus upon a few elements of the ritual and their significance for uncovering the relation between ideology and *praxis* developed in this chapter.

First, Galaty correctly rejects a merely "referential" dimension or "propositional function" for the ritual (or any other ritual for that matter). He notes (1983:365–366) that "ritual . . . is an aesthetic form which is both persuasive and transformative, and preeminently relates to society in the pragmatic rather than the referential mode. . . . Through semiotic means ritual participants are identified with the institutional order of society, so in their ritual actions, society acts and is itself transformed."

Second, during the course of *eunoto*, the junior *ilmurran*, with their internal divisions into sub-sets, become *olaji*, "the great house," members of a single major age-set or division (*olporror*), for the first time. Simultaneously (Galaty 1983:377), "it amalgamates the members initiated throughout its dispersed country. The rite of response to the evocation of the name is a classic performative speech act by which the name is given. The response of recognition by the entire age-set marks its constitution as a symbolic entity in Maasai history and as a social group with corporate responsibilities and prerogatives."

Finally, the *eunoto* ceremony itself "involves the construction of progressively smaller-scale spatial models of Maasai society upon which the ritual acts" (Galaty 1983: 376). It is a means whereby "social order is transformed," and in which "concrete images of the historic and cosmic processes are not just expressed but are *created*

(Galaty 1983:380, 368). Elsewhere, I have stated for Ilparakuyo (Rigby 1985:87):

> [Although] . . . I emphasized the real and symbolic role of age-sets in social reproduction, it should be stressed here that the succession of age-sets through the age-grade system should not be thought of as merely a repetitive cycle, the life-cycle writ large; Ilparakuyo certainly do not think of age-sets as such. Each age-set, the circumstances of its formation, and the creativity and originality of its actions, are emphasized, making it unique in the annals of Ilparakuyo historical consciousness as well as a referent for historical interpretation and, ultimately, the future of the social formation itself. If Ilparakuyo have any "identity" as a social formation, it lies not merely in an endless repetition of the past (despite a strong emphasis upon adherence to certain basic social practices and their associated values) but in a consciousness of a developing entity, with a definite historical beginning, and moving in a specific historical manner. This movement is not towards a "destiny," but embodies both the relations of the past and present in the creation of a future.

Ilpuli (meat feast ceremonies), *eunoto*, and other rituals are embedded in the age-set organization, functioning as relations of production at community, and sometimes "national," levels. As Feuchtwang reminds us (1975:68), "Ideological production, the production and communication of ideas, is no more purely ideal practice than economic production is purely material." Thus, "only by means of ideology are individuals constituted as subjects, that is to say, as sources of action able to relate to the whole of which they are a part." If Ilparakuyo and Maasai *ilmurran* are able in *eunoto*, *ilpuli*, and other rituals to "create" (and therefore to "correct" or "act upon") perceived changes in the historical social formation, they also have never been reluctant to translate their apperceptions into politico-economic practice to resist unwanted intrusions, such as the penetration of wage labor, even when the latter is disguised under the Christian doctrine of the "dignity of labor" (Rigby 1985:118–120).

◆ **IV**   It is evident from what has gone before that the sporadically "elder-aided" policy to control (that is, to destroy) the *murrano* system continued throughout the colonial period in the form of forced labor policies and forced recruitment into the military and educational institutions, resulting in fluctuating but generally increasing tensions between those occupying the *ilmurran* age-grade and their elders. As each age-set passed through the system of grades from junior warriorhood to senior warriorhood (at *eunoto*) and thence to elderhood (at *olng'esher*), the solidarity established for each age-set at the earlier period in both real and symbolic terms by sharing and such rituals as *ilpuli, eunoto,* and the institution of *enturuj,* declined; patrilineal, matrilateral, and other kinship and affinal bonds became more important (Rigby 1985:156–161). Since control over property is inherited through patrilineal descent, it is hardly surprising that certain elders who wish to take advantage of the process of commoditization, first of livestock, then of land, and finally, of labor, have since early colonial times attempted to limit the power generated by junior warrior age-set solidarity and, at the same time, to erode the control by women of the process of production (Rigby 1985; cf. Oboler 1985:238–251 on a similar process among the Nandi of Kenya).

The historical evidence adduced in this chapter and elsewhere in this book shows clearly that at each crisis, it is the *ilmurran,* acting in local groups of varying size and bolstered by ritual and ceremony, who have consistently resisted the processes of commoditization and external political and economic control and, hence, from our analysis, have ensured the overall reproduction of the Ilparakuyo and Maasai social formations, albeit in considerably altered form. *Ilmurran* at *eunoto,* and other rituals, represent not only their own age-set but the entire age-set system as well as the social and symbolic reproduction of the whole social formation *and* its cumulative historical adaptations, in contradiction to the immediate interests of some elders.

The crucial point here is that the colonialist administrators and their successors seem eventually to have realized this and, as a result, began to concentrate their efforts on destroying the *ilmurran* category, attempting in both real and symbolic terms to weaken the ability of these social formations to reproduce themselves by manipulating the *eunoto* ceremony (cf. Baxter and Almagor 1978:23–24).

These attempts, which have failed for the reasons outlined above, continue in similar form today as capitalist penetration becomes increasingly effective, particularly in Kenya, through the commoditization of land. In 1983, a news broadcast over the Voice of Kenya declared that, at a meeting with the district commissioner at Kajiado (Olkejuoado), the District Council and leading elders had decided that the "time had come to dismantle 'moran-hood,' " since it no longer had any "functions."[8] Banning *eunoto* was proposed as one method of achieving this. The news that this policy was to be put into effect nearly two years later reached even the relatively parochial news media in the United Sates. A report by David Crary, Associated

Press correspondent in Nairobi, was published in the *Philadelphia Inquirer* of 31 August 1985:

> A centuries-old rite of passage in which young men of the Masai tribe serve stints as warriors is dying a graceful, government-ordered death on the plains of southern Kenya. Local authorities announced in June that the Masai warrior class would be banned in three months. They said the young men, known as Morans, were missing education and job training that would help them contribute more to their tribe and to Kenya. . . . With Kenya's government preaching nationhood and denouncing tribalism, the warrior class of the proud Masai have become obsolete. This summer, Masai elders meeting in Kajiado district south of Nairobi resolved to comply with the government order, although a minority argued that the ban would deprive future generations of their cultural heritage.

Nationally prominent Maasai also disagreed over the value and validity of the ban. Phillip Odupoy, elected by a Maasai constituency to parliament in 1985, asserted that the "elders and mothers" of *ilmurran* "all seemed to agree that this [warrior age-grade as well as the *eunoto* ceremony] should be the last. . . . They are concerned about their sons." Professor Geoffrey Maloiy, however, a Maasai elder and principal of Nairobi's College of Agriculture and Veterinary Science, felt that the "Moranism ban may be too sweeping"; he suggested instead a "modified form of ceremony," referring presumably either to circumcision (*emurata*) or *eunoto*, or both. Maloiy also said that "Moranship" should be "reduced to a year or two," during which "Morans could join a local version of Kenya's National Youth Service, engaging in projects useful to their clan or tribe." The report went on to discuss the impact of the "ranches and farms" now established in Kenya Maasailand as a "problem" for *ilmurran*, causing some young Maasai to "drift into Nairobi, mainly seeking jobs as security guards."

As with the colonialist governments, the real reason for the ban lies in the fact that the *murrano* system and the present *ilmurran* continue to gain new functions and appear to constitute a threat to the ability of some current elders to profit (literally) from the government-mandated process of land commoditization, and hence its sale or accumulation. *Ilmurran* are accused of interfering with nationally and internationally sponsored "development" policies that are fundamentally geared to a capitalist model of development in keeping with national ruling class interests and their international backers in the drive to capitalist accumulation and control.[9] *Eunoto* and other rituals serve as "reminders" of other forms of production, that is, pastoral *praxis*, as well as providing an arena for the reproduction and transformation of what we might call "*ilmurran*-power" and the assertion of new types of relationship with "elders in authority," still within the overall practical ideology and age-linked power and responsibility.

The real power of the ideological and religious productions of these rituals, which are still internal to the social relations of production, both reclaim the past and adapt to the present with an eye to the future, enabling individuals or categories of individuals to act politically and economically to counteract capitalist penetration; *that* is the reason they must go. The experiences of *ilmurran* at each stage described must have influenced, and probably still do, but did not determine, their actions as the elders of the future. For the present *ilmurran*, particularly in Kenya, things may really be out of their hands when they reach the stage of *eunoto* and then *olng'esher*. I return to these and related issues in both Tanzania and Kenya in Chapter 7.

5   Pastor   Egalita   the State

Erisio Ilmaasai
o enkai.
Equal are the Maasai
and God.

◆   It is not my assumption that pastoral social formations are "inherently" egalitarian (*pace* Goldschmidt 1965, 1971);
they vary a great deal in relation to actual as well as ideological forms
of equality or inequality, and hence differ in their processes of class
formation, or lack of them. As I have noted in many places above, and
have also demonstrated elsewhere (1985; cf. also Chapter 7 below),
Ilparakuyo and Maasai social formations have, until their enforced
incorporation into the global capitalist system by imperialism and
neo-colonialism, exhibited a relative lack of internal differentiation;
and their response and resistance to the penetration of commodity
relations and capitalist forms of wage labor and their ideological
concomitants have, characteristically, been complex (Rigby 1985:
92–175).

Neither do I subscribe to the notion that the category of male
elders among Ilparakuyo and Maasai, or among other non-stratified
African social formations (Bonte 1978), both East and West African, such as Turkana, Samburu, and Fulani (Peul; cf. Riesman 1977;
cf. Dupire 1962, 1970; Stenning 1959), automatically embodies the
"class function" of exploiting male juniors and all women (cf. Meillassoux 1978; Rey 1979). Neither do I uncritically accept the description of age-set systems universally as "gerontocracies" (*pace* Spencer
1965), an issue succinctly explored upon a comparative level by
Bernardo Bernardi (1985:30 *et passim*). I would, in fact, concur with
Bernardi that the "structural tendency toward the ideal of equality

asic trait of age class systems" (1985:147; Alma-
ch are characteristic of, but not universal in, pas-
ic social formations.

ortant issue in this chapter is to explore how egali-
these societies is embedded in the formal structure of
set systems, as well as embodied in the dominant "practi-
ology" of pastoral *praxis*, and how these undergo transforma-
in particular historical circumstances. The dominant ideology
which I refer, it will be seen, is a crucial factor in the formation
of the (individual) subject, through the mediation of oral literature,
political language and song, ritual discourse, and, of course, language as speech, in what Raymond Williams has called "the living
speech of human beings in their specific relationships in the world"
(1977:17).

♦ I   It is not a new idea in anthropology, linguistics, philosophy, or comparative political economy that the diverse
cultures and social forms that have been created by humankind are
closely linked to the historically grounded formation of the social
beings and personalities who inhabit those cultures and who are
also instrumental in their transformation. However, many theories
of "culture and personality" are locked into a relatively untheorized
"psychologism" that lacks a historical dimension, leading to a futile
search for a universal "human nature" whose locus is a biological or
philosophically idealist reductionism (cf. Seve 1978:68–69; Woolfson 1977:233). Norman Geras (1983) and Lucien Seve (1978) have
pointed out how a truly historicized concept of the formation of subjects may be derived by commencing with Marx's sixth, seventh, and
eighth "Theses on Feuerbach" (Marx 1975:423):

> (vi) . . . The human essence is no abstraction inherent in each indi-
> vidual. In reality it is the ensemble of social relations. Feuerbach, who
> does not enter upon a criticism of this real essence, is consequently
> compelled: (1) To abstract from the historical process and to fix the reli-
> gious sentiment as something by itself and to presuppose an abstract—
> *isolated*—human individual. (2) Essence, therefore, can be compre-
> hended only as "genus," as internal, dumb, generality which *naturally*
> unites many individuals.
> (vii) Feuerbach, consequently, does not see that the "religious senti-
> ment" is itself a social product, and that the abstract individual whom
> he analyses belongs to a particular form of society.
> (viii) All social life is essentially *practical*. All mysteries which lead

theory to mysticism find their rational solution in human practice and the comprehension of this practice.

In this historical and social formation of the subject, language and ideology play a major role. Marx and Engels noted (1976[1845–46]:44): "Language is as old as consciousness, language *is* practical, real consciousness that exists for other men as well, and only therefore does it exist for me; language, like consciousness, only arises from the need, the necessity, of intercourse with other men. . . . Consciousness is, therefore, from the very beginning a social product, and remains so as long as men exist at all." It follows, then, that "real consciousness" of individuals varies from one kind of social formation to another (and hence from one kind of dominant mode of production to another), and that their variations can be grasped *through* the articulation of language and ideology. Ideology, in fact, is given *material substance* in language as the utterance, "the real unit of verbal communication" in a "continuous chain of speech performance" (Woolfson 1977:234; Voloshinov 1986:72).[1]

The notion of language as both practical and material is strongly emphasized by Raymond Williams, who expresses it most succinctly (1977:38):

> Signification, the social creation of meanings through the use of formal signs, is then a practical material activity; it is, indeed, literally a means of production. It is not, as formalism would make it, and as the idealist theory of expression had from the beginning assumed, an operation of and within "consciousness," which then becomes a state or process separated, *a priori*, from social material activity. It is, on the contrary, at once a distinctive material process—the making of signs—and, in the central quality of its distinctiveness as practical consciousness, is involved from the beginning in all other human social and material activity.

Voloshinov's position, then, with which both Woolfson and Williams would concur, is "a decisive theoretical rejection of mechanical, behaviorist, or Saussurean versions [of language as] an objective system which is beyond individual or creative use," as well as a "theoretical rejection of subjectivist theories of language as individual expression" (Williams 1977:40; Voloshinov 1986:96; Woolfson 1977:234).[2]

Voloshinov (1986:19) establishes the crucial notion that language also illuminates the *diversity* of possibly conflicting ideologies that characterizes all social formations and, therefore, that "the word is the most sensitive *index of social changes* and, what is more, of changes still in the process of growth, still without definite shape and not yet accommodated into already regularized and fully defined ideological systems." A sign, in the sense of a "signifying element of a language," which Voloshinov strongly distinguishes from a "signal" (Williams 1977:40)

> has, like the social experience which is the principle of its formation, both dialectical and generative properties. . . . The true signifying element of language must from the beginning have a . . . capacity [different from a signal]: to become an *inner sign*, part of an active practical consciousness. Thus in addition to its social and material existence between actual individuals, the sign is also a part of a verbally constituted consciousness which allows individuals to use signs of their own initiative, whether in acts of social communication or in practices which, not being *manifestly* social, can be interpreted as personal or private. This view is then radically opposed to the construction of all acts of communication from pre-determined objective relationships and properties, within which no individual initiative, of a creative or self-generating kind, would be possible.

Social and historical consciousness is "materially embodied in signs which are themselves impregnated with ideology" (Woolfson 1977:237). Hence, in class society, "differently oriented accents intersect in every ideological sign . . . [and the] . . . sign becomes an arena of the class struggle" (Voloshinov 1986:23). This view of the historical contextualization and role of language is very close to that advanced by Gramsci, a position that is also "diametrically opposed to those of contemporary structuralist and positivist linguistics" (Salamini 1981:192). Leonardo Salamini continues:

> Gramsci's notes on linguistics and the study of language . . . must be analysed in relation to the central theme of the "Prison Notebooks," the notion of hegemony and the socialist construction of a new socialist order. He is concerned with the political context of language, the place of the study of language in a general historicist theory of knowledge, and the role of language in socialist transformation.

In the work of Marx and Engels, Voloshinov, and Gramsci, then, we have a historical materialist conception of language (developed by such contemporary scholars as Williams and Woolfson) in which it is *not* an abstract, reified "reflection" of material reality in the form of a synchronic *langue*, but an "active *social language*," of speech (*parole*). Williams sums this up admirably (1977:38):

> What we have, rather, is a grasping of this reality through language, which as a practical consciousness is saturated by and saturates all social activity, including productive activity. And, since this grasping is social and continuous (as distinct from the abstract encounter of

"man" and "his world," or "consciousness" and "reality," or "language" and "material existence"), it occurs within an active and changing society. It is of and to this experience—the lost middle term between the abstract entities, "subject" and "object," on which the propositions of idealism and orthodox materialism are erected—that language speaks. Or to put it more directly, language is the articulation of this active and changing social *presence* in the world.

We may conclude from the theoretical discussion so far that the link between the structural features of a particular social formation and the conditions for the formation of the subject is accessible, at least partially, through linguistic forms and discourse, particularly discourse that comments upon, and is embodied in, the "political language" (Parkin 1984), public rituals, and symbolic manipulations crucial to its reproduction (Galaty 1983). Such discourse, particularly in an "oral culture," would also be both an indicator of change and a vehicle for influencing and controlling the forces of transformation.[3]

◆ II   I have already noted that Ilparakuyo and Maasai social formations are characterized by a strong adherence to notions of egalitarianism. These ideological concepts are embedded in the age-set and kinship structures and are materialized in all forms of speech and discourse, whether in the everyday *praxis* of pastoralism or in the rituals that mark crucial periods in the lives of boys and girls, women and men. Inevitably, much of this discourse is about power and influence, their legitimate evocation, and their transformations. Referring to Voloshinov's (1986) and L. S. Vygotsky's (1962) work, Williams links the historical, social structural aspect of the sign with its individual expressive nature when he writes (1977:41) that "what has really to be said is that the sign is social but that in its very quality as a sign is capable of both being internalized—indeed, has to be internalized, if it is to be a sign for communicative relation between actual persons, initially using only their own physical powers to express it—and of being continually available, in social and material ways, in manifest communication."

For Ilparakuyo, I have shown elsewhere (Rigby 1985:44–66; see Chapters 3 and 4 above) the ambiguity inherent in the relationship between circumcised young men who have satisfied certain other ritual conditions and who are known as *ilmurran* (sing. *olmurrani*, usually translated as "warrior"), on the one hand, and "elders in power" (*ilpayiani*, sing. *olpayian*), on the other, especially in the changing circumstances under which Ilparakuyo struggle to reproduce their society. Galaty has shown the conative and poetic functions of the most important of Maasai and Ilparakuyo rituals and symbols in his analysis of the *eunoto* ceremony, "by which events generated from aesthetic line and figure bear the power of social transformation" (Galaty 1983:363, 380). And Bernardi has perceptively commented on the comparative level that "the application of the structural-age [rather than the physiological-age] concept to age class systems produces two contrasting effects, the one homogenizing and the other diversifying. The ambivalence between equality and inequality is, in fact, one of the fundamental problems that age class systems must confront and deal with. Manipulation of structural age is the instrument used to correct and contain the negative aspects of the differentiation built into the system" (Bernardi 1985:169).

For our present purposes, I want to discuss some of the fundamental concepts embodied in Ilparakuyo and Maasai culture that are central to an understanding of the link between the social structural aspects of egalitarianism embedded in pastoral *praxis* and the formation of individual subjects in their capacity to comment and act upon their constantly changing economic, political, and social universe. The "wider" universe includes the political economy of the post-colonial states of Tanzania and Kenya, which in turn cannot be fully understood without reference to their colonial predecessors and the struggle for political independence in the 1960s.

Apart from the complex of contradictions in the systems of production and exchange that relate to the process of class formation already discussed, and to which I return in Chapter 7, a central anomaly facing Ilparakuyo and Maasai is the one that has arisen between a commitment to the pre-colonial unity of pastoral *praxis* and egalitarian practical ideology and the authoritarianism of the state and its policies for "economic development." This contradiction *implies* the transformation from pre-class to class structures through progressive incorporation in the state, and its concomitant "struggle of hegemonies" (Gramsci 1971). The utility of examining the Ilparakuyo and Maasai concepts is established not only by the preceding theoretical discussion of a historical materialist approach to language, but also by the explanatory power of such a method in what may be called "reflexive ethnographies" and "reflexive theory," so crucial to the construction of a historical materialist phenomenology.[4]

The Ilparakuyo/Maasai proverbs that serve as an epigraph to this chapter and the previous one do not, as may appear at first sight, imply that Maasai raise their own cultural distinctiveness or their age-set system to some elevated spiritual plain upon which "god" (*enkai*) may be thought to exist. On the contrary, they convey the opposite notion that, although *enkai* is creator and giver of all humankind's gifts (land, grass, water, salt, cattle, etc.), gifts that are accessible to all (Rigby 1985:48–66, 92–122), god is not remote and held in awe, but is thought of as a part of everyday life and discourse. For example, Ilparakuyo and Maasai women regularly invoke god's intervention for rain, good health, and fertility in day-to-day contexts (cf. Hollis 1905:345–348; Kipury 1983a:205–222).

The first concept I examine is embodied in the verb *aarisio*, which may be translated as "to be equal."[5] This is to be distinguished from another verb, *aanyanyuk*, which denotes "to be the same as" or "to resemble." A noun derived from the former is *erisioroto*, which can correctly be understood as the abstract notion of "equality"; the instrumental form of the verb is *arisiore*, "to be equal with." The causative "to make equal," or "to level," is *aitoris*. Among some pastoral Maasai sections, another noun derived from this verb is *erisiori*, denoting a *sub-set* of an age set (*olporror*), that is, a group of age-mates who are circumcised at the same time in the same locality, but who belong to one age-set (*olaji*) together with other similar subgroups; but there is a great deal of variation in such usages from one area of Maasailand to another, represented by the different "sections" of the Maasai peoples. Among Ilparakuyo, *erisiori* is not commonly used for these localized age groups, the term *esirit* (pl. *isirito*) being employed instead to denote a "local company" or "division" of *ilmurran* ("warriors"); this word is now also recruited to mean "a ladder."

Aarisio may be contrasted with the verb *aitore*, which means "to command" or "to control" (it is also sometimes translated as "to rule," which is incorrect). *Aitore* is represented in the age-set system by the influence and authority all "elders in power" have over all juniors, but most particularly over the alternate age-set below them, linked to them by the ritual firestick bond (*olpiron*: see Rigby 1985:22, 56, 61–63). In the system of kinship and descent, it denotes the authority of the male head of the patricentral polygynous family over wives, sons, daughters, and so on, but *not* all women as a category (see also Chapter 7 below).

Thus to be "in control" is to have *enkitoria*, and such a person can be referred to as *olaitoriani* (pl. *ilaitoriak*) or *enkaitoriani* (fem. sing; pl. *inkaitoriak*). The root-*aitore* does not *necessarily* have any gender connotations, and is distinguished from "strength," "power," or "bravery," which is *engolon*. Paradoxically, a strong and brave man is *oloing'oni* (lit. "a bull"; pl. *iloing'ok*) which, of course, does have a gender referent; yet *enkoing'oni* ("female bull"; pl. *inkoing'ok*) is a brave or strong women. But not only may women have the qualities of strength and bravery (*enkoing'ono*, the quality of "bullness," if I may coin a term) or *engolon*, a quality that may be possessed by both men and women, but also these qualities are less imporant than those of cooperation and unity. Ilparakuyo and Maasai have a proverb that says, *Meitululung'ayu enkoing'ono*, "Bravery (or strength) does not make itself complete" (or, bravery is not enough; however brave a person may be, two are better).

But perhaps most importantly, the ambiguity in the juxtaposition of equality and inequality that is the inescapable result of the age-set system ("inequality" inhering in a relation of "authority" and "power") is represented for the individual in the all-embracing concept of *enkanyit*. This word means a number of things, depending on context. It may thus be translated as "honor," "respect," or even "obedience"; but it applies with the same force to those attitudes that govern the relations between equals, as well as those that "inferiors" must show toward their "superiors." Elders constantly try, through lengthy and often repetitive lectures and harangues, to instill this quality in the members of their younger alternate (*olpiron* firestick) age-set; elders, however, must also demonstrate their own adherence to the norm of *enkanyit* by respecting their juniors, age-mates, kinsmen, kinswomen, and affines.

I have already explored the nature and importance of sharing among Ilparakuyo and Maasai (Rigby 1985:48–66), especially when they are in the junior warrior age-grade (*ilmurran*), who must adhere strongly to the injunctions of *enturuj* (or *entoroj*). This sharing, I indicated, was inseparable from the notion that at meat-feast ceremonies (*ilpuli*), *ilmurran* are both really and symbolically re-creating the movement from "community" to "structures" of influence and authority, functions that in other pastoral Maasai sections are located in the warrior villages known as *imanyat* (sing. *emanyata*; see Jacobs 1965a:299–308). During these periods, young men are also expected to form especially strong individual friendships (*shoreisho*), particularly with a close friend (*olchore*, pl. *ilchorueta*) with whom everything is shared.

All mature people, however, must show a commitment to being generous, which is an essential feature of having a "sense of honor" or "respect" (that is, *enkanyit*; see Spencer 1965:26). Among *ilmurran*, the sharing is often explicitly directed towards equalizing access to the basic things such as milk (i.e., "food"). Ilparakuyo and Maasai say, *Keng'ar 'lmurran ndaiki enye pookin, metaa ore 'lmurran aisinak neitoti 'lkulikai*, "Ilmurran share all their food, so that even [those without many cattle] are fed by their fellow age-mates" (Mpaayei 1954:13).

Spencer's excellent and detailed account (1965) of the concept of *enkanyit* among the Samburu (Isampur, sing. Osampurri, who use the same word) is valid *pari passu* for Ilparakuyo and other pastoral Maasai. In general, he notes (1965:26), the "worthy man has a marked sense of respect (*nkanyit*) and he is generous to the point of self denial." This "social value . . . embodies almost everything that the Samburu expect of a mature person," says Spencer, who continues (1965:xxii): "This value, *nkanyit*, acquires different shades of meaning in different contexts: it may be rendered variously as respect, a sense of shame, honor, a sense of duty, politeness, avoidance, or decency."

But above all, the ambivalence of authority and equality in the same and successive generations who, ideally, belong to alternate *olpiron*-linked age-sets (what Spencer calls "the tension of successive generations") is overcome by the power of *nkanyit*, which seems to have at times the ontological status of a "thing," although it can only be manifested in the *praxis* and discourse of individual persons. *Enkanyit* is inculcated into young men and women equally, and from an early age. Spencer quotes a Samburu elder who says, "*Nkanyit* is a wonderful thing. When the other elders see that a man has *nkanyit*, they all respect him [whatever his age-set status], for his heart and his stomach[6] are good. . . . He may not be rich. He may not be a skilled debater. But he is a worthy man, and no one will curse him. God [Nkai] likes *nkanyit*."

Ilmurran at meat-feasts among Ilparakuyo, or in the *imanyat* camps among other pastoral Maasai sections, therefore, have a "sense of community by creating the principle of *enturuj*, of sharing everything as equals in a world of love and emotion. *Enturuj*, however, is only the beginnings of community, it is not yet 'structure'—it is not authority in a system of 'ordered relations between structures,'" as manifested in the hierarchy of age-grades. But both are controlled by the mutual respect evoked by the concept of *enkanyit* (Rigby 1985:60).

Thus, the juxtaposition of equality and authority, the "tension" that arises in the age-set system, is transformed into action (or *praxis*), which, in this context, is constantly adjusting to changing circumstances. Ilparakuyo and Maasai say, *Etudung'oyie osinka olchekuti* (lit., "the worker has substituted for the shepherd" or "the wrong person or thing may show up at a time when you need him, or it, and prove to be very useful"; Kipury 1983a:165–166). Under these changing circumstances, the surplus labor generated by *ilmurran*, both junior and senior, is essential for the reproduction of the contemporary Ilparakuyo and Maasai social formations, negating the commonly voiced complaint by previous colonial administrators as well as contemporary governmental bodies in both Kenya and Tanzania that "moranhood" no longer has any relevance, since its "military functions" have disappeared, and therefore must be abandoned. But *ilmurran*, for Ilparakuyo and Maasai, still have *enkanyit*, both in themselves and for their elders, who return the respect by entrusting *ilmurran* with the marketing of livestock and the purchasing of veterinary medicines and heifers to reproduce the home herd: grave responsibilities involving huge sums of cash (Rigby 1985:160–161 *et passim*).

However, other factors caused by colonial and post-colonial interventions by government have also promoted, as we have seen, severe ambiguities in relations between elders in power and junior and senior *ilmurran*. To re-capitulate briefly, the colonial administration initially used Ilparakuyo and Maasai *ilmurran* to overcome other intransigent groups in the early stages of imperialist penetration, rewarding them with cattle they had raided during military engagements. Having achieved their ends, the colonialists then tried to control Ilparakuyo and Maasai by destroying the *ilmurran* age-grade and its ceremonies. At the same time, the colonial administration tried to influence the elders in power at various points, seriously jeopardizing amicable relations, particularly with the junior *ilmurran*.

Relations between the sexes are also embodied in the powerful notion of *enkanyit*, and the changing nature of these relationships are manifested in legends, myths, and songs commenting upon precolonial, colonial, and contemporary interventions in Ilparakuyo and Maasai society (cf.Kipury 1983*a*, 1989; Beidelman 1980; Burton and Kirk 1979; Llewelyn-Davies 1978, 1981; Spencer 1965; etc.). Two points may be noted here, although it is not possible to explore their full implications. The main issue again is the presence of ambiguity and respect, parallel to the juxtaposition of age-set equality and inequality already examined.

First, gender relations among Ilparakuyo and Maasai are reflected upon by an inconsistent yet persistent reversal of linguistic gender indicators (*Olmaa*, the language of Ilparakuyo and Maasai, is one in which nouns and syntax are gender-related, as opposed to all the Bantu languages of many of their neighbors, which are not) in words denoting sexual organs and other human and animal anatomical features. Thus, penis is "feminine" *enjabo* (pl. *injabon*), the singular and plural feminine prefixes being *en-* and *in-* respectively; among Ilparakuyo, the clitoris is "masculine" *oltolu* (pl. *iltoluo*), the singular and plural masculine prefixes being *ol-* and *il-*. Elsewhere in Maasai, the clitoris may be referred to as *olmouo* (pl. *ilmouoshi*), literally "the cow horn"; the feminine forms of this noun (*emouo* and *imouoshi*) may also be used. Nipples are (masculine) *ilki* (sing. *olkina*) but vagina is (feminine) *enkomos* or *embalishi* (Ilparakuyo; the slang words *enking'opi* and *entunde*, both feminine, may also be used, as are other various slang terms), and testicles are (masculine) *ilterege* (sing. *olteregeli*).

These reversed, as contrasted with non-reversed, usages are, however, consistent with some myths of the origin of cattle and the institution of marriage, and they embody yet another ambiguity about the relative logical status of male and female. Furthermore, circumcision ceremonies, the healing period after them, and other rituals also involve symbolic sex reversal, usually expressed in dress and ornaments but including forms of behavior.

Second, since English is the language of external domination (as well as Kiswahili, a basically Bantu language), the sexist, racist, and class dominance embodied in its usage and vocabulary (as *opposed* to Olmaa) became vehicles for new forms of categorical inequality. These implications of English in other contexts have been extensively remarked upon (cf. Lakoff 1980; Spender 1980; Parkin 1984).

Enkanyit encapsulates all the qualities that a mature person of either sex must have among Ilparakuyo and Maasai, and its evocation expresses the mutual respect required between categories of kin, affines, and members of age-sets, as well as the individual subject's responses to, and impact upon, everyday relationships, which are themselves constantly undergoing transformation. The latter, at least partially, is predicated upon the authoritarian nature of colonial, as well as some elements of post-colonial, administrations and their "development" schemes. The ultimate alienation inseparable from wage labor, however, does not yet affect the majority of Ilparakuyo and Maasai, although, as we have seen, the inroads of commoditization are universally evident. But now, especially in Kenya, there is a rapid increase, particularly among young men, in the drastic effects of separation from pastoral *praxis* and the means of production (the herd, land, grazing, and so on), intermittent wage employment, and overall under-employment in Nairobi and other urban areas. The struggle of hegemonies between the two levels of quotidian practices and their ideological supports is thus engaged (Gramsci 1971:333). It is to some aspects of this that I now turn.

◆ **III**   The characteristics of the colonial and post-colonial states of Africa and in other parts of the underdeveloped world have been elaborated in a number of recent works (Saul 1979; Leys 1975; Kitching 1980; Thomas 1984). The main features of the colonial state, from which the post-colonial, frequently authoritarian, state arises and with which it shares a number of features, have been admirably stated by Clive Thomas (1984:39). At the crucial point of transition from colonialism to neo-colonialism, "three great revolutionary streams" appear in the post–World War II period. These are "the nationalist, anti-imperialist movement in the periphery, the capitalist-worker conflict in the main capitalist countries, and the struggle between socialism and capitalism for dominance" at the global level.[7] In this context, and although nationalist independence movements constitute one of these streams, Thomas notes (1984:43) that "nationalist independence settlements were based on the exclusion of the masses from effective control of their society." This exclusion suited both the local petit bourgeoisie in power in the periphery, as well as the neo-colonial forces and intentions of previous or newly generated centers of capitalist growth.

The "backward" capitalist states of the periphery obviously share a number of characteristics with the advanced states of the center, but there are crucial differences. Although ideology and hegemony play an important role in the latter, they take on additional force in the post-colonial states in that a "hegemonic position *must be created*, and created within territorial boundaries which often appear as quite artificial entities since the powerful force of direct colonial fiat has been removed." John Saul (1979:70), expanding upon Hamza Alavi's earlier work (1972), states correctly that:

> Peripheral capitalism, like advanced capitalism, requires territorial unity and legitimacy, and the post-colonial state's centrality to the process of *creating* these conditions (like its centrality in promoting "economic development") further re-inforces Alavi's point about the state's importance. Indeed, when viewed from a Marxist perspective, this is what all the fashionable discussion of "nation-building" in development literature is all about.

Similarly, the ideological hegemony of the post-colonial state's ruling class includes the manipulation of "ethnic" and "tribal" identities, forging them into a weapon of ideological control, usually in the name of "anti-tribalism" and "nation building." As Leys perceptively remarks (1975:199), "modern tribalism" both is a creation of colonialism and provides the comprador ruling class with an excuse for labeling any dissension as "anti-nationalist." "Tribalism," says Leys, "consists in the fact that people identify other exploited people as the source of their insecurity and frustrations, rather than their common exploiters."

Capitalist "development" is always uneven, whether at a global, regional, or national level, and is particularly acute in peripheral social formations. As a result, in both Kenya and Tanzania, Maasai and Ilparakuyo, as well as other pastoralists, are caught in a double bind of external hegemonic control. For, as a result of their peripheralization *within* the national social formation (Hedlund 1979) and relative non-participation in commoditization and wage labor in the colonial state, they are singled out for the heaviest dose of "development interventions" in the post-colonial state. The latter are almost always top-down policies carrying a very strong authoritarian component, couched in a language and form of discourse that is entirely alien, if not antithetical, to the structural features of these social formations and their individual subjects, as well as the ethos of egalitarianism embodied in the concepts and forms of discourse presented in this chapter.

One further example will suffice. While it is quite evident from a historical materialist analysis that the herd, apart from the necessarily commoditized segment demanded by articulation with the state's political economy, is not a product but a means of production (Rigby 1985), development strategists still treat livestock as the "target" for development interventions, under the title of "livestock development"; that is, the herd is treated as a commodity produced by pastoralists. This makes the discourse of the agents of development entirely incomprehensible and hostile to pastoralists and their interests, just as pastoralists considered the discourse of imperialist-related Christianity as essentially alienating (Rigby 1985: 92–122).

In post-colonial authoritarian states, as Thomas ironically indicates (1984:120–121):

> Development is promoted as an end in itself and as a principal objective of all social and economic activity. To be sure, such development is deliberately divorced from any consideration of social justice, equity, or democracy, and is instead measured in terms of new constructions, the growth of gross national product, the degree of literacy, and in some cases the extent to which the security forces carry modern equipment.[8]

Little wonder, then, that Ilparakuyo and Maasai, who had previously welcomed individual missionaries into their midst, and even some colonial administrators, broke off relations and dialogue as soon as these intruders wished to dominate them politically, economically, and intellectually. So too they have viewed with suspicion and mistrust the interventions of post-colonial states, thereby earning the label "conservative." The authoritarian nature of development strategies exists irrespective of the capitalist or socialist leanings of the state (Thomas 1984:121). And although there are significant differences in the penetration of commoditization and capitalist relations of production as between Kenya and Tanzania (see Chapter 7), "development" is in both cases presented in an authoritarian and frequently arrogant manner, definitely lacking in the subleties and nuances of *enkanyit*.

In late capitalist societies, the state plays a hegemonic role by penetrating *all* classes (and hence affecting the social formation as a whole), mystifying the nature of exploitative relations, as Gramsci (1971) and Nicos Poulantzas (1973) have indicated. Observers who are sensitive to the role of language and ideology realize the distorted nature of communication and discourse that results in class societies (Jameson 1981). Sartre, for example, in *Les Mots* (1963:151), observed that "having discovered the world through language, [he] assumed for a long time that language was the world." And in his illuminating interpretation of Sartre, Joseph McMahon elaborates (1971:18):

> This is where a fundamental but tempting misapprehension, both of the functions of language and the nature of the world, begins. If the language through which one discovers the world is defective, and if the systems devised through use of that language are incomplete or ultimately impertinent, then both language and the systems—philosophical as well as social systems—will be defective and will produce unfortunate consequences.

The distortions in language engendered by class relations in advanced capitalist society are obviously alien to the classless, egalitarian Ilparakuyo and Maasai formations. Thus the materialization of ideology in the language and discourse of pastoralist *praxis*, a discourse in which the relations of production are relatively transparent, *demands* a hegemonic struggle with the authoritarian language of national development strategies, their associated class ideologies, and the social scientists who promote them. This is particularly so since the egalitarianism embodied in the formation of the individual Olparakuoni or Olmaasani subject is inseparable from the structures and processes of age organization and, to a lesser extent, of kinship (Chapters 4, 6, 7). The "universalistic" or "global" nature of age-set systems resists processes toward class formation. The resulting antagonism at the structural and ideological levels is well formulated by Bernardi in his comparative study of "age class systems" when he notes (1985:167):

Colonial impact pitted two global social and political systems against each other. There is no doubt that age class systems constitute a global social system for those societies where they represent the major eth-neme. In the one case, as in the other, that is, in the case of the colonial system and the age class system, all social life is involved—from the cognitive and ideological to the political and economic.

The inherited, albeit transformed, authoritarianism of national state intervention in these pastoral social formations guarantees a continuing confrontation between their pastoral *praxis*, its associated practical ideology, and their materialization in language, discourse, and ritual, on the one hand, and the imposition of legal, economic, and moral constraints by the state, on the other.

6   Some Ilparakuyo Views of Peripheral Capitalism

*Miaru inkishu
ilking'arana.*
They do not procure
cows, those who fight
among themselves.

◆   The concept of alienation in historical materialist theories of capitalism has been the subject of intense debate and elaboration (e.g., Meszaros 1970; Ollman 1971; Mandel and Novack 1970). But it is, without doubt, Stanley Diamond (1974, 1980, *et passim*) who has done most to develop the concept, in a comparative context, to encompass its utility in understanding pre-capitalist formations as well as capitalist ones, and the violence of the transition from one to the other. I use "violence" here in all its complexity of meaning, not only in its "physical" sense. The alienation engendered by capitalist forms of "development" was of central concern to Marx, not only (as is commonly supposed) in his earlier philosophical writings, but also in *Capital* and his subsequent attempts to theorize the revolutionary socialist and communist society of the future (cf. Dupré 1983).

Although Marx had on a number of occasions seen the development of capitalism as a necessary (albeit cruel and inhuman) historical phase, creating the conditions for revolution and social transformation, his and Engels's later studies of pre-capitalist formations were leading to altogether different conclusions that, unfortunately, were never fully pursued. As Eric Hobsbawm phrases it (1964:50), Marx "found himself increasingly appalled" by the inhumanity of capitalist society. The corollary of this was that Marx and Engels "always admired the positive social values embodied, in however backward a form, in the primitive community," and this led them to a deeper study of the "backward" Russian peasantry, from which, ironically, the Narodnicks later derived their position (1964:50, 49; Shanin 1983).[1]

At any rate, with the rise of a contemporary, critical, and comparative political economy, I have suggested throughout this book that "capitalist development" as proposed for underdeveloped countries by international and national agencies of various kinds is inherently contradictory in its recommendations and, hence, a lie. That it is productive of forms of alienation unparalleled in history is documented by economists and other social scientists who are by no means all representatives of a historical materialist position. The violence it does to pre-capitalist formations is succinctly expressed by Diamond when he notes (1974:345), "Obviously, the Marxist notion of alienation as social pathology flows from the assumption that there is a nucleus of possibilities in human nature which the ensemble of social relations in [capitalist bourgeois] society distorts."

This does not mean, however, that Marx, Engels, Diamond, or myself advocate a "return" to some idyllic, pre-capitalist, and pastoral (in its original sense) "golden age," in which exploitation and alienation never bared their fangs (Bourdieu 1977:177; cf. Bhalla 1986 for an interesting literary gloss). What it does mean is that the "benefits" of capitalist development strategy in the Third World are non-existent and, more pointedly, reactionary. It is the latter notion that lies behind the theory of underdevelopment as a retrogressive *process* entailed by the penetration of capitalism into non- (or pre-) capitalist formations over the past four hundred years or so, and not merely as a comparison between more and less "developed" countries (cf. Rodney 1972; Wolf 1982; Worsley 1984).

But the process of increasing alienation engendered by the penetration of capitalism involves not only the loss of land and the commoditization of labor but also the loss of indigenous technologies, cultural production, religions, and philosophies—in short, the loss of the unity of theory and practice, leading to social and political estrangement in pre-capitalist social formations. The Ilparakuyo and Maasai social formations with which I am here concerned are no exception (Rigby 1985:25–47 *et passim*). Yet not all pre-capitalist societies are affected in the same way, a phenomenon that results in multiple transitional forms.

The purpose of this chapter is to examine how Ilparakuyo and Maasai have observed, and continue to observe and comment critically upon, the relatively unique form taken by the processes of their violent incorporation into peripheral capitalism. This critical commentary is manifested in Ilparakuyo and Maasai use of language in politics, economics, ritual, and symbolic forms of *praxis*. Following Bakhtin (1981), whose dialogic is essentially a social philosophy and theory of language, we may note in preliminary fashion that terms referring to the physical representatives of colonial intervention and power (settlers, administrators, and missionaries), not to mention those of post-colonial governments, and embedded in a wholly Maasai form of utterance and discourse, are given poetic and conative power directed toward rejection of the commoditization of herds, land, and labor, and their concomitant forms of objectification and alienation.

The dialogue is always among Ilparakuyo and Maasai, whether age-mates, elders, women, uninitiated girls, uncircumcised boys, or the like. Addressees respond in uniquely Maasai fashion, but differently according to who they are and what the context is; the terms referring to concrete representations of intervention are invested with new meanings, responding to the context and the historical processes that bring them about. The "power" of language "lies not in the identity of the form but in that new and concrete meaning it acquires in the particular context" (Voloshinov 1986:67–68). Voloshinov/Bakhtin continues (1986:68,86):

> The task of understanding does not basically amount to recognizing the form used, but rather to understanding it in a particular, concrete context, to understanding its meaning in a particular utterance, i.e., it amounts to understanding its novelty and not recognizing its identity. . . . In point of fact, *word is a two-sided act.* It is determined equally by *whose* word it is and *for whom* it is meant. As a word, it is precisely *the product of the reciprocal relationship between speaker and listener, addresser and addressee.* Each and every word expresses the "one" in relation to the "other." I give myself verbal shape from another's point of view, ultimately, from the point of view of the community to which I belong. A word is a bridge thrown between myself and another. If one end of the bridge depends on me, then the other depends on my addressee. A word is a territory shared by both addresser and addressee, by the speaker and his interlocutor.

In this chapter, I must restrict my analysis to only a few examples of utterances in a total field of discourse; first, however, a number of other theoretical issues must be addressed.

✦ I   I have referred previously to the pertinence of Jean-Paul Sartre's understanding of the "role" of language in history and in the historical conditions that create alienation. Although

Sartre does not examine this question on the basis of a comparative political economy of social formations, restricting his investigations to bourgeois culture in the capitalist mode of production, there is, I suggest, a comparative methodology embedded in his intellectual *praxis* and its consequences for other forms of political *praxis*. It is this that enables us to deal with non-capitalist societies in terms of his theoretical framework, which includes a discourse on colonialism and racism (Sartre 1976b:716–734).

In answering the fundamental question in historical materialism, "What does it mean to *make* History on the basis of earlier conditions?" Sartre turns to the problem of language. First, language is *material*, representing both "interiority" in relation to the individual subject, and the "exteriority" of the "public" domain. This is the way he puts it in *The Critique of Dialectical Reason* (Sartre 1976b:98–99; hereafter the *Critique*):

> Words are matter. . . . Every word is, in fact, external to everyone; it lives *outside* as a public institution; and speaking does not consist in inserting a vocable into a brain through an ear, but in using sounds to direct the interlocutor's attention to this vocable as public exterior property. From this point of view, the totality of language as a set of *internal* relations between objective senses is given, for and to everyone; words are simply specifications expressed against the background of language; the sentence is an actual totalization where any word defines itself in relation to the others, to the context and to the entire language, as an integral part of the whole.

Hence, "languages are the product of History; as such they all have the exteriority and unity of separation. But language *cannot have come to man*, since it presupposes itself."

Second, however, in certain historical circumstances and senses, language is inert, denying the dialectical *praxis* of human beings in history, and thus declining into a reification of the *status quo* of bourgeois society.[2] Sartre connects these circumstances when he notes (1976b:97), "If we do not distinguish the project [the making of History], as transcendence, from circumstances, as conditions, we are left with nothing but inert objects, and history vanishes. Similarly, if human relations are a mere product, they are in essence reified and it becomes impossible to understand what their reification really consists in." He continues (1976b:98):

> Nor can there be any doubt that speech separates as much as it unifies; or that it reflects cleavages, the stratifications and inertias of the group; or that dialogues are partly dialogues of the deaf. Bourgeois pes-

simism decided long ago to rest content with this observation; the original relation of men to one another would be reduced to the pure and simple exterior coincidence of immutable substances.

These are the conditions in which language both generates, and is generated by, alienation, a situation in which, "for an individual to discover his isolation, his alienation, for him to suffer from silence or, for that matter, to become integrated into some collective undertaking, his relation to others, as manifested in and by the materiality of language, must constitute him in his own reality" (1976b:99).

And, finally, what of this "original relation of men to one another" that has been reduced and reified in bourgeois society? For Sartre, the latter condition of isolation and alienation is a particular aspect of the wider dialectical context, a condition in which the subject/object dichotomy and analytical reason predominate. I must quote the *Critique* again *in extenso* to get the full flavor and impact of his remarkable insight (Sartre 1976b:99):

> If the *praxis* of an individual is dialectical, his relation to the other must be dialectical too and it is contemporary with his original relation to materiality both inside and outside him. And this relation should not be seen as a potentiality present in everyone as a kind of "opening to the other" which is actualized in a few particular cases. This would be to shut up these relations in "natures" like boxes and to reduce them to mere subjective dispositions: and then we would relapse into analytical reason and molecular solipsism. "Human relations" are in fact [originally] inter-individual structures whose common bond is language and which *actually* exist at every moment in History. Isolation is merely a particular aspect of these relations.[3]

Two further issues remain before we can proceed to the historical commentary that Ilparakuyo and Maasai peoples have upon the intrusion of colonialism and capitalism into their social formations. They can be dealt with fairly briefly. The first one raises the problem of the relation between our understanding of the contexts in which certain structural processes occur historically, on the one hand, and the language and forms of discourse involved both *in* those contexts and also *about* those contexts, on the other. The second is to explore the relevance of Sartre's work for three discourses, which may be called Western Marxism, Third World Marxism, and their respective forms of intellectual and revolutionary *praxis*. Let me deal with them in reverse order; and there is no better place to begin than with Perry Anderson's penetrating critique of the first of the three discourses, at the very least, in his *In the Tracks of Historical Materialism* (1984).

Sartre claimed on several occasions that his *Critique* was not a

"Marxist book," but sometimes also said that it was "close to Marxism" (Catalano 1986:5,n.9). Joseph Catalano's gloss on this is important: "But of course, Sartre could very well be wrong in his judgment about his own work." Sartre never joined the French Communist Party and, as Anderson phrases it (1984), "Sartre in his last years followed his own trajectory from denunciation of [Stalinist] communism to formal renunciation of Marxism."[4]

Anderson's exposition of the reasons for these actions and positions taken by Sartre is totally convincing, and cannot be repeated in detail here. While the major figures of Sartre's generation in European Marxism had developed "lateral links to bourgeois culture" and to "philosophical legacies anterior to Marx himself" (in Sartre's case to the work of Heidegger and Husserl), Sartre "did try to develop a consequent practice of Marxist political intervention and theoretical interpretation of the course of class struggle in France and the world outside it" (Anderson 1984:16, 70).

Furthermore, Sartre and his European coevals "pioneered studies of cultural processes . . . as if in glittering compensation for their neglect of the structures and infrastructures of politics and economics." Anderson concludes (1984:17): "At the same time, within its newly constricted parameters, the brilliance and fertility of this tradition were by any standards remarkable. . . . Above all, art and ideology were the privileged terrain of much of this tradition, sounded by thinker after thinker with an imagination and precision that historical materialism had never deployed before." Somewhat ironically, the two elements of Sartrean Marxism—a theory of certain cultural processes and a discourse upon the *necessity* of violent revolution to overturn the violence of imperialism and neo-colonialism—became the basis of his relevance to Third World Marxism and revolutionary *praxis* in the underdeveloped world, and in particular, Africa.

In his highly concentrated and remarkably brilliant exposition of the rise and transformation of a contemporary African philosophy and its relations with the Negritude movement, African literature, and criticism, as the "groundwork" for an African revolution, V. Y. Mudimbe considers the historical pertinence of Sartre in a section entitled "J-P Sartre as an African Philosopher" (Mudimbe 1985:167–174, 1988:83–87). First, he notes, in qualification, that despite the fact that Sartre, in *Black Orpheus* (1976a [originally 1948]), thwarts "in a sovereign manner some possible orientations of the [Negritude] movement . . . [it is] a major event, perhaps most important, ideologically. It displays the potentialities of both Marxist revolution, and the negation of colonialism and racism. . . . What Sartre did was to impose philosophically the political dimension of negativity against

colonial history, which was a compelling undertaking for Africans"
(Mudimbe 1985:169). Sartre states in *Black Orpheus* (1976a:59) that
"the African" "creates an anti-racist racism. He does not at all wish
to dominate the world; he wishes the abolition of racial privileges
wherever they are found; he affirms his solidarity with the oppressed
of all colors. At a blow, the subjective, existential, ethnic notion of
Negritude passes, as Hegel would say, into the objective, positive,
exact notion of the proletariat."

In relation to African cultures, then, "by rejecting both the
colonial reason and the set of socially external values as the basis
of society, [Sartre's] brief treatise philosophically founded a relativist perspective in African social studies" (Mudimbe 1985:170); this
was not, however, a reductionist relativism. For at the same time,
it justified the grounds for a violent revolution to overthrow colonialism and racism as well as to re-shape the post-colonial states. It
remains to note at this point that, although Sartre did have an enormous impact upon the *littérature engagée* of the Negritude and African liberation movements, he was not accepted uncritically by such
seminal writers as Césaire, Leopold Senghor, Cheikh Anta Diop,
Bernard Dadie, Rene Depestre, Frantz Fanon, Keita Fodéba, Camara
Laye, Ferdinand Oyono, and others (Mudimbe 1985:169 *et passim*). I
return to the central points of this debate in Chapter 8.[5]

In relation to the issue of the reflexivity of language demanded
by a dialectical reason, Sartre was fully aware of being trapped by
the very categories (and hence alienation) of the referential and positivist terms he himself had to use in the *Critique*. Catalano deals
admirably with this problem in his highly illuminating commentary
on the *Critique* (Catalano 1986:158):

> Although Sartre does not mention it here, it is clear that the writing
> and reading of the *Critique* can reveal the same seriality, alterity, and
> impotence of any collective *product*. It is a commodity whose fate de-
> pends upon the practico-inert field it critiques. More than this . . . the
> language of the *Critique* is not above the specific alienations that it
> attempts to reveal. Terms like "study", "experience", "alienation", and
> "refer" all exhibit the alienation of our everyday lives, in which the
> product of our labor is a commodity to be bought and sold within the
> milieu of scarcity. . . . Sartre is well aware that his attempt to escape
> his French, intellectual, bourgeois heritage is but a fulfillment of his
> class being as bourgeois. Still . . . there is a crucial difference between
> struggling in good faith against inhumanity and directly aiming to
> increase it.

And here we must end this overextended struggle to gain the grounds
of a discourse upon which we *may* have the capacity to attempt,

in turn, an understanding of Ilparakuyo Maasai discourse upon the colonialist (and peripheral capitalist) penetration of their societies and history.

◆ **II**   In his paper on "Theory, Practice, and Poetry in Vico," Diamond (1980:313) notes that G. Vico's only real contribution to critical anthropology is his "unprecedented understanding of the 'primitive' character of poetic language ultimately in conflict with the 'higher' development of civilization, which Vico himself considered his single, most struggled-for achievement." We have already noted Marx's own search for the attributes of the communist society of the future in at least some aspects of the classless, communal societies of the past. The unity of theory, practice, and poetry can be seen in such societies; for Marx, as Diamond indicates (1974:104):

> Prehistory (the period of primitive, classless, communal society) and the post-historical societies (presumably, free of alienation) are hardly the subject of conventional Marxist analysis. The historical materialist terms of reference grow more cogent as class societies mature and harden, as states emerge, as civilization develops. . . . It follows, therefore, that only in primitive societies can we begin to understand the full potential of the generic-symbolic capacities of man.

Engels waxed eloquent in similar fashion in his interrogation of the "gentile constitution" of the Iroquois gens, Nubian society in Sudan, and the Amazulu of southern Africa. "There can be no poor and needy" in such societies, says Engels correctly (1970[1884]:266–267). "The communistic household and the gens knew their obligations towards the aged, the sick, and those disabled in war. All are free and equal, including women."

I have previously pointed out that the unity of theory (and/or practical ideology) and pastoral *praxis* among Ilparakuyo and Maasai informs *all* aspects of their social relations, from age-set organization, through kinship and affinal bonds, to gender relations and the ritual and symbolic contexts in which they are periodically manifested (above and Rigby 1985: *passim*). Contradictions do, of course, arise as political and economic transformations occur, stimulated by numerous historical forces both large and small in scale; but—and this is the crucial point—until very recently, these contradictions assumed a multiplicity of changing forms, unlike those associated with the rise of two antagonistic classes (Chapters 3, 4, and 5).

In an Ilparakuyo text recorded for Hollis in about 1905 by Justin

Lemenye (whose real name was Sameni ole Kipasis; see Rigby 1985: 108–110 *et passim*; Lemenye 1956; Fosbrooke 1956*b*), the "arrival of the Europeans" is commented upon in the idiom of Ilparakuyo cosmogony and prophesy:

> When Maasai see a comet (*olakira lo 'lkidong'oi*, lit. "star of the tail"), they know that a calamity will come to them (*eibung'u*, lit. "will take hold"). The cattle will die, there will be famine (*olameyu*, also "drought"), and their people will defect to their enemies.
>
> It is said that a comet was seen before the Europeans arrived, and one day when some Maasai children were herding cattle, they went to water them at a pond. When the cattle had finished drinking, a thing resembling a cow came out of the water, and the children were afraid. So they killed it, and found that it was full of caul fat (*enkipa*) instead of blood (*osarge*). When they reached home, they told the news.
>
> When the prophet (*oloiboni*) heard the news, he said: "If we see such a thing as a comet again, there will come into the land green people who have come out of the water. If they are killed, blood will not come out, only caul fat will issue."
>
> Soon after people had seen the next comet, the Europeans arrived. It was said that Europeans do not have blood, but only caul fat in their bodies.[6]

This commentary upon the arrival of the Europeans not only is recounted within the context of Ilparakuyo cosmology, as already mentioned, but is also associated with the signs of the worst kind of disaster that may befall Ilparakuyo and Maasai: the death of livestock and subsequent famine. But more important, it coincides closely with pivotal historical events that had serious consequences for Ilparakuyo and Maasai. The comet mentioned in the text is undoubtedly Halley's comet, which appeared in 1835 and 1910. Let me consider the two dates in sequence.

In 1835, there was a great deal of instability, population movement, and internecine strife among pastoral Maasai and other eastern African peoples. After some forty years of conflict, leading up to this date and caused largely (but not entirely) by external depredations, in about 1835 Ilparakuyo section broke away from Ilkisonko section of Maasai in what is now Tanzania (Rigby 1985:82–87, where I give the date as 1832 for the break; see also Chapters 1–5 above; cf. Thomson 1885:240–242; Beidelman 1960:249). Arab and European trading caravans were growing in number, causing increasing demands for food from the areas through which they passed. Since these caravans were frequently composed of two to three thousand people, their depredations were enormous, quite apart from those of the slave trade (see Kjekshus 1977:122–125).

Elders and warriors during a ceremony for a young man who killed a lion that was attacking the herds. Photo by Toreto ole Koisenge.

Ng'oto Toreto, the author's adoptive mother. Photo by Richard Cross.

The children of Shomet, the author's age-mate. Photo by Richard Cross.

Moyiyoi, an olmurrani *warrior. Photo by Richard Cross.*

Seis, the wife of Toreto ole Koisenge, the author's youngest brother, with her son. Photo by Richard Cross.

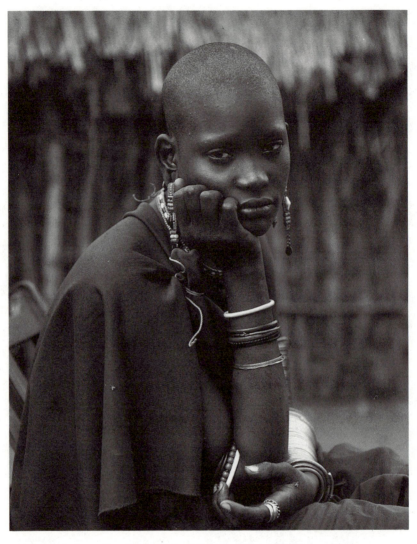

"Nakerai," the wife of Katau ole Koisenge. Photo by Richard Cross.

Lesinka and Siparo, **ilmurran** *warriors, with Toreto's motorcycle. Photo by Peter Biella.*

Saisi, an olmurrani *warrior, with Tanzanian currency in his earlobe. Photo by the author.*

Koisenge, the author's adoptive father. Photo by Richard Cross.

Warrior and uninitiated girls at a mutai at Koisenge's homestead, feasting and dancing after an olpul meat-feast ceremony. Photo by the author.

Saidi and Jani ole Maasai playing enkeshui, a traditional board game. The cigarettes are a local Tanzanian brand called Kali. Photo by the author.

Melkiori Matwi (seated) with a government driver and Shomet's children, at Koisenge's homestead. Photo by the author.

Toreto ole Koisenge repairing his motorcycle, at Koisenge's homestead. Photo by the author.

119

Kaisuse and Kone ole Kipalisi, **ilmurran** *warriors, with Koisenge's herd. Photo by the author.*

But the disasters and conflicts of the time also coincided with other crucial transformations "internal" to Ilparakuyo and other pastoral Maasai social formations. The most important for the present discussion is the rising influence during this period of the great prophets (*iloibonok kituaak*), which generated new contradictions and conflicts within these societies. The prophet Mbatiany ole Supet, who, like his father Supet, was one of the most influential prophets in the entire history of the prophetic lineage in Maasailand, succeeded his father in about 1851. Mbatiany belonged to the Iltwati age set, who were *ilmurran* ("warriors") from 1836 to 1856 (Jacobs 1968:16).[7]

Ilparakuyo and Maasai recognize that the time of the greatest "domination" by the great prophets, which covers the period from Supet (about 1806–1851) through the incumbency of Mbatiany (about 1851–1890) to Olonana (1896–1911) and Senteu (1890–1933), was the result of the penetration of merchant capital—not, of course, described as such, but in the form of foreign traders, up to the end of the nineteenth century. Then there was direct colonial intervention in the area by Germany and Britain, and all that came with it (Rigby 1985:67–122, Chapters 3, 4, and 5 above; cf. Fosbrooke 1956a; Jacobs 1968, 1979, *et passim*; Waller 1976; Lawren 1968; Mungeam 1970; etc.).

Among the disruptions caused by colonial penetration, upon which some Maasai historical texts reflect, are those directly linked to the changing role of the great prophets. Not only are the prophets given in these texts the capacity to interpret "omens" (*iltiloi*, sing. *oltilo*), and hence the powers of prophecy, but their relationships with, and influence upon, these prophesied external interventions are considered highly ambiguous. In one of the more formalized texts available to us, J. Tompo ole Mpaayei (1954:4–5) records the following:[8]

> Maasai . . . have prophets who foretell the future for the cattle, provide rituals [and give protective charms, *intaleng'o*, sing. *entaleng'oi*], send out the "warriors" to the wars [*nereu lmurran njorin*, lit. "drive—as of driving cattle—the *ilmurran* to the wars"] and bless the warriors' peaceful delegations [*nemayian lamala*], and do many other things besides. But prophets are *not* spokesmen [*ilaiguenak*, sing. *olaiguenani*, "age-set spokemen"]; their "track" *orrekie*, viz. "role" is different in forms of authority over the people [*inkishu*, lit. "cows"]. But the power [*engolon*] of the prophets is no longer as great as before, because [things] have changed and new knowledge [*eng'eno ng'ejuk*] has come in, of "papers" [*impala*, sing. *empalai*, lit. "subcutaneous tissue"] from the Europeans, [and] there has also come in [new ways] of praying to god [*omono ng'ejuk e nkai*]. . . . The powerlessness of Maasai today,

since the coming of the Europeans, is [because] they had weakened
themselves in internecine wars, after they had finished defeating their
[nineteenth-century] enemies [*ilmang'ati*, sing. *olmang'atinta*].

I must note here that, although the "warriors" are referred to
in this context by the descriptive word *ilmurran*, the "people in general," who elect age-set spokesmen and fall under the ritual influence
of the prophets, are consistently and metaphorically identified as
"cattle" (*inkishu*). Mpaayei's elders continue:

> It was pleuro-pneumonia [*olkipiei*, lit. "lung"] and rinderpest [*olodua*]
> of the cattle and smallpox [*entidiyai*, also called *enkeeya nemeipoti*,
> "the disease that should not be mentioned," because it killed so many
> people in the 1890s] which finished off Maasai, and so they were few
> when the Europeans arrived.[9] But it was the previous wars which were
> brought by the quarreling [*olong'oling'oli*] and jealousy [*olom*] of the
> prophets, it was they who brought low the people, and it was the rea-
> son why Maasai "went for each other" over the jealousy of the sons of
> the prophets, over the cattle medicines of Maasai.

The elders here are clearly referring to, and commenting upon,
the disastrous effects of a number of linked events. The rising power
of the prophets *prior* to actual colonial control at the end of the
nineteenth century, with their subsequent eclipse from official recognition later in this century once they had lost their usefulness to
the colonialists, is commented upon as well. This is predicated as a
cause of internecine warfare among Maasai sections, during which
some "break away" as did Ilparakuyo, while others, such as Iloogolala section, are "exterminated." Later, yet other sections, including
Ilaikipiak, are destroyed by white settler machinations and colonial
government policy; I return to this below.

But there is another subject of the discourse embodied in
this text: the frequently ambiguous *relationships* between the great
prophets on the one hand and the structures of age organization,
kinship, and affinity, as well as the protective medicines and blessings thought essential for *ilmurran* in war and cattle raiding, on
the other. The discourse reflects here upon the division of influence
and power betwen the religious and ritual (the prophets) and the
secular (age-set spokesmen, *ilaiguenak*, and age-set organization).
The tension betwen these two elements lies at the heart of Ilparakuyo and Maasai political and economic organization, as reflected
in their history since the rise of the prophets in the middle of
the seventeenth century (Rigby 1985:67–91 and Chapters 3 and 4
above). The influence of the former rises and falls as a result of
historical forces largely outside Ilparakuyo and Maasai control; the

latter remain more or less intact, although continually adjusting to new circumstances. And the idiom of a dialectical discourse upon these processes, embodying the unity of pastoral *praxis* and the ideological elements of ritual versus secular authority and their inevitable ambivalence, is anchored in the metaphor used—the term "cattle" (*inkishu*) for "persons" (*iltung'ana*, sing. *oltung'ani*) over whom these variant forms of influence and authority are exercised.[10] This text also links the two time periods we have mentioned (the early nineteenth century and the early twentieth century), and it is to the second of these that I now turn.

The reappearance of Halley's comet in 1910 coincided with further highly significant and dangerous events in Maasai history. The sons of the great prophet Mbatiany, Olonana (Lenana) in Kenya and Senteu (Sendeyo) in German East Africa, were deeply involved in the politics of the very strained relations between Ilparakuyo and Maasai and the intruding settlers and colonial governments, as well as the Christian missionaries,[11] so much so that Olonana was, at one time, made "paramount chief" of Kenya Maasai by the British administration. Most immediate for Kenya Maasai, as we have seen, was the loss of enormous areas of their most valuable dry-season grazing, and that most coveted by the settlers, as a result of the two "treaties" they made with the British colonial administration in 1904 and 1911. The "northern reserve," which had been cut off from the southern part of Maasailand by the 1904 agreement and settler appropriation of land, was abolished by the 1911 agreement, coinciding with the "rising desire among the settlers for an opportunity to appropriate the broad expanse of the Laikipia plateau" (Low 1965:36; cf. Sorrenson 1968; Leys 1926; etc.). Both "treaties" were later unilaterally abrogated by the British colonial government.

Olonana, now playing the dual role of *oloiboni kitok* (great prophet) and mediator between Kenya Maasai and the colonial administration and settlers, found that the Ilaikipiak section of Maasai in the north were "now acting without regard to his authority" (Low 1965:37). From the Maasai point of view, however, not only was Olonana "selling out" by acquiescing, in a meeting with the British governor Girouard in May 1910, to colonialist demands to abolish the Ilaikipiak section by absorbing them into the southern sections, he was also conforming to the pattern of "jealousies and quarrels" between him and his brother, Senteu, in German East Africa, as well as with Legalishu in Laikipia, a situation adversely commented upon as causing war and death to Maasai. Whatever Olonana's motives were at this stage, neither Ilaikipiak themselves nor the rest of Maasai were in favor of this loss of grazing and a whole section of Maasai in Laikipia. Maasai still refer correctly to this unfortunate event by a seldom-used phrase, *enkidaaroto oo 'Laikipiak,* which implies the "*extermination* of Ilaikipiak section."

But there was yet another operative factor. Owing to the enormous livestock losses Ilparakuyo and Maasai had suffered in the pleuropneumonia and rinderpest epidemics of the 1890s, some groups of *ilmurran* found it expedient to ally themselves with British expeditions to "pacify" neighboring peoples, such as the Nandi (see Chapter 2 above; cf. Mungeam 1970; Waller 1976; but cf. King 1971*b*), in the period between 1895 and 1905. This was because they were allowed to raid for cattle, which they desperately needed to replenish their herds, during these expeditions.

Needless to say, just as the colonialists had elevated the great prophets Olonana and Senteu to positions of secular political authority hitherto unknown in Ilparakuyo and Maasai history only to demote them later, so too the British used Maasai *ilmurran* for their own purposes and then tried to destroy their organization for fear that it might be used against them.

In German East Africa Maasailand, as it was then (later Tanganyika), policies encouraging settler agriculture and peasant production of commodity crops also led to an attempt to confine pastoral Maasai to an area south of the Arusha-Moshi road, bounded on the west by the Kondoa-Mbugwe road and lying between these and Ukaguru and Ugogo in the south, with centers at Kibaya and Kiteto. The areas demarcated for settlers contained numerous and extremely valuable seasonal grazing lands. Despite the fact that German colonial policy generally failed in this area, partly because there were not enough settlers but also because the Germans took longer than the British to establish military and administrative ascendency in Maasailand (cf. Huntingford 1969:103; Fosbrooke 1948; Parkipuny 1983), pastoral Maasai and Ilparakuyo were deeply and adversely affected. Kaj Arhem correctly observes (1985:19–20): "Yet agricultural encroachment and piecemeal land alienation for agricultural development took on considerable proportions in Tanganyika Maasailand during German rule. The Tanganyika Maasai soon lost the rich land around Mt. Kilimanjaro and Mt. Meru to white settlers and indigenous [petty commodity producing] farms."

An Ilparakuyo/Maasai "warriors' song" about a raid to Kikuyu country, transcribed by Lemenye as an *osingolio loo 'lmurran* for Hollis in about 1905, indicates the ambivalence *ilmurran* felt about the military relationship they had with the colonialists for the brief period during which they tried to replenish their devastated homestead herds. The song both praises an individual *olmurrani,* ole

Lang'oi, for his skill and bravery in war and livestock raids, and admits that the *ilmurran* needed the "permission" of a British administrator (Sub-Commissioner Ainsworth of Ukamba Province in Kenya) to take confiscated livestock home. The relevant parts of the song are as follows (Hollis 1905:354; my re-translation):

> Ole Lang'oi, the red [with blood] *olmurrani*
> Who went ahead to spy the country
> Returning in the evening to his fellows
> I say he has killed
> (how many times?)
> Thrice in a month!

> The cows in the cattle byre
> With downward twisted horns (*arroi*)
> Were shown to Encowaine [Ainsworth]
> And which we captured
> Because he climbed up to Kimara [a place in the country of the
>   Wakikuyu people].

The need to seek permission from an outsider to carry out an action that would normally be taken for granted is outrageous and deeply disturbing for *ilmurran*, even today. And this raises a further question about the status of this song in the discourse of Ilparakuyo and Maasai *ilmurran*.

A "war song" is normally called *enkipolosa*; war songs are central to the discourse through which Ilparakuyo and Maasai *ilmurran* assert their Maasai-ness, and they should never be sung near the homestead or be heard by women there, or even by the elders (Rigby 1985:57, 59; cf. Kipury 1983a:222–225). There are two possible reasons that Lemenye described this song to Hollis by the generic term for all songs, *osinkolio* (pl. *isinkolioitin*), rather than the more correct *enkipolosa*. For in Maasai discourse it would surely not have been merely a "Freudian slip": either it was not considered a "proper" war song by *ilmurran* who sang it or Lemenye did not want, for political reasons at that time, to classify the song correctly. I would tend to favor the latter explanation, although, of course, we will never really know.[12]

The year 1910, however, was not only the year of Olonana's "sellout"; it was also the year of the re-appearance of Halley's comet, an omen that presaged other calamitous events. The 1911 agreement forcing the northern sections of Kenya Maasai to move to the "southern reserve" was negotiated in 1910. I have already noted that representatives of Ilaikipiak section as well as other Maasai had rejected this plan. But in March 1911, Olonana died at Ngong (correctly

Enkong'u, "Eye" or "Spring"), and his "deathbed wish that the north-
erners should move south was skilfully exploited, with the result
that eventually, on the 4th April, 1911, the second Maasai agreement
was signed" (Low 1965:37).

In two other Ilparakuyo texts of 1905, pastoral Maasai peoples
again reflect upon the association of the prophets with the disasters
brought by colonial and settler occupation of Maasailand. At the
same time, they express a nostalgia for the earlier, less complicated,
capacities of these prophets' ancestors. The relevant parts of these
texts are as follows (my translation; cf. Hollis 1905:326–327)

> When the Europeans (*Ilaisungun*) came to these countries and Maa-
> sai first saw them, they [Maasai] used to spit, because they said, "We
> have not yet seen people like these." And they also said, "These people
> are prophets [themselves]." And if a European gave a person medicine
> (*olcani*, denoting actual, physical medicine, as "tree" or "plant"), the
> latter asked him to spit upon him to heal him.[13] And the former was
> given the name *olojuju*, "the hairy one" [from *aju*, "to be hairy"].
>
> Of all the prophets of the past, Mbatiany was the greatest one. Now,
> it is said that, before the Europeans came to these countries, he told
> the people, "Sometime in the future, white people [*iltung'anak ooibor*]
> will arrive among these [Maasai] sections (*iloshon*)." And then again,
> before he died, he told the people, "Move [away], because the cattle
> will die! You will first also see that which make hives like bees. And
> then the wild animals will die, and afterwards, the cattle." Both these
> prophecies have come about: the Europeans arrived and the cattle died.
> And when the cattle died, so also did Mbatiany himself [in the 1890s].

It is difficult to convey the metaphorical power and subtle inferences of other texts, songs, and poetic recitations that reflect upon
these various issues. But it *is* possible to generalize that, in all of
them, there are, first, the linking of Maasai cosmology with the presaging of events that occurred in the early nineteenth and the early
twentieth centuries. The bad omen (*oltilo torrono*) of Halley's comet
in both its appearances in 1835 and 1910 establishes a continuity between the beginning of each period of major upheavals, followed by
severe diseases of both humans and animals, drought, devastation,
and death. Second, the rising secular power of Mbatiany in the nineteenth century is reflected upon, especially his capacity to prophesy
major events. But third, the apotheosis of Mbatiany is replaced by
the fission of his prophetic powers (and thus their weakening) when
they become divided among his sons, Olonana and Senteu. These two
presided over the period of formal colonial penetration, the expropriation of vast areas of grazing land, and the fragmentary political

and ideological underpinnings, confirmed even further for Maasai by the Anglo-German conflict of 1914–1918.

Finally, in one sense, the prophetic capacity to foretell the future, coupled with the descent of the prophets into petty quarreling and jealousy, becomes the cause of the disasters of the 1890s to 1911, and beyond. While alluding to these dire consequences of history, certain forms of discourse juxtapose their prophesied inevitability with the continuing adherence of *ilmurran* to their role, not only as "warriors" but also as the locus of the physical and symbolic "regeneration" of pastoral Ilparakuyo and Maasai society (Rigby 1985:48–66, 87–89 and Chapters 3, 4, and 5 above).

These juxtapositions and allusions in turn engender a conative force in their re-telling and continual emendation. They constitute a series of performances, most particularly when *ilmurran* are speaking or singing their war songs, ballads, and poetic recitations for a specific audience; or when elders are nostalgically remembering their songs and recitations when they were *ilmurran*. Through them, the continuity yet transformation of Maasai history is re-affirmed, while the disruptive power of alien (and alienating) institutions of production and the ideological baggage they bring with them is controlled: the commoditization of the herd, land, and labor and the inroads of mercantile capital itself.

It is widely known that Ilparakuyo and Maasai have largely refused to engage in wage labor, religious conversion, and modern education until very recently. This rejection has been more successful among Ilparakuyo than other pastoral Maasai sections, particularly those in Kenya (see Chapter 7 below; cf. ole Sena 1981, 1986; Kipury 1983*b*, 1989). I have also indicated elsewhere (Rigby 1985:157–163) that the category of *ilmurran* (erroneously translated commonly as "warriors") is still essential for the social reproduction of Ilparakuyo and Maasai societies, both because they have assumed new economic and political duties in a transformed political economy and because they have retained *de facto* control (albeit modified) in certain rituals thought necessary for this social reproduction to occur.

The discourse proper to the time, when young men are *ilmurran*, embodies the struggle of Ilparakuyo and Maasai against total domination by external forces, both colonial and post-colonial. First, as we have seen, there is the commentary and reflection upon externally generated events, commentary that "records" and hence appropriates the essential consequences of these events for Maasai, by incorporating them into on-going pastoral *praxis*. Second, and parallel to this process of incorporation, war songs and poetic recitations continue to record, praise, and enhance the (ostensibly unchanging) qualities of *murrano,* or "warriorhood," juxtaposing in the process and hence linking dialectically these two "levels" of time, neither of which can be fully understood without the other (cf. Rigby 1985:67–91 *et passim*).

◆ **III**   In this chapter, I have been able to examine only one side of this dialectic; the other requires a much more detailed and careful textual analysis of the stories, songs, and recitations learned or composed and performed mainly by Ilparakuyo and Maasai men when they are *ilmurran.* These are frequently recalled by elders who wish to testify to certain historical events or look back nostalgically to their own days of glory as *ilmurran* themselves. Women too compose and sing historical songs, as well as those extolling the virtues of their clandestine lovers (Kipury 1983*a: passim*). Meager as it is, I have presented here sufficient textual evidence to make some preliminary assertions.

First, these texts are grounded in the idiom and metaphor of the Maasai language (*Olmaa,* or *enkutuk oo 'lMaasai*) *and* its instantiation in pastoral *praxis.* To this extent they are concordant with Sartre's definition of dialectic discourse (1976*b*:828) as "the intelligibility of *praxis* at every level." But second, and of equal significance, this discourse encompasses the historical reality and oppressive danger of colonialist intervention, embodied in merchant and trader, missionary, settler, and administrator. The individual composer, interpreter, or performer of a text expresses the contradictions, yet "inevitability," of the wholesale destructiveness of these intrusions, again in the context of pastoral *praxis.* This "other" dialectical element is again illuminated by Sartre's insight when he states (1976*b*:220) that the "only concrete basis for the historical dialectic is the dialectical structure of the individual action"; it is also elucidated by Bakhtin's notion of "dialogic."

The "time" expressed in these Ilparakuyo and Maasai discourses is, in a sense, "transcendental," expressing the continuity of Ilparakuyo and Maasai history; but this is a continuity punctuated by the temporal dimension of "significant" events that constitute an irreversible historicity. The concept of the irreversibility of events is neither foreign nor new to Ilparakuyo and Maasai (Rigby 1985:67–91). But the temporality of these events is controlled through the dialectical relations between historical discourse about them on the one hand and the continuing transcendental unity of pastoral *praxis* and discourse about it on the other, itself expressed as a historicity.

In the previous chapter I noted the authoritarian nature of the colonial and post-colonial state; indeed, the latter derives its initial structure, at least, from the former. As with advanced capitalist states, and differing from them more in degree than in form, ruling class ideology in peripheral states is inseparable from hegemonic control, in which distorted forms of communication play a major role. However, in both colonial and post-colonial states, the languages of state and national policy are often different from the multiplicity of local languages that are still the basis for everyday discourse. As in other forms of polity, language differences and policy may provide the arena for internal conflict and secession; they most certainly provide the context for frequent contradictions. Most people, even in the rural areas of Africa, know two or more languages, and sometimes even as many as seven or eight. For this and other reasons, hegemonic control in peripheral states is elusive, yet still necessary for the state's reproduction; it is therefore much more evidently strengthened by the very real threat of physical force, used by the ruling class to maintain its position.

In the context of developing a contemporary African philosophy, the *structure* of the so-called "Bantu languages" (lit. "people languages") has, on occasion, been identified as a "window" into African philosophical ideas (see the commentary upon the work of A. Kagame, N. Tshiamalenga, and others in Mudimbe 1985:187–192, 1988:145–52 *et passim*). While some of this work constitutes "deductions of a really solid and impressive linguistic analysis" (Mudimbe 1985:192), one cannot help wondering how such a procedure could be extended to other African language groups such as the "southern Nilotic," of which Maa is one, which are totally different in structure from the Bantu languages. I take this up more systematically in my conclusion (Chapter 8).

Nevertheless, commencing with a Gramscian view of a Marxist theory of language, I return to the necessity, already gleaned from Sartre, of viewing language as material, historical, and dialectical. Thus, we may agree with Salamini when he states (1981:191): "Teaching a particular grammar means teaching about a particular phase of the history of language, from a certain class position. And learning a grammar means learning a particular interpretation of the past. . . . With no hesitation [Gramsci] states that a normative grammar is a political act."

It is not in contradiction with certain phenomenological and existential views of language (views that also stress the historicity and materiality of language, speech, and discourse) to suggest that language is closely related to the dialectic of technology and the social relations of production, that is, of a *particular* mode of production. Marx and Engels make a clear distinction between the natural role of language "at first" in human "pre-history," as *opposed* to its later alienating (and alienated) function in class society, a point already made in reference to the work of Diamond and Sartre (cf. also de Certeau 1984:133 *et passim*). In the *German Ideology*, Marx and Engels maintain (1976:36, cf. 44; also Paci 1972:207–208):

> The production of ideas, of conceptions, of consciousness, is at first directly interwoven with the material activity and the material intercourse of men—the language of real life. Conceiving, thinking, and mental intercourse of men at this stage still appear as the direct eflux of their material behavior. The same applies to mental production as expressed in the language of the politics, laws, morality, religion, metaphysics, etc., of a people. Men are the producers of their conceptions, ideas, etc., that is, real, active men, as they are conditioned by a definite development of their productive forces and the intercourse corresponding to these.[14]

The language of Ilparakuyo and Maasai, as I have tried to show, is *poetic*. Stanley Diamond (1980:310) asks the question, "Does [Vico] mean, ultimately, that any man can become a poet of words and things (primitive man is said to be a poet by nature . . .), but only a few may understand what men make?" And his answer is (1980:320): "The origins of language—its metaphorical, connotative, associative, and yet concrete character, are in poetry. Myths are imaginative, not abstract, universals, the poetic personification of history."

How better to end this discussion than with an excerpt from a Maasai poetic recitation (*eoko*), half sung and half spoken, by an *olmurrani* from Ilpurko section of Kenya Maasai in 1976, in which the transcendental and historical discourses are conjoined in one glorious epic (Kipury 1983a:226–227):

> I would never have thought I would have come this far
> Before telling you that I am ole Kores [son of Kores]
> The legs of whose beautiful heifers are branded
> As they move on the green landscape.
> There goes Maroroi [name of a cow] with the spotted ochre color
> Then that ox of mine that is dressed in blue
> Who takes a quick flight up to the high country of ole Polos
> Where we, the brave sons of ole Dikir live
> Whose cattle are used to paddock grazing.[15]
>
> Are they the ones of there or not?
> I know it is they the red heifers with brown ears

Though they have not been smeared with ochre
Ones that are well suited with patches
And whose hearts are too soft to permit them delay.

Are those others mine, or are they not?
I know they are the ones all of the same color
Looking like the Kanga cloths [16]
The country of cool air
And where my patterned ox stretches his legs.

7   The Dynamics of Contemporary Class Formation

Etejo enkiteng':
"mikintaaya,
nchooyioki!"
The cow said, "Do not
lend me out, give
me away."

✦   It is neither desirable nor possible to provide a comprehensive history of development strategies in Tanzania and Kenya Maasailand; much of the voluminous literature on this topic is admirably surveyed in L. M. ole Parkipuny (1979 *et passim*; cf. Hoben 1976; Jacobs 1978; Ndagala 1978, 1982, etc.) for Tanzania, and Evangelou (1984) for Kenya. We have noted that national policies for rural development since independence have been radically different in Kenya and Tanzania. The latter is ostensibly committed to a socialist path while Kenya, despite a now forgotten nod toward "African socialism" in 1965, is generally open to capitalist forms of development strategy, whatever they may be. But does this difference in national commitments really affect what happens at the *local level* in Tanzania and Kenya Maasailand? I attempt in this chapter to deal with some aspects of this question.

There are, however, other levels upon which answers to this problem must be sought. One of these relates to the question of international aid toward development. Here, both Kenya and Tanzania Maasailand have been the object of internationally funded "interventions" of various kinds, both before and after the national independence of each country. In Kenya, Maasai have been subjected historically to both poles of governmental attitudes toward pastoralists identified by Galaty (1980). During the colonial period, the attitude has been decribed as one of "benign neglect" but only, as we have seen, after settlers and colonial government had stolen much of the best grazing areas. Since the late 1960s, however, the Kenya government has adopted the second pole, which involves "radical governmental intervention in the process of nomadic pastoralism" (Galaty 1980:159). Galaty goes on: "While in the first case, the land rights of nomads are generally recognized, in the second case, pastoral lands are often viewed as relatively unoccupied, unowned, and unused, and thus represented as *national* rather than regional or group resources" (1980:160).

In Tanzania, "the idea of bringing development to the Maasai dates back to the arrival of the Europeans in the area in the second half of the nineteenth century" (Parkipuny 1979, cf. 1983; Fosbrooke 1948; etc.). The Germans tried to alienate the entire northern part of German East Africa Maasailand for settler occupation, but did not have enough settlers to complete the job before they were defeated in the 1914–1918 war and removed, leaving Tanganyika to British mandate under the League of Nations. Since before Tanzanian independence, however, Maasailand has also become the object of development interventions, both under the Range Management and Development Project (funded initially by the United States Agency for International Development; see Hoben 1976) and the villagization policy, whose most recent variant in Maasailand was called "Operation *Imparnati*" (or "Operation Permanent Settlements": cf. Ndagala 1978, 1982; Parkipuny 1979, 1983), whose implementation began in September 1974.

There are three hypotheses that dominate the study of class formation among the pre-capitalist and previously egalitarian social formations of East African pastoralists; all three have relevance, but not necessarily conclusive answers, for the study of Ilparakuyo and Maasai society. The first claims that pervasive ecological, economic, and social processes result in inevitable inequalities between livestock-holding units in the numbers they have at their disposal, this leading in turn to "rich" and "poor" classes of pastoralists. The second is that an incipient ruling class, derived from the unique position held by the descent group that provides the prophetic lineage of ritual and religious leaders, was already present in these social formations prior to the penetration of merchant capital and, later, formal colonization. I have dealt with these arguments in Chapter 3. The third hypothesis proposes that these social formations were not egalitarian in the first place, and that exploitation was inherent to their social reproduction and involved the appropriation of surplus value by male elders from male juniors and all women.

These three hypotheses are not, of course, mutually exclusive; they all focus upon characteristics that are inseparable from the very nature of these social formations; as such, they postulate that, even without the global expansion of capitalism, imperialism, and colonialism, these societies would have inevitably become class societies, with the inevitable formation of states. The latter conclusion does not concern me here; it is based upon an "if/then" view of history, and we shall never be able to decide the issue one way or the other. And since part of the third hypothesis, that which proposes that exploitation based upon gender was a property of these societies, is the subject of Naomi Kipury's doctoral dissertation (Kipury 1989; Kipury is from Kenya Maasailand), I shall refer to this aspect only in a cursory manner. This chapter, therefore, is largely concerned with a critical appraisal of the first hypothesis, and is an attempt to place it in historical perspective for Ilparakuyo as well as other Tanzanian and Kenyan sections (*iloshon*) of pastoral Maasai.

✦ I   Neither Ilparakuyo nor Maasai pastoralists are truly nomadic, although they move their homesteads (*inkang'itie*) frequently, not only within the local community of which they may have been members for some years but also over long distances, either to establish new communities or to join already established ones (Beidelman 1960, 1962a; Ndagala 1974; Rigby 1985). In the former case, two or more homestead groups, which are usually related to one another by descent, matrilateral kinship, affinal bonds, or age-set bonds, often move together, although long distance movements may also be the result of fission within one three-generation domestic group. In the latter case, moves are made primarily to communities where persons in such categories of relationship already reside.

Descent and kinship ties in Ilparakuyo and Maasai society are always converted into livestock exchange relationships when they are "in operation"; individuals, both male and female, then refer to each other by "livestock terms" and not kinship ones (cf. Hollis 1910:477–478 *et passim*). In fact, the use of livestock exchange terms between closely related people, affines, age-mates, and friends indicates that their relationship does not merely exist, but is active in cooperation and sharing in the day-to-day tasks of pastoral production and life. Some relationships among heads of domestic groups in

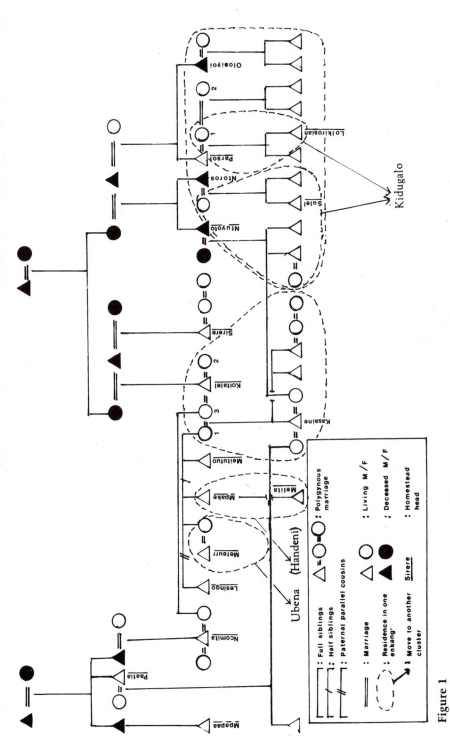

Figure 1
Some Relationships among Ilparakuyo Homestead Heads, West Bagamoyo District, c. 1980
(see Sketch Map 1)

one community between 1978 and 1980 are represented in Figure 1; the rough location of their (unidentified) homesteads are provided in Sketch Map 1.[1] This diagram does not represent *all* kinship ties: this would not be possible; individuals are often related through more than one kinship category, and indications of this are given in the figure. Neither does it indicate age-set ties, which are just as frequently the basis for common residence and cooperation.

Many of these homestead heads had moved about 120 miles into this area from Kiberashi in Handeni District, beginning in the late 1930s, where there had been a drought at that time. Most of them had come with their parental or grandparental generation: a few of the former are still alive as "retired elders" (*iltasati*). By 1987, several of the homestead heads in West Bagamoyo District had moved away to Kisarawe and Morogoro districts, to the south and southwest, following the general pattern of Ilparakuyo movement from the northeast to the southwest, over several hundred years (see Rigby 1985:9–11; Beidelman 1960, 1962*a* and *b*; Ndagala 1974, 1986; Mustafa *et al.* 1980). Ilparakuyo now live scattered among numerous cultivating or agro-pastoral groups, as far south as Mbeya, Rungwe, and Njombe districts.

I have discussed in some detail elsewhere the value of conceptualizing Ilparakuyo and Maasai social formations as representing a specific form of the "Germanic" mode of production (Rigby 1985:9–24, 123–167, *et passim*; cf. Bonte 1978) This implies that there are two "basic" levels of the mode of production, although it cannot be reduced to these two levels; among Ilparakuyo, we have distinguished at least three levels (see Chapter 3). In this, Ilparakuyo differ from other pastoral Maasai sections. Ties of patrilineal descent, matrilateral kinship, and affinity are given more emphasis in domestic group organization among Ilparakuyo than among, for example, Ilkisonko and other sections. Thus the term "camp," used for larger associations of domestic groups among the latter, is not as important in conceptualizing Ilparakuyo production and consumption units (cf. Bonte 1981: 26–32 *et passim*). Instead, I use the concepts "domestic group" and "homestead" to indicate the first level of production relations and local organization, at which direct appropriation of the means of production occurs. In this, Ilparakuyo are more akin to the Wagogo than to other pastoral Maasai formations (Jacobs 1965*a*, 1965*b*; cf. Spencer 1988).

From the complex of relationships represented in Figure 1, it is clear that almost all the domestic group heads in the area are related to one another. Thus, Koitalel and Sirere are paternal half-siblings; Koitalel and Meitutuo are brothers-in-law. Koitalel's son Kasaine is

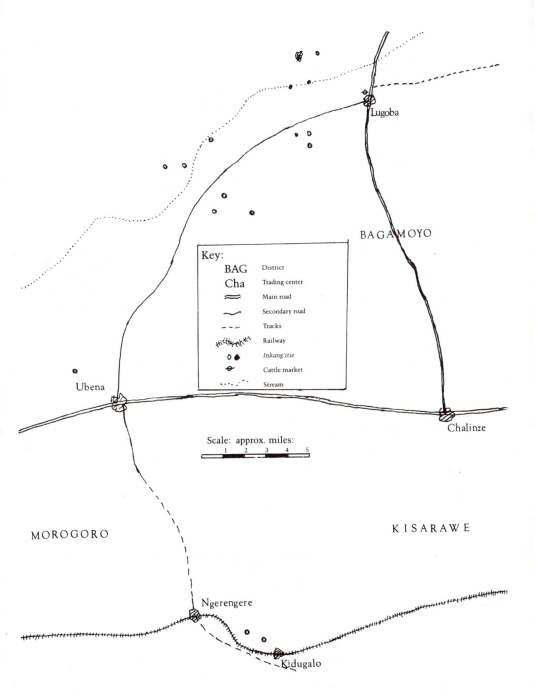

Sketch Map 1
Some Ilparakuyo Homesteads (*inkang'itie*), West Bagamoyo District,
c. 1980 (unidentified)

married to Ncomita's classificatory sister (the daughter of Ncomita's father's brother, Paatia); his second wife is also Parsoi's paternal half-brother's daughter, Manang'oi, making Parsoi and Koitalel classificatory father, and father, respectively of married children; thus, Kasaine married his classificatory FMZSD; and so on. As opposed to the forces of fission and conflict that may arise between agnatic full- and half-siblings, who have close interests in decisions and divisions of the herd, relations between cross-cousins, especially if they belong to the same age-set and neighborhood, are very close and cooperative. This extends to all matrilateral kin, and is related to the strong mother's brother–sister's son bond in this patrilineal society. Thus, Hollis is quite correct when he notes (1910:478):

> A maternal uncle (*olapu*) exercises great influence over his nephews, as it is believed that if he were to curse them they would die. He can at any time stop a fight in which one of his nephews is engaged by merely calling on his nephew to desist, as the nephew would be afraid of his right arm withering if he were to disobey. This power is to a certain extent reciprocal, and if a man were to start beating his wife he would have to stop if his maternal nephew ordered him to do so.

This religiously and ritually sanctioned reciprocity between mother's brother and sister's son extends to the relationship between cross-cousins (who are also, reciprocally, *olapu* or its cognate *ole'nkapu*), and is contrasted with the relatively weaker power of a father to curse his son; it also implies reciprocity in access to livestock. Cross-cousinship is, of course, derived from an affinal relationship in the preceding generation; thus reciprocity in livestock rights also applies to close affines. Given the crucial importance of these relationships in the local community, I quote Hollis again, both to reinforce my analysis and to demonstrate its validity for the wider Maasai community. He accurately states (Hollis 1910:479):

> If the uncle desires anything that is the property of his nephew's father the nephew must [get] it from his father, who will at once give it up when he knows for whom it is required. This power of taking property is reciprocal, and in fact applies to all persons who address each other as *ol-apu*, *ole'ngapu*, etc. A nephew, for instance, can go to his maternal uncle's kraal, and if his uncle is absent, he can slaughter a goat or drink his uncle's milk, and nothing would be said. He cannot, however, drive off a cow without his uncle's sanction, but permission would not be refused.

And so on.

For our present purposes, it is not relevant to pursue such inter-domestic group relations any further, save to note that local communities of Ilparakuyo are based upon a network of kinship and age-organization. These ties reinforce local community decisions about pastoral *praxis*, provide the context of age-set rituals such as meat feasts (*ilpuli*: see Rigby 1985:48, 66), circumcisions (*imurat*), marriage (*enkiyama*), and so on, and establish the conditions for mutual support among "better-off" and "worse-off" domestic groups at any particular point in time. As I have noted, they almost all involve bonds of livestock exchange, which is the basis of such mutual support.

Until the early 1980s, the dynamics of homestead movements, relationships among domestic groups at the local community level, and the internal fission of the latter were based largely upon these relationships of descent, kinship, affinity, and age-organization (Rigby 1985:123–167). Fission *within* domestic groups provided (and still provides) a major basis for the creation of new and relatively independent homestead groups, either nearby in the same locality or in other localities. This fission takes place almost exclusively along the lines of cleavage between the semi-autonomous, matricentral "houses" (*inkajijik*) in the polygynous extended family, sometimes delayed until the third generation. Thus Parsoi's deceased elder *full*-brother Olosiyoi's sons, Shapara and Kurratany, lived with him until his death in 1985. But his (also deceased) paternal *half*-brother's sons, Sulel, Masaika, and others, had moved away, as one domestic group, to Kidugalo in Kisarawe District, some forty miles to the south. This did not, however, prevent continuing contact through regular visits, livestock exchanges, marriage arrangements, and other activities among these kin. Ilparakuyo travel frequently and extensively throughout the scattered areas they inhabit, as well as into the areas of other pastoral Maasai sections in Tanzania and Kenya (see Figures 2 and 3).

In another case, fission began to appear in Koitalel's agnatic polygynous extended family in the late 1970s. In 1975, he had moved his homestead of five houses (*inkajijik imiet*: three of his own wives and one each of the wives of his two married eldest sons), as a still intact group, a few miles to a new locality to avoid having to enter the government-created *ujamaa* village, established in the area specifically for Ilparakuyo pastoralists. By 1979, his senior (first) wife, Ng'oto Toronkei, and her three adult married sons had left her husband's *enkang'* (homestead) and gone to live some four and a half miles away, still within the same pastoralist community. She still retains a physical "house" (also called *enkaji*) in her husband's homestead, but no longer has her herd there and does not live there. Koitalel is thus left with his two junior wives and their children. This form of "terminal separation," usually commencing with the senior wife's house, is characteristic of domestic group fission among Ilparakuyo. It does not dismantle the marriage, the mutual rights and obligations of husband and wife; but since the wife is usually no longer capable of having children, the husband abandons control of her sexuality and procreative abilities.

At the community level of the relations of production then,

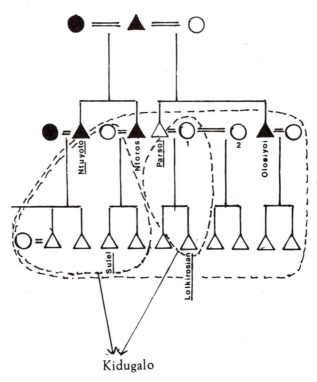

Kidugalo

Figure 2
Fission in Parsoi's Homestead

although there always are significant disparities in livestock holdings from one domestic group to the next, mutual rights in livestock, continual exchange, and trusteeship arrangements ensure the redistribution of cattle and small stock (especially cows in milk) among homesteads, providing all with at least some access to the major means of production. Homestead migration and internal fission are normally based upon the exigencies of good herding techniques and general

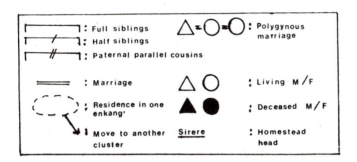

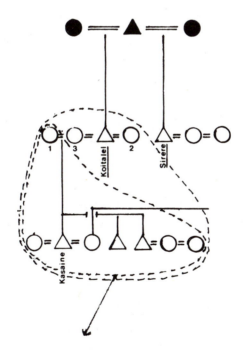

Figure 3
Fission in Koitalel's Homestead

pastoral *praxis*. Although Ilparakuyo and Maasai have a noun for the notion of "witchcraft" (*esakutore*) and a verb that means to practice sorcery (*asakut*), mutual accusations based upon these notions were, until the recent past, very rare, and the movement of domestic groups away from each other for reasons associated with these beliefs virtually non-existent.[2] But this, as we shall see, is changing.

◆ **II**   Almost all recent studies of Ilparakuyo and Maasai communities show great variations in the size of herds belonging to different domestic groups at any one point in time. There is little doubt that such variations were also true of the pre-colonial situation in these social formations; but it is also certain that these differentials in access to the major means of production of domestic groups have been aggravated by commoditization of the herd, loss of grazing lands and water resources, and other "external" factors such as the introduction of animal and human diseases previously unknown to Maasai (such as rinderpest, bovine pleuropneumonia, and smallpox). Before I consider the implications of these inequalities for the dynamics of class formation, I present some numerical data for Ilparakuyo herds and those of other Maasai sections in both Tanzania and Kenya, at varying periods in time.[3]

Unfortunately, most of the data available on Ilparakuyo and Maasai livestock holdings use different parameters for stratifying domestic group samples into "rich," "middle," and "poor" pastoralist families. While the gross figures allow of some direct comparisions between different pastoralist communities, there are insufficient data for re-analysis upon common parameters for comparative stratification for all Ilparakuyo and Maasai sections in which some numerical data are available. Nevertheless, through dint of some statistical manipulation, I have arrived at very rough stratification figures for the Ilparakuyo community in which I live, and the East African Range Livestock Systems Study (EARLSS; see Chapter 1, above) site in Ilkaputiei section of Kenya Maasai (see the Appendix, Table 1).

It is apparent that, although the distribution of domestic groups through the categories is skewed (there is a far larger percentage of domestic groups in the "poor" category among Ilparakuyo than Ilkaputiei, as there is a far higher percentage in the "middle" category among Ilkaputiei than Ilparakuyo), the figures do indicate drastic differences in livestock holdings within each community.[4] The fact that the "rich" domestic groups in Ilkaputiei have approximately twice the per capita livestock holdings of the same groups among Ilparakuyo is in keeping with the generally lower holdings among the latter; but this comparison does not hold for *all* other pastoral Maasai sections. There are even greater variations among the various pastoral Maasai sections than between them and Ilparakuyo, as we shall see.

Even with these figures, however, if we divide both samples into the "rich" and "the rest" (middle + poor), we get a very similar picture among "the rest." They constitute 73.9 percent of Ilparakuyo and 70.8 percent of Ilkaputiei domestic groups. Among Ilkaputiei, these domestic groups average 7.6 LSUs per capita; among Ilparakuyo, the figure is 5.8 LSUs.

If we turn now to comparisons, at specific times, between Ilparakuyo and other Maasai sections in terms of global figures for non-stratified samples, we may illustrate inter-community and inter-section variations. Average figures for livestock units per capita among Ilparakuyo, Komolonik Ranching Association, and Ngorongoro Maasai in Tanzania, and Ilkaputiei Maasai in Kenya, are given in the Appendix, Table 2.[5]

It is evident that, taken at one point in time, although pastoral Maasai sections have on average more livestock per capita than Ilparakuyo, there is considerable variation among the latter. The very low figure for the Komolonik Ranching Association in Monduli Juu, northern Tanzania, when compared with Ilparakuyo and other pastoral Maasai in Ngorongoro and Ilkaputiei, needs some explanation. It may be associated with a number of factors, all of which are important for this analysis (see Ndagala 1978, 1982; cf. Parkipuny 1975, 1979, 1983). First, there are a considerable number of non-Maasai in this area. Second, Komolonik was a ranching association associated with the *ujamaa kijijini* of Monduli Juu, created for development purposes under the national villagization scheme for socialist development in Tanzania (Ndagala 1978, 1982), which began in earnest in Tanzania Maasailand in 1975. Finally, almost all the Maasai domestic groups in this community cultivate food crops for themselves, or cash crops that they sell for money to purchase agricultural products (Ndagala 1982:36). I return to these issues later.

In terms of variations and trends in overall herd size, some time-depth gross figures are available with which we may begin. Figure 4 represents graphically the overall herd size for the Ilparakuyo community in West Bagamoyo District, for the period 1966–1978. These are for homesteads that later became part of the pastoralist "village" (*kijiji cha wafugaji*) in this area, under Tanzania's villagization development plan. Previous figures (Ndagala 1974, 1986) indicate that the rapid increase in the total herd in the area, demonstrated for the period 1966–1969, had been going on since Ilparakuyo began moving into West Bagamoyo from Handeni District in the late 1930s. This trend can be illustrated for the years 1935–1937 (see the Appendix, Table 3). Not all these cattle, however, were in Ilparakuyo herds at this time. In 1937, only 50.4 percent of the total herd in Bagamoyo District belonged to Ilparakuyo; by 1954, the total herd had increased more than seven times over the 1937 herd, and the percentage of it controlled by Ilparakuyo rose from 50.4 percent to 85 percent.

Between 1954 and 1957, however, the total herd controlled by Ilparakuyo declined slightly, while their percentage of the total remained constant (see the Appendix, Table 4). The herds of non-Ilparakuyo continued to decline: the predominantly agricultural Wakwere controlled 7.8 percent of the district herd in 1954, and only 4.4 percent in 1957, the rest belonging to other immigrants into the district. But none of these gross figures mean very much unless we look at herd composition for the periods discussed.

As with other pastoralists, Ilparakuyo herds are periodically beset with droughts, tsetse fly infestations, and epidemic livestock diseases; several of the latter also appear in endemic form, their inci-

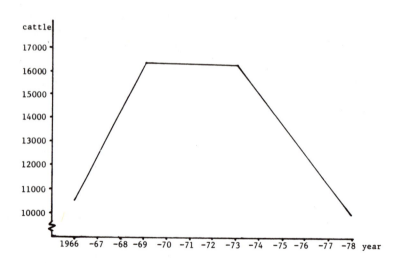

Figure 4
Total Ilparakuyo Cattle Population, West Bagamoyo District, 1966–1978.
From Mustafa *et al.*, 1980

dence rising and falling with varying climatic and ecological conditions. Contemporary Ilparakuyo and Maasai communities adjust to these conditions by such measures as increasing sale of surviving livestock, direct trading of livestock for agricultural products, or the purchase of the latter. They sell off what is now explicitly considered to be a "commoditized" part of the herd, composed largely of males and no longer productive females, as well as a disproportionate number of small stock. The aim, crucial to good herding decisions and pastoral *praxis*, is to maintain, even in bad times, a high proportion of productive, or potentially productive, females. This is accomplished by constantly adding to the portion of the herd composed of heifers.

For the entire period under discussion among Ilparakuyo of West Bagamoyo (1935–1978), and using the materials from Ndagala's earlier study (1974) as well as later figures from Mustafa *et al.*(1980), the latter admirably sums up the nature of this pastoralist strategy, and I quote in full (Mustafa *et al.* 1980:67):

> According to Ndagala [the] drop in cattle numbers between 1954 and 1957 . . . can be explained by the opening up of the Lugoba cattle market in 1955 [see Sketch Map 1], as well as by food shortages in the area caused by drought. . . . We can demonstrate that Ndagala's argument is basically correct on the basis of the following analysis. If we examine the percentage decreases in the period 1954–1957 among the different categories of livestock making up the Ilparakuyo herd in Bagamoyo District we find the following features. Small stock such as goats decreased by 33.8%, while sheep decreased by 57.3%.[6] Apart from natural deaths these could have been slaughtered for consumption or sold for cash [probably the latter]. In relation to cattle we see that bulls decreased by 52.1% and steers by 25.9%. These two categories could have been consumed for cash. In contrast to these relatively large percentage declines we find the number of cows only decreased by 9.9%. In absence of mortality rates it is difficult to be precise, but apart from natural deaths it is likely that only a small number of old and unproductive cows were sold for cash. The significance for pastoral peasants of preserving a high ratio of female to male stock is to ensure herd reproduction [and, I may add, to ensure a supply of milk, particularly for children] [and] is brought out all the more clearly when we see that while there was a 18.8% decrease in the number of male calves during this period, there was a corresponding increase of 18.5% in the number of female calves and heifers.

All of this is in keeping with a continuation of sound pastoral *praxis* by Ilparakuyo, despite the pressures of commoditization of the herd and natural conditions. By 1957, the 1,183 Ilparakuyo who lived in Bagamoyo District had 23,650 cattle, giving a figure of 20 head per person, considerably higher than the figure given by Jacobs and others for non-Ilparakuyo Maasai sections in the 1960s as 14 head per person (Jacobs 1965a, 1975:408). For the internal composition of these herds, Jacobs gives an overall figure of 57–60 percent "adult milch cows on which the family depends for daily subsistence." The comparable figure for Ilparakuyo was 60.5 percent adult cows in the herd in 1954, and 62.7 percent in 1957. These figures place Ilparakuyo at that time as being among the "wealthiest," if not *the* "wealthiest," pastoral peoples in East Africa.[7]

However, as we have seen from Figure 4, the years 1973–1978 saw a drastic decline in the Ilparakuyo herd. There was a gross reduction of 41.7 percent in the total herd, representing a decline from 307.94 cattle per domestic group to 135.82, and a drop from 20 to 8.81 cattle per capita. Despite the fact that, by 1978, Ilparakuyo controlled 91.2 percent of the cattle, 65.6 percent of the sheep, and 39.8 percent of the goats in the Lugoba Ward of West Bagamoyo District, they plunged from being the "wealthiest" cattle herders to being well below many other pastoral Maasai sections in terms of livestock holdings. Part of the reason for this catastrophe was the enforced movements Ilparakuyo had to make under the provisions of the villagization policy for national development in Tanzania (Rigby 1985; Parkipuny 1975, 1979; Ndagala 1974, 1986).

Among pastoral Maasai of the Ngorongoro Conservation Area in northern Tanzania, the dwindling pastoral herd size is reflected in livestock units per capita for the period 1960–1978 (Appendix, Table 5). Between 1960 and 1978, the overall drop in livestock units per capita is a shocking 32.32 percent; there is, however, a characteristic increase/decrease pattern between each of the successive periods. These figures must also, therefore, be viewed first in terms of the ratio of cattle to small stock (there are insufficient data for cattle herd composition): the loss of *cattle* was 53.38 percent, the decline in overall livestock units per capita being kept more constant by a substantial increase in goat and sheep flocks.[8] Although the human population of Ngorongoro Conservation Area was higher in 1980 than in 1960, Arhem's figures confirm a generally recognized *lower* rate of increase in the *pastoralist* populations of pastoral areas, as compared with non-pastoral, predominantly agricultural, populations.

The question arises: do we have, among all these average and gross figures, any data that can really be useful in postulating that inter-domestic group differentials in herd size, which are characteristic of Ilparakuyo, Maasai, and other pastoralists, are the basis for class formation, or even general socio-economic change in these societies? None of them deal with variations over time in the livestock holdings of the same domestic groups; and this is where the real reason for the great discrepancies lies. Unfortunately, this is also where the numerical evidence does not help. All is not in vain, however; by combining qualitative data with overall figures, we are able to discern at least some patterns and trends that relate to the issue of class formation and the three hypotheses indicated at the beginning of this chapter.

We must note that, although numerical corroboration is unavailable for Ilparakuyo and other Maasai sections under discussion, the domestic groups that are the primary units of real appropriation of the means of production exhibit a pattern of periods of relative prosperity in livestock holdings, interspersed with periods of severe hardship. These fluctuations, both for periods of disastrous decline in livestock numbers and in the time it takes to rebuild a herd, are often extremely precipitous. In one homestead of which I have detailed knowledge, the domestic group in 1975 was composed of four married women's houses (*inkajijik ong'uan*); by 1987, it had split into two homesteads, with three and five houses respectively (rows A and B in Table 6). Herd fluctuations over this period are set out in the Appendix, Table 6.

Although there is again the long-term decline in the animals available as means of production in this kin group (a trend accompanied by a gradual rise in the consumption of agricultural foods), the fluctuations both up and down of livestock units per capita are also evident. The enormous loss of livestock between 1980 and 1987 was occasioned by a serious epidemic of cattle disease between 1985 and 1987, combined with a chronic lack of accessible veterinary medicines. Had the medicines been available, this disaster would have been avoided; Ilparakuyo, like other Maasai, make extensive use of modern veterinary interventions when they are accessible. Although the domestic group split in two in 1980, the resulting homesteads were only about five miles apart. The combined figure for both units in 1987 was only 3.88 livestock units per capita, down from 27.34 in 1975. But since 1987, there has been evidence of a general recovery of livestock holdings in the two homesteads, as well as in the areas as a whole; several groups in the community, however, have moved long distances away.

As I have noted above, radical variations between domestic groups in terms of livestock holdings, particularly in regard to milk cows, were at least partially leveled out by mutual access rights among kin and affines, and livestock trusteeship arrangements between age-mates, friends, and even neighbors (cf. Rigby 1985:133–

136). With such arrangements in the past, inequalities between domestic groups within one locality or community at one point in time
did not lead to class formation. The only exception to this was the
extremely large and spatially stable domestic establishments of the
great prophets (*iloibonok kituaak*; see Chapter 3). A "balance" was
constantly restored and reinforced by the dominance of *giving* livestock over the lending and borrowing of them, as the epigraph to
this chapter indicates. We may summarize these various forms of
redistribution as a central aspect of good pastoral *praxis* as follows:
Rapid fluctuations in herds of specific domestic groups is consciously
recognized; inter-homestead reciprocity is a partial, short-term solution; migration to better pastures and other ecological adjustments
aid in rapid herd build-up after disastrous losses, as does the judi-
cious use of modern veterinary medicines when available; and herds
are subject to multiple rights and duties, expressed in what may
be called "inclusive control" of most livestock (Rigby 1985:142 *et
passim*; cf. Ndagala 1982:38,n.5; Lindstrom 1977).

This pattern of sharing between those who happen to be well
off at a particular time and those who are less lucky, always with
the anticipation that the reverse may be true at any moment in the
future, precluded this factor alone from being responsible for class
formation in pre-colonial Ilparakuyo and Maasai social formations.
More recently, however, these inequalities are *combined* with the
loss of land (grazing and water resources) together with the commoditization of the herd, land, and, eventually, labor. The latter are the
results of the penetration of peripheral capitalism, creating the basis
for class differentiation: and yet not on the grounds of these inter-
domestic group inequalities alone; they must be associated with the
other factors of an economic, political, and ideological nature. Before I illustrate these processes of class formation with specific cases,
I must deal briefly with what others have said about this element
in class formation and the impact of the continuing losses in the
resource base of Ilparakuyo and pastoral Maasai communities.

◆ **III**   In the contemporary context, other observers
who are conscious of the issue of class formation have tended to be as
cautious as I am on this matter, at least until further detailed information on the contemporary situation among Ilparakuyo and Maasai
is available. Thus, while remarking upon the "marked inequality in
the distribution of livestock between homesteads" in the Ilparakuyo
community of Mindu Tulieni in 1978, Mustafa *et al.* state (1980:77):
"However, we are not yet in a position to analyze the process of class

formation among the Ilparakuyo, since we lack systematic data on the relations of production and modes of surplus extraction." Mustafa and his colleagues mean *numerical* data, and I fully concur with their conclusion for the situation up to about 1978 or 1980. Since 1980, however, detailed qualitative information I obtained in 1987 provides considerable insight into the processes of class formation in the Ilparakuyo community of West Bagamoyo. I return to these cases later.

A similar argument may be made for the situation in Ilkaputiei section of Kenya Maasai until the early 1980s. Lack of suitable numerical data with which to demonstrate the rise of stratification among pastoral Maasai in the Olkarkar, Merueshi, and Mbirikani group ranches is clearly presented in an ILCA report (1981:19):

> In discussing the purpose of the study, it was clear that all members of the team felt that wealth greatly influences the strategy of production and therefore households within each group ranch should be stratified by wealth before sampling in order to increase precision and to enhance the researchers' ability to analyze various phenomena according to wealth rank. Unfortunately the varying interests and approaches of the team scientists as well as limitations in quantitative data available, precluded the determination of a true wealth parameter for stratification.

So much for the possibilities of a "holistic" approach by inter-disciplinary teams (see Chapter 1). But it is clear that, even where research resources involve a large team and strong financing, the difficulties of obtaining suitable time-depth data on the relation between livestock holdings and class formation are intractable.

Ndagala, while concurring broadly with my position (Ndagala 1982:35), sees forces at work in northern Tanzania ranching associations and among Ilparakuyo that could be called the "functional correlates" of class formation associated with the *dissolution* of the pastoral mode of existence. Commenting upon the stratification figures on Ilparakuyo from Mustafa *et al.* (1980), which I have reproduced in Tables 1 and 2, Ndagala draws a number of pertinent conclusions. The "rich" group among Ilparakuyo, with 14.86 livestock units per capita, could relatively easily survive on a purely pastoral diet. The "middle" and "poor" domestic groups, however, with averages of 8.39 and 3.17 livestock units per capita respectively, would have to incorporate increasingly large amounts of agricultural produce in their diet.[9]

Ilparakuyo domestic groups, especially the poorer ones, are turning increasingly to regular incorporation of agricultural foodstuffs in their diet; they nevertheless look forward to returning to an almost purely pastoral regime when "things get better," and they still attempt either to buy such produce with money obtained from live-stock sales (where in the past they may have bartered pastoral prod-ucts for agricultural ones directly) or to hire non-Ilparakuyo labor to cultivate fields obtained on the same basis as their immediate agri-cultural neighbors. Migration to new areas is sometimes a path to returning to a predominantly pastoral regime.

Ndagala also mentions Ilparakuyo of the "poor" group in the sample as selling *their* labor to richer members of the community, since the former would experience a "relative surplus of labor in respect of pastoralism" (Ndagala 1986:15). I have not yet seen this myself. But, as we shall see, I have come across Ilparakuyo who have literally become "kulaks" by diversifying their economic activities as rich peasants, a practice that includes the hiring of non-Ilparakuyo labor for agricultural work on a full-time basis.[10] In fact, abandoning commitment to return to a "purely" pastoral regime is often an in-dicator of economic "diversification" by richer, "better off," pastoral peasants, creating the conditions for the solidification of class dif-ferences as well as a decline in the position of women vis-à-vis the production process (cf. Talle 1987; Kipury 1989).

Among pastoral Maasai in the ranching associations of northern Tanzania, however, it seems the reliance upon agriculture has be-come considerably greater than for Ilparakuyo as well as Ngorongoro Maasai in Tanzania and Ilkaputiei in Kenya. Ndagala eloquently sum-marizes the situation for Maasai in Monduli Juu Ujamaa Kijijini in 1980 (Ndagala 1982:36):

> Over the years . . . circumstances have changed. The pastoralists con-sume large quantities of agricultural goods which they either grow themselves or have to buy for cash. Most people in Monduli Juu pro-duce less crops than their actual needs due to rain failures and vermin. Stock sales become the alternative source of cash with which to buy food. The new type of house which has been adopted [after governmen-tal pressure for permanent dwellings] by the people of Monduli Juu demands materials, particularly poles, which they have to buy. Since agriculture even without its attendant problems is meant [again under government policy] for subsistence needs[11] the only dependable source of cash short of selling one's labor is sale of stock. The role of cattle and livestock in general has thus changed. Livestock have increasingly become *exchange values* so that giving one head of cattle or goat to a friend [customary, as we have seen, in the traditional reciprocity of re-distribution], for example, means parting with the ability to acquire goods and services which have now become important.

We might also add that the latter "goods and services" are not merely "important," but essential for the reproduction of the domestic group caught in the "simple reproduction 'squeeze'" (Bernstein 1977:64–65). At any rate, it is clear that the necessary commoditization of the herd among Maasai in Monduli Juu destroys the network of livestock exchanges that, in the past, prevented the development of enduring inequalities between domestic groups, creating the conditions for the rise of a "rich peasant" class, ready to diversify their economic position through the process of "kulakization." That this feature of contemporary Maasai ranching associations in Tanzania is also true of Ilparakuyo communities, although not in as advanced a form, will emerge later. Among Kenya Maasai in group ranches in Ilkaputiei and other sections, while relevant statistical data are hard to come by, the process of class formation is alive and growing.[12]

Put in slightly different terms, in these Tanzanian Maasai ranching associations, livestock have not only been transformed from having predominantly use values to representing predominantly exchange values, as Ndagala suggests; they have been transformed from being the dominant form of the means of production (the major products being milk, meat, blood, and hides) into commodities themselves, which have to be exchanged for money if the pastoral peasant community is to reproduce itself. Little wonder, then, that the figures for livestock units per capita are so low in this community (4.58 LSUs per capita: see Table 2).

The general point that I have established is that inequalities in livestock holdings between domestic groups cannot be considered as the basis of class formation among Ilparakuyo and Maasai, until they are associated with commoditization of the herd, with a consequent decline in the ability of pastoral social formations to reproduce themselves purely through pastoral *praxis*.[13] The next stage in the penetration of capitalist relations of production takes the form of the commoditization of land. And this phase is brought about by two factors: the loss of land (represented as grazing, water, and salt for Maasai) and "development interventions."

As we have remarked on several occasions, Maasai in both Kenya and Tanzania lost enormous areas of land, especially the crucial upland dry-season grazing areas (*isupuko*, sing. *osupuko*), during the period of colonial penetration and expansion (cf. Rigby 1985:21, 109, 111, 114–116; Sorrenson 1968: *passim*; Jacobs 1965a; Arhem 1985:16 *et passim*; Leys 1926; etc.). This initial loss, one that was to be permanent, is the single most important factor in the peripheralization of pastoral Maasai. Commenting upon the pressures being experienced by both the human and livestock populations of Kenya

Maasailand, Isaac Sindiga, a Kenyan geographer, admirably sums up the overall situation (Sindiga 1984:36–37):

> In essence the problem of populations pressure in Kajiado and Narok [the two districts comprising almost all of what is left of Kenya Maasailand] is the loss of dry-season herding resources and overexploitation of ecologically fragile lands. Insensitive land and economic policies in the colonial time undermined the subsistence basis of life in Maasailand. These combined with European settler opposition to frustrate the Maasai from joining Kenya's emerging colonial spatial economy. There were no linkages with the colonial system. Maasai spatial economy turned inwards. But even here, the absence of modern infrastructure hindered development. . . . Overcrowding and loss of self-reliance that characterize Maasailand today were both inherited from the colonial days.

But, one may correctly add, there were "linkages" with the colonial system, all of a "negative" kind; nothing "positive" has really been done about it since.

Add to this the lands lost to arable farming, a deprivation that continues today as the result of both official and unofficial encroachment of cultivation into pastoral Maasailand in both Kenya and Tanzania, and to the creation of game-parks and reserves, and the situation looks desperate indeed (see Parkipuny 1975, 1979, 1983, and Arhem 1985:19–22 for Tanzania). Sindiga notes for Narok District in Kenya (1984:35):

> The Kenya government is committed to arable farming in the high potential land in western Narok district and the adjoining areas. . . . When the planned Narok Agricultural Development project is completed, some 320,000 hectares of land will be brought into commercial farming use. The project will also open up 13,000 hectares of new land for wheat and barley production. Virtually all the high potential land in Narok district will be covered in this program.

Ilparakuyo pastoralists, since they do not occupy an area of contiguous and "bounded" territorial units, are not faced with exactly the same emergency. Their response to resource shortages is frequently to move away to other parts of central and southern Tanzania, to create new communities among other agriculturalists and agropastoralists. But the policies of *ujamaa* villagization have often seriously affected this alternative strategy; formal permission to move from one *ujamaa* village to another is technically required, tending to create permanent or semi-permanent *ujamaa vijijini* and exacerbating the effects of decreasing grazing, water, and salt resources. Although, as I have already indicated, by 1987 many domestic groups in West Bagamoyo were either moving *in toto*, splitting up into more than one homestead, or leaving for areas to the south and south-west in search of better conditions, the "pastoral village" (*kijijini cha wafugaji*) of Mindu Tulieni is still the focus of government development strategies.[14]

Ndagala demonstrates how government projects in Bagamoyo District up to 1973 not only directly alienated large areas of dry-season grazing and other essential resources from Ilparakuyo (Ndagala 1974, 1986), but also caused displaced cultivators to move into pastoralist grazing areas (see Sketch Map 2). These processes of alienation continued after 1973 and are still a problem today (Rigby 1985: 36–39 *et passim*). Ndagala comments concisely on the implications for Ilparakuyuo of these land alienations, and I quote him *in extenso* (1986:10):

> All the displaced cultivators were compensated [as pastoralists were not] and had to look for new land elsewhere. The projects marked 1, 2 and 3 . . . were established in the most densely populated part of the district and displaced hundreds of families. . . . [Many of these families moved into Ilparakuyo-occupied territory.] . . . Projects 5, 6 and 7 were established in the area hitherto used by Ilparakuyo and occupied 61,000 acres. There were hardly any agriculturalists in this area thus giving the impression that it was unutilised land. However, this "take-over" was on the contrary a big blow to the pastoralists because this was a very excellent grazing area during the dry season due to the presence of Ruvu and Msua rivers.

Out of a total of 79,000 acres alienated for these government projects, about 61,000 (or 77.2%) were occupied by Ilparakuyo pastoralists; cultivators, on the other hand, were removed from 18,000 acres (or 22.8%). The Tanzanian government's argument that this loss of Ilparakuyo territory was excusable because it gave the "impression that it was unutilised land" is highly reminiscent of earlier British and German colonialist explanations for the alienation of vast areas of Kenya and Tanzania Maasailand.

A combination of all these factors—loss of resource base, commoditization of the herd, commoditization of land for "development" purposes, "Western-style" education (particularly in Kenya: see ole Sena 1986), and the eventual commoditization of labor (see below)—has conspired to create the conditions for class formation among Ilparakuyo and pastoral Maasai in contemporary Kenya and Tanzania; the processes in each case, however, are somewhat different in the two countries. I now turn to some recent case materials to illuminate these similarities and differences.

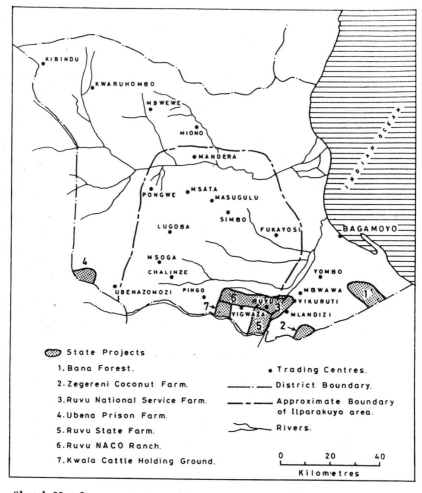

Sketch Map 2
Government Projects in Bagamoyo District, 1973.
From Ndagala 1974, 1986

♦ **IV**   Of a total of 20,015 square kilometers of trust lands (in which "traditional" land use forms are operative) in Kajiado (Olkejuoado) District in southern Kenya, over 9,000 square kilometers were made available for adjudication by 1979, and almost all of the grazing areas so adjudicated were destined for occupation as "Group Ranches" (ILCA 1981:7 *et passim*; cf. Galaty 1980). The group ranch in Kenya Maasailand was formally advanced as the "principal entity by which [pastoral trust lands in Kajiado and Narok] would be transformed into deeded holdings, with rights and responsibilities of land ownership devolving to specific household heads, namely, the group ranch members" (Evangelou 1984:113).

The group ranch concept as the basis for development in Kenya Maasailand was consolidated legally by the Land (Groups Representatives) and the Land Adjudication acts of the Kenya parliament in 1968. The concept was specifically designed to promote forms of development based upon private property, particularly in land. This property, it was maintained, would allow the World Bank to "facilitate the shift from subsistence milk production to meat production for the market, by establishing the collateral conditions for major loan investments" (Evangelou 1984:113). There is, of course, no record of any widespread consultation with the Maasai community beyond its formal representatives at the district and national level, comprising individuals who had already taken advantage of opportunities available for capital accumulation (see Chapter 4).

Unfortunately, none of the resulting land units in Kajiado or Narok are ecologically or economically viable under existing forms of pastoral *praxis*, a fact that Maasai immediately perceived. If the new "owners" of these demarcated and designated areas were to enforce their legal rights, for example, by fencing off their ranches to ensure their exclusive use of them by barring non-members from bringing in their herds, not only would those excluded suffer losses and probable ruin but also the members themselves would fail either to support their families or to produce any surplus for the market.

Maasai responses to this imposed strategy of development have been based upon the continuation of their traditional practice of allowing free movement of livestock through ecological zones on the basis of continued reciprocity of access for all Maasai to grazing, water, and salt. And this strategy of scuttling the very purpose of the group ranches themselves is followed even by many Maasai who are prominent in politics and government at the district and national levels, sometimes to their own unfair advantage. For example, during a drought in Kenya Maasailand in 1983, the people of one Kenya Maasai section were understandably upset when a prominent politician from another area moved about 3,000 head of cattle from his ranch, where the drought was more severe and grazing almost gone, into their area, where conditions were a little bit better.

Despite these various subterfuges to circumvent the full impact of policy, the non-viability of group ranches has led to developments that ensure the growth of established class interests. While some Maasai attempted to beat the system by gaining rights of access (through kinship, age-set, and other livestock exchange relationships) to areas of more than one designated group ranch, others have pressed to create individual ranches within each group's area. This has further decreased the viability of ranches, and is leading to individual accumulation and even more rapid commoditization of land in numerous areas of Kajiado and Narok. That these processes were evident as early as 1982, and even before, is illustrated by Dyson-Hudson's absolutely accurate and prophetic conclusion (1982:11):

> To judge from present conditions, it would be . . . accurate to conceive of the group ranch strategy as a phase which Maasai producers are passing through on the way to further individuation of their production. In that process of individualising their resources it is likely that many of them will cease to be independent producers, many will have to move out of livestock rearing of any specialised kind, and many may have to leave the area or seek different careers at emergent urban centers within it. A great diversity of individual strategies is likely to be visible, and a high failure rate is to be expected before it becomes evident which combination of responses will work best for which sets of people.

The drive to individual ownership of land, which has in fact been officially recognized from the start of group ranch policy, is largely beneficial to Maasai who already have status, power, and class position by virtue of their role in the local and national petit bourgeoisie. This is illustrated in Case 1.

Case 1: The Disillusioned Bureaucrat

In 1983, I had a long and illuminating conversation with a sub-chief in Kajiado District (let us call him Lekoyian). Our conversation began at his house, and ended up many hours later at the local bar. Despite the fact that he was initially somewhat suspicious of my unannounced arrival, he gave me a fairly detailed account of how the group ranch in which his homestead was located was adjudicated and registered, a narrative that does not concern us directly here.[15] The fact that we soon got to know that we belonged to the same clan (*olgilata*: Ilmolelian) also helped break the ice. Lekoyian had been a sub-chief for almost fifteen years; he is fluent in Kiswahili and able to communicate in English. He attributes his becoming a sub-chief at a relatively early age to the fact that he was a protegé of a prominent Maasai elder who had been active in national politics since before Kenyan Independence in 1963. Lekoyian is of the Ilnyankusi age-set, whose *eunoto* ceremony (promotion to senior warriorhood and assumption of proper name) took place in 1959; he would have been a senior *olmurrani* (warrior) or junior elder (*olpayian*) when he joined the Kenya administrative service.

While we were talking at a local bar, two young men of *ilmurran* (warrior) age-grade came in. After they had greeted Lekoyian and myself, he told me that they were the sons of his first wife; he has three wives. He then went on to tell me that, although his area had been adjudicated as a group ranch, he had later established his own individual ranch within it. This process is very common (cf. Evangelou 1984:113; Dyson-Hudson 1982:9).

When I asked him what would happen to his individual ranch when he died and left the children of the three houses (*inkajijik uni*) of his three wives to inherit, he told me that he had two options. The first was to use his influence, of which he is very conscious, in the government in Nairobi to get more rights in land for all his children, including those of his first two wives, whose houses he referred to as "those other houses" (*inkajijik 'nkulie*), an expression he employed because of his second and only other option. Of this he said, "Look at my two sons here: neither they nor their full brothers or half brothers from my second wife will inherit any land from me." This was because, he added, the ranch was already too small and could not be further subdivided. The inheritance would go to the children of his third house, that of his youngest wife.[16]

In response to my question, "What will the others do?" he said, "They will have to go to Nairobi to work, of course." These other sons, however, were still to be responsible for the herd, as he indicated by his orders to them about their duties that evening (it was almost dusk). He seemed overassertive in his authority over these two young men, which may have indicated a contrary lack of control, or it may have indicated that, although they would not inherit his land, they would still inherit the livestock allocated to their houses, which was the case. (Although where they would herd them was still a moot point.)

Lekoyian is conscious that his administrative position makes him somewhat unpopular among some of his age-mates and other Maasai elders, although his status in the government keeps him relatively secure, both for the present and for the near future. He told me, in a conspiratorial whisper though, that he keeps abreast of political and economic developments in other parts of his area and Kenya Maasailand as a whole through what he called the "Maasai newspaper" (*ilomon loo 'nkuapi*, lit. "the news of the countries/lands").

In this case, the ideology of power invested in local government officials emanates from the center, Nairobi; there is little difference here between the hegemonic control of the colonial state at this level (whose "absolute authority" derived from outside the state itself) on the one hand and the contemporary ideology of "national unity" on the other. To question the structure of the latter is tantamount to being anti-nationalist and, therefore, treasonous, as well as "anti-development." For it is the local government official who can encourage or stifle dissent among the local population; his local position is authoritarian, since his constituency is not behind, but "above" him. The local citizen experiences "development" and government from the same source (see Chapters 5 and 8).

That many Maasai in Kenya are now losing all rights of access to land for grazing, water, and salt is attested to by their becoming entangled in wage-labor—a fate they had long escaped by dint of expert pastoral *praxis*, despite continual losses in their resource base. Many Maasai and other pastoralists are now employed by the government, while others have to struggle at less than minimum wage in Nairobi, often as security guards for the estates of foreign residents or the comprador bourgeoisie (Kipury 1983*b*). Some Maasai have set themselves up in business in Nairobi, sometimes as cattle traders to urban butcheries; still others have become hairdressers to fashionable Nairobi women who have come to like the tight plaiting of hair that only *ilmurran* (junior warriors) do for each other when creating and ochering their traditional "pigtails" (*iltaikan*, sing. *oltaika*). But other ideological forces are generated by, and also become necessary for, the processes of class formation, and it is to a discussion of them that I now turn.

◆ V   I have already indicated in some detail that the specificity of Ilparakuyo and other Maasai social formations does not encourage a notion that supernatural powers are used to create evil such as poverty, sickness, infertility in people and animals, and death (Rigby 1985:92–122 and Chapters 1 and 4 above; cf. Baxter 1972). I have also elaborated the theoretical grounds for this ideological distinctiveness in Chapter 1, above.

This relative lack of credence in the efficacy of sorcery and witchcraft among pastoralists generally is in contrast to the comparatively high incidence of such beliefs among neighboring cultivators. Ilparakuyo and Maasai represent something of a clearing in the middle of a forest of symbolically evil supernatural powers. While it is important to place witchcraft and sorcery beliefs not only in a framework of specific structural forms but also in the context of related beliefs such as those characterized as religion, magic, medicine, art, and science (Ndeti 1972:113), it is precisely the elaboration of such beliefs that Ilparakuyo and Maasai lack.[17] Spencer confirms this for Ilmatapato section of Kenya Maasai when he notes (1988:267):

> Neither Matapato as a society nor their meat feasts are dominated by an excessive concern over sorcery; but insofar as it is always felt to be a remote possibility with its own cosmological niche, sorcery belongs to the area beyond the feasting circle. The belief in sorcery as an expression of a vague unease whose shadow is cast over feasts of celebration, and more especially when a feeling of general misfortune is the pretext for the sacrifice in the first place.

Although Spencer does not mention it, since his study lacks any real historical dimension, I am inclined to think that these "feelings of general misfortune" among Ilmatapato are at least partially the product of their devastating historical experience of pre-colonial and colonial penetration of their society by the disruptive forces of merchant capital and, later, commoditization and wage capitalism, as the following Ilparakuyo cases demonstrate. This, I have argued, is because in the Ilparakuyo and Maasai social formations, the social relations of production are not originally based upon class and are characterized by a relative transparency (see Chapter 1). The corollary of this argument, then, is that, when classes do begin to form and consolidate, they are accompanied by an increasing opacity in the relations of production. For Ilparakuyo and, by extension, other Maasai sections, this growing opacity is represented in the mystification of productive relations by burgeoning beliefs and accusations of sorcery and witchcraft and an increasing use of the "curse" (*eng'oki*) by both men and women. The former are illustrated in Cases 2 and 3.

Case 2: The Ungrateful Senior Warrior

Toronkei and Seronke were very best friends for many years, having exchanged cattle when Toronkei was just about to be circumcised and enter the age-grade of junior warriors (*ilmurran*); Seronke, however, was soon to be a senior warrior and was therefore one age-set (called Ilmedoti) above that of Toronkei (an Oltaretoi). Such friendships between young men of proximate age-sets are unusual; there is considerable tension between them (Rigby 1985:60–63 *et passim*). In this case, the friends were matrilaterally related, Seronke being Toronkei's father's mother's sister's daughter's son (FMZDS: classificatory cross-cousin, or *oleng'apu*); later, Toronkei also became Seronke's classificatory brother-in-law (class. BWB).

Until the early 1980s, this friendship persisted, Toronkei the junior benefitting initially from the help of his older friend; later, he himself gained the position to help his senior, rather than the other way around. By 1987, the friendship had become very strained, and whenever they met, Toronkei and Seronke would cover up this strain by continual ribald joking, which, although forbidden by their age-set positions, is permitted by their kinship and affinal bonds.

In 1979, Toronkei and Seronke had moved their homesteads to the same local cluster, becoming, in fact, immediate neighbors. Seronke, however, had obtained a loan in cash from Toronkei, who was involved in trading livestock and veterinary medicines, an activity now frequently pursued by junior warriors (see Rigby 1985:157–163). Seronke did not return the loan, becoming instead a much "richer" person through his own economic activities.

During the period 1984 to 1987, Toronkei lost three children still in their infancy, probably due to endemic and chloroquin-resistant malaria, even though he had taken them to government hospitals, the one nearest the community as well as the major hospital in Dar es Salaam. All three children died suddenly, while in apparently good health. As a result of these misfortunes, Toronkei had gone as far as Ngorongoro in northern Tanzania, a distance of some 480 miles, to consult with a ritual expert (*oloiboni*) who has gained a pan-Maasai reputation as a very powerful healer and prophet, almost the status of the hereditary great prophets of the past (*iloibonok kituaak*; see Chapters 3, 4, and 6 above). This was despite the fact that the recognized great prophet for this part of Ilparakuyo section of Maasai lives much closer by, in the Morogoro District, a prophet who has to be consulted for all major rituals of this sub-section. As the hereditary great prophets are seldom consulted upon individual matters, Toronkei's long journey to Ngorongoro was very unusual.

At any rate, the Ngorongoro *oloiboni* determined that Seronke had been using "bad medicine" (*enaibon torrono*) against Toronkei and his family. This was because, he said, Seronke was "jealous" and afraid that Toronkei might exceed him in status, although the latter is now a junior elder, both in terms of livestock holdings and family size, as well as in terms of "modern" indicators of style of house and possession of such consumer items as radio–cassette recorders and, in this case, a motorcycle. Seronke reinforced the apparent validity of this interpretation by twice intercepting parcels and letters addressed to Toronkei while the latter was nearly 350 miles away away in Arusha town. Part of the solution suggested by the *oloiboni* was to move away to another locality; Toronkei, however, did not wish to demonstrate that he was afraid of Seronke, so he did not move. Instead, he obtained medicines to protect his homestead and cattle byre, which included the wives, children, and livestock of his full brother.

After the death of his third child in 1986, however, Toronkei decided with his brother Kasaine, who himself has a reputation for being an expert in the use of both modern veterinary medicines and "traditional" ones (although he is not of the prophetic clan and lineage, the Ilaiser Inkidong'i), to strengthen the protection of their joint homestead (*enkang'*) by getting medicines from non-Maasai sources. For this, Toronkei and Kasaine both went to the city of Tanga, on the northern coast of Tanzania, and twice brought back Waswahili diviners (*waganga*). One of the latter was originally from the island of Pemba, whose diviners have an excellent reputation for power and success. The homestead was again supplied with medicines to be placed at all the entrances to it.

Prior to about 1983, Ilparakuyo used medicines, often obtained from diviners from among the local cultivators' community, to "close" their homesteads and cattle byres to livestock thieves. Such elaborate interpretations of misfortune and death as manifested in this case, and what to do about it, are, however, quite new. In this case, I maintain, this interpretation is related to the fact that Seronke now has status in the contemporary local political economy, not only because of his age-set status (he is my age-mate, now junior elders: *ilpayiani*) but also because he has prospered in contemporary terms. He has, for example, built a permanent house with bricks and corrugated iron (*bati*) roof and has several bicycles and three wives; he has also adopted a poor youth, who had lost his own relatives among the local cultivating community, and promises to help him marry when he is ready. Seronke has, most important for our present purposes, become a purchaser of wage labor in his diversified economic activities.

A final case involved another age-mate of mine, who combines

his status in several different political and economic arenas to ensure his own security in what are, for him, highly unstable politico-
economic conditions, and drawing to himself in the process accusations of sorcery and witchcraft.

Case 3: The Ambitious Son of a Prophet

Lesingo belongs to the prophetic clan (Ilaiser) and sub-clan
(Inkidong'i, lit. "the horns"); not only that, but he is also the
son of the current great prophet (*oloiboni kitok*) of our section of Ilparakuyo (Rigby 1985:10–11). Lesingo is also, however,
chairman of the local branch of Tanzania's governing party,
Chama cha Mapinduzi (CCM, "The Revolutionary Party"), as
well as being a senior official in relations between Ilparakuyo
pastoralists and the local government. (I cannot be more explicit
than that.)

Lesingo therefore represents success in all three systems of
power. He is a paragon of excellent pastoral *praxis*: he has one
of the largest herds in the local community, spread among numerous homesteads of kin and livestock associates, and nine
wives. His *enkang'* (homestead) is, as a result, one of the largest
in the area. He has enough children to send several to school,
some now reaching secondary (high) school; he can also provide
for children of less fortunate kinsmen, some of whom he also
supports in school.

Although he still lives in "traditional" style houses, he is
constructing a "hotel" (guest house) in a nearby trading center,
and is reputed to have used "medicines" (*enaibon*), traditionally
associated with the prophetic lineage, to dispossess a business
partner in this venture. Nevertheless, in local age-group meetings (*inkiguenaritin*, sing. *enkiguena*) he is still subject to the
authority of the senior elders' age-set.

Lesingo is thought to be able to use his "traditional" medicines (*inaibonereitin*) both for good, in "traditional" contexts,
and also for bad in the context of modern commercial transactions and commodity relations.

The qualitative data presented in these three cases illustrate
the form that class differentiation is taking in both Tanzania and
Kenya Maasai communities, for different reasons and in subtly different ways. I conclude with a brief discussion of these similarities
and differences.

◆ **VI**   Although continuing loss of the resource base is common to pastoral Maasai in both Tanzania and Kenya, the advanced state that the alienation of *land* has reached in Kenya is the primary factor in economic differentiation and class formation there (Kituyi 1990, particularly ch. 7). The history of colonial interventions, initially the theft of large areas of the best grazing and water sources from Maasai, and of post-colonial "development" interventions leading to much the same thing, has manifested itself in all aspects of Maasai social organization: the transhumant grazing patterns, densities of human and livestock populations, age-set and kinship structures, ideology, and overall pastoral *praxis*.

These factors "freeze" the previously fluid patterns of re-distribution of the livestock, the major means of production, among "better-off" and "worse-off" domestic groups, creating necessary but not sufficient conditions for class formation. Under contemporary conditions of commoditization, however, the children of the "better-off," because of the latters' much more plentiful supply of labor, go to school and university, gaining positions in the national hierarchy and class structure. The children of the "worse-off" and poor, like Lekoyian's older sons in Case 1, may have to become nightwatchmen in Nairobi or enter other semi- and un-skilled jobs at minimum wages. While they may still have livestock, they may have no place to herd them, and thus lose control over them. The dominant ideological forces in Kenya Maasailand emanate from the process of commoditization of land inseparable from the group and individual ranch system that form the basis of current "development" policy in that country, a process necessarily rooted in the power structure of the authoritarian state. Sale or renting out of land for agricultural production is another form of commodity manipulation of land, particularly in Narok District (cf. Sindiga 1984; Doherty 1979a, 1979b); even the latter often leads to total loss of that land through sale.

In Tanzania, on the other hand, the commoditization of pastoral resources is retarded by a national policy prohibiting private ownership of land, either by individuals or corporate "persons." Here, the impetus for class formation is primarily *political*, in which the manipulation of ideological forces other than those of capital accumulation and wage-labor are dominant. These ideological forces combine a number of elements: Evidence of the success of particular persons in "traditional" pastoral *praxis*; association with pre-capitalist sources of power, such as those still held by the prophetic clan; position in the political hierarchy of local government as well as the local and national political party structures; and, almost least, involve-

ment in the processes of individual economic diversification among
the small category of "rich" peasants. The last has become both
more feasible and more desirable with very recent easing of restric-
tions upon private enterprise in Tanzania, together with an increased
potential for the hiring of wage labor for cultivation by pastoralists,
often of crops for sale at local markets, and sometimes even with the
use of irrigation in pastoral areas.[18] These new forms of "success" in
a context of declining pastoral *praxis* by others draw accusations of
witchcraft and sorcery and the manipulation of medicines normally
used for the benefit of the entire community.

Ilparakuyo, as we have seen, also have the option, which other
pastoral Maasai in both Kenya and Tanzania do not have, of moving
out to new areas and setting up new pastoral communities among
other cultivators and agro-pastoralists. This possibility was more or
less suspended by the enforced villagization policy from the mid-
1970s to the mid-1980s, compelling some Ilparakuyo to adopt the
other "solutions" already described. As of 1987, a relaxation of enforced residential stability in pastoralist *ujamaa vijijini* seems to be
re-opening this option for some Ilparakuyo.

The egalitarian Ilparakuyo and Maasai social formations are
currently facing almost insurmountable pressures toward increasing
differentiation and class formation in both Kenya and Tanzania; the
actual *forms* these pressures and consequent changes take are different in each case, largely as a result of the explicit differences in rural
development strategies in the two countries. The dominant ideological forms generated in each case, as I have suggested, have different
emphases; but both result in the increasing opacity in the social relations of production, endangering the very core of the pastoral *praxis*
that characterized these societies in the past.

Several studies have shown the increasing importance of witchcraft and sorcery beliefs and accusations in the local (as well as
the national) levels of power relations in colonial and post-colonial
states (e.g., Fields 1982; Rowlands and Warnier 1988; Geschiere 1988;
Mesaki 1988). Geschiere admirably encapsulates the ambiguity of
belief in such mystifying forces in political action among the Maka
of southeastern Cameroon, where "state officials see sorcery as the
main obstacle to 'Le Development' and as a form of subversion of
government projects." But he concludes (Geschiere 1988:55):

> [The] ambiguous attitude of the new state elite makes popular beliefs
> in witchcraft and sorcery a problematic issue in the crytallization of
> new relations of domination. On the one hand, sorcery appears to be a
> force from below, a popular reaction against the new forms of domina-

tion. Consequently, African state regimes feel obliged to lash out, just as European regimes did three centuries ago, against local manifestations of witchcraft. These official interventions often lead to a chaotic disruption of ancient sanctions and control over the occult forces. On the other hand, certain aspects of the same popular beliefs and practices provide opportunities to reinforce relations of authority and to broaden the consensus on the new forms of domination. The elite's rejection of witchcraft is therefore seldom complete. Certain aspects of these popular ideas fit in very well with the new elite culture and can even complement the national hegemonical project.

I deal with some aspects of the last point in this quotation in my final chapter.

Despite the emergence of forms of contradiction and conflict in Ilparakuyo and Maasai society that were not characteristic of these formations before colonialism and capitalist penetration, many Ilparakuyo and Maasai still adhere to the elements of pastoral *praxis* that have enabled them to change and yet survive for the past three hundred years or so. In this adherence they challenge the forms of "development" designed for them by outsiders, together with all the ideological baggage that comes with these forms. They still manage, in other words, to wage a counter-hegemonic struggle to retain a relative transparency in the relations of production among themselves, in their relations with the national states of which they are a part, and, finally, in their unique form of appropriation of the physical world they inhabit.

8   Ilparakuyo Maasai Transformations: African Episteme and Marxian Problematic

*Meidip oltung'ani
endapana
enkiteng' enye.*
The hide of his own
cow cannot suffice a
person.

◆   The aim of "African philosophy," or, better still, "African philosophies," is not merely to "Africanize" philosophy but to create a discursive space in which an epistemology and problematic related to the historical experiences of Africa can be constructed (Mudimbe 1988:164–165 *et passim*). It is not just to make philosophy an object of research and study in Africa; it is to provide a reflexive and critical theory for truly revolutionary action.[1] It is to go *beyond* Negritude and "Afrocentricity" in order to create a future free from class, gender, or any other kind of exploitation and oppression. It is both theory and practice.

It might seem ambitious, presumptuous, and even obnoxious for a non-philosopher to begin a *conclusion* in this fashion; I have my reasons, which, I hope, will appear as we proceed. And I can perhaps justify such an opening by saying that my position is not at variance with V. Y. Mudimbe's claim for the "unity in diversity" of contemporary African philosophy (Mudimbe 1983); in fact, this chapter may be taken as an affirmation of African philosophy as a continuing process within which often heated debate is its most characteristic feature, indicating "the creative power of African self-criticism" (1983:147).

My main concern is that, if a future anthropology (and perhaps

166

any other social science) is to be of any help at all in realizing "development," cultural and social transformation, and "true freedom" in Africa, it must be a force in heightening "awareness" of what is involved in "development," and hence in political mobilization toward these ends. Such an accomplishment would engender a process of development in all four aspects of a comprehensive political economy: namely, economic disengagement and internally generated transformation; free political *praxis* toward this end; cultural independence in all its senses; and their accompanying discourses free from the *categories* of thought and dialogue of past and present colonial domination.

It is, therefore, quite obviously not my intention here to summarize or evaluate the extremely diverse views expressed by African philosophers, theologians, and social scientists, even if I were capable of it. This task has been most penetratingly and comprehensively achieved by Mudimbe (1983, 1985, 1988, *et passim*). What I attempt in this chapter is to suggest a direction in which a truly radical and subversive African theoretical framework (and, as a result, a basis for political, economic, and cultural *praxis*) might be derived from a convergence of African philosophy and a particular *form* of historical materialist theorizing.[2]

During this excursus, I will address the issue of the "Africanization" of Marxist theory, as well as the "Marxistization" (if I may coin a term) of African historical, social, and reflexive studies. This is necessary, I believe, because neither a Marxist theoretical position nor an African philosophy, on its own, is capable of creating the conditions in which the struggle for freedom in Africa (or elsewhere in the Third World) can proceed and fulfill our expectations. It is immediately clear, of course, that this is no easy task, since the diversity of opinion within Marxist theorizing is as great as the almost intractable controversies that bedevil African philosophical discourse.

◆ I   In many places, but perhaps most eloquently in his *Decolonizing the Mind* (1986; cf. 1977, 1981*a*, 1981*b*, 1982, 1983), Ngugi wa Thiong'o states his position on the relation between class struggle and cultural liberation, a struggle in which the problem of language plays a central part. While I adopt a position on language as a material force in the liberation struggle that is broader than Ngugi's, the elemental point that the theory and practice of class struggle and liberation must occupy the *same* discursive space as that occupied by African history, cultures, and languages is brilliantly made by Ngugi, and I quote him *in extenso*:

> Imperialism, led by the USA, presents the struggling peoples of the earth and all those calling for peace, democracy, and socialism with the ultimatum: accept theft or death. The oppressed and exploited of the earth maintain their defiance: liberty from theft. But the biggest weapon wielded and daily actually unleashed by imperialism against that collective defiance is the cultural bomb. The effect of a cultural bomb is to annihilate a people: belief in their names, in their languages, in their environment, in their heritage of struggle, in their country, in their capacities and ultimately in themselves. It makes them see their past as one wasteland of non-achievement. . . . Amidst this wasteland which it has created, imperialism presents itself as the cure and demands that the dependent sing hymns of praise with the constant refrain: "Theft is holy!" Indeed, this refrain sums up the new creed of the neo-colonial bourgeoisie in many "independent" African states. (Ngugi 1986:3)

The class struggle, then, is inseparable from a cultural struggle, through which revolutionary *praxis* unites the past and the present in the *creation* of a future (cf. Rigby 1985:81–87 *et passim*). The forces and strategies of the ruling class, manifested in cultural hegemony, *become transparent* to the "actors" (the historical subjects) in an alliance of peasants and urban proletariats and lumpenproletariats, through recourse to the forms of language and discourse of the people themselves. This constitutes a rejection of cultural imperialism and neo-colonialism; awareness, engendered by a re-inspired language and discourse, includes an apprehension of the hegemonic control exercised by the post-colonial state. The latter has a power more tenuous than in mature capitalist formations, and is more likely to have recourse to physical coercion and cultural censorship. Ngugi concludes (1986:3): "The classes fighting against imperialism even in its neo-colonial stage and form, have to confront this threat with the higher and more creative culture of resolute struggle. These classes have to wield even more firmly the weapons of the struggle contained in their cultures. They have to speak the united language of the struggle contained in each of their languages." In Ngugi's terms, Ilparakuyo and Maasai are not *conservative*; they are positively *revolutionary*.[3]

Before we proceed, I must insert a caveat. As I point out elsewhere (Chapters 4, 5, and 6 above), by emphasizing the subversive use of African languages and linguistic categories, a *prise de parole* including diverse cultural elements, I am not referring to the phenomenon known generally in anthropology as "revitalization movements," or "millenarian cults"; on the contrary, I am referring to the conative power embodied in specific forms of *parole*, not as in Saussure's *parole*, but as in Bakhtin's sense of the speech act as "made specifically social, historical, concrete, and dialogized" (Bakhtin 1981:433 *et passim*; cf. Clark and Holquist 1984:10–15).

I begin with a brief consideration of the debate about African philosophy, conducted by African philosophers, writers, and social scientists; I then turn to its implications for the social sciences, for Marxist theorizing, and, finally, for Ilparakuyo and Maasai studies.

◆ **II**   There are two questions of fundamental importance in what follows: what constitutes the specificity of *African* philosophy; and what, if any, is the relation between African philosophy and Marxism. As we shall see, these two questions are intimately linked. But another caveat: As I have noted, I am not a philosopher, and therefore my excursion into the territory of African philosophy is fraught with hidden perils. My justification for so doing is twofold: first, the intention and logic of this book demands that anthropology, in its broadest sense, *must* cease to define itself on the basis of a reified (and spurious) object; second, this necessary re-definition must involve the production of a knowledge that is both temporally and spatially congruent (or as congruent as possible) with its subject of discourse (cf. Fabian 1983).

The first question involves Paulin Hountondji's work in African philosophy. Hountondji has been described as "perhaps the best known of the 'professional philosophers'" (Owomoyela 1987:79; cf. Irele 1983:8). His position is highly controversial, since he rejects what has come to be called "ethnophilosophy" in Africa. Because such "ethnophilosophies" are the historical basis for the initial thrust in generating the interest in African philosophy, it is not surprising that his views have been sharply criticized. And, partially because Hountondji was a student of, and influenced by, Louis Althusser, a prominent French philosopher of Marxism, the rejection of Hountondji's position is sometimes taken as a simultaneous repudiation of any possible *rapprochement* between African philosophy and Marxism.

One of the most recent and strongest critiques of Hountondji comes from Kwame Gyekye, of the University of Ghana. He is quite unequivocal in his condemnation of Hountondji's position (Gyekye 1987:36). Hountondji's rejection of a philosophical basis for "traditional" African thought and his proposal for a "new concept of African philosophy" are, according to Gyekye, a "tissue of errors. . . . The so-called new concept of African philosophy may be 'radically new', but it is equally radically false and radically unacceptable."

Gyekye is very concerned about Hountondji's criticism of what Hountondji calls "culturalism." While admitting that Hountondji is not alone in denying the link between culture and philosophy, and hence negating "ethnophilosophy" (Gyekye includes P. O. Bodunrin and Kwasi Wiredu in his critique), he makes a strong case (I think correctly, for reasons that will appear) for deriving African philosophy from its cultural context. Philosophy, however, cannot be reduced to culture; if it is, it ceases to exist. This entails another point of contention: that of the collective nature of a culturally derived African philosophy versus the individual production of philosophies in the Western tradition (Gyekye 1987:24–29). Gyekye also makes a good case for the collective provenance of ancient Greek philosophy, from which Western philosophy is said to descend, as interpreted by such eminent scholars as F. M. Cornford. And to Gyekye's argument we can now add that the "collectivity" from which Thales and Aristotle probably derived their philosophical systems was African and Asian, rather than "pure Greek," whatever that may be (Bernal 1987:207, 233 *et passim*).

What Gyekye does *not* deal with is one of the major reasons given by Hountondji for his trenchant critique of "culturalism" in African philosophical discourse. Hountondji's argument is powerful (1983:162): "Culturalism is an ideological system because it produces an indirect political effect. It eclipses, first, the problem of effective national liberation and, second, the problem of class struggle." Not only this, however; for Hountondji, culturalism is a weapon of class oppression, as are anthropology and ethnology (Hountondji 1983:162):

> In independent countries culturalism takes the form of a backward-looking cultural nationalism, flattening out the national culture and denying it its *internal pluralism* and *historical depth*, in order to divert the attention of the exploited classes from the real political and economic conflicts which divide them from the ruling classes under the fallacious pretext of their common participation in "the" national culture.

Hountondji then proceeds to ethnology and political anthropology, noting that culturalism is "characteristic of Third World nationalists and Western ethnologists: it is the locus of their objective complicity." He continues (1983:163–164):

Ethnologists . . . tend to isolate the cultural aspects of society and to stress it at the expense of the economic and political aspects. Even when dealing with politics, ethnologists will generally be concerned with the traditional kind, arbitrarily reduced to its pre-colonial dimension, petrified, ossified and emptied of its internal tensions, discontinuities and confrontations. The political problem of colonial or neo-colonial domination is never posed. . . . Moreover, when they investigate this pre-colonial past, they refuse to see the evolution, revolutions, and discontinuities that may have affected it, and the precarious balance which has made these civilizations temporarily what they are today. Anthropologists need to play with simple units, univocal totalities without cracks or dissonances. They need dead cultures, petrified cultures, always identical to themselves in the homogenous space of an eternal present.

How true this is will become more evident as we proceed, particularly when I return to recent work on Kenya Maasai by anthropologist Paul Spencer, already mentioned in the Introduction. It is quite reasonable to suggest that Hountondji here (and elsewhere in his book) is being deliberately polemical in suggesting an epistemological and politico-economic origin in common for the ethnophilosophies so carefully constructed by so many African philosophers on the one hand and the notoriously alienated forms of bourgeois social science on the other. For the moment, however, I propose to follow Gyekye's broad suggestion (1987:9), which is one among many similar statements by other authors: "The denial of the philosophical component of African thought cannot really be accepted. The reason is that philosophy, as an intellectual activity, is universal; it cannot be assumed to be confined to the peoples of the West and the East. Philosophy of some kind is involved in the *thought and action* of every people and constitutes the sheet anchor of their life in its totality."

I have emphasized the words "thought and action" because this statement, perhaps paradoxically, is not as odds with Hountondji's position and can easily be conjoined with a historical materialist problematic. It is precisely Marx's task, in "clearing the philosophical decks" in order to construct a radical political economy, to do away with the introspective musings of "the philosophers" and thus re-insert philosophy into history and materialism, and hence into culture. But this must be theorized; it cannot be taken for granted, and this is my longer-term task. For the time being, I note that, in his *Economic and Philosophical Manuscripts of 1844*, Marx states (1975:357): "But since for socialist man the *whole of what is called history* is nothing more than the creation of man through human

labor and the development of nature for man, he therefore has pal-
pable and incontrovertible proof of his self-mediated *birth*, of his
process of emergence." Colletti, in his gloss upon key terms in these
manuscripts (1975:431), also points out that for Marx, *praxis* "is also
the foundation of the 'science of man', which supersedes both traditional speculative philosophy and political economy, abolishing the
opposition between them" (cf. Dupré 1983: *passim*).

Some of the peculiarities of Hountondji's thinking, which provide the major targets for his critics, are possibly linked to his (mostly
silent but continuing) dialogue with Althusser, with whom he had
studied at the École Normale Supérieure in Paris, although I would
not go so far as to say that he is a "disciple" of Althusser's (Mudimbe
1988:160).[4] In his introduction to the English edition of Hountondji's
African Philosophy: Myth and Reality, Abiola Irele notes (1983:28):

> The charge of elitism is often linked to what is also perceived as the
> "theoricism" of Hountondji, ascribed to the influence of his former
> teacher, Louis Althusser. . . . It is possible to consider that Hountondji's
> emphatic tone betrays him into the occasional simplification or over-
> statement of his case; to discern a preremptoriness which, while it
> corresponds to the strength of his conviction, obscures the finer points
> of his argument and therefore leaves room for its misinterpretation.

It is also important to note that both Irele and Mudimbe feel some of
Hountondji's critics go beyond the bounds of intellectual propriety,
although I doubt very much if this would worry him. Mudimbe says
that Hountondji's critics are "sometimes a bit raucous" (1988:160),
and Irele suggests that "there is often a tendentious character to the
criticisms levelled against Hountondji's ideas" (1983:28).

Whatever the case, this discussion is intended to set the scene
for the second of my two initial questions: What is the relation between African philosophy and Marxism? For my present purposes,
the construction of an epistemology grounded in Ilparakuyo history
and experience as well as in historical materialism, this question has
two levels. The first (and most obvious) concerns the way in which
various African philosophers read and use (or reject) Marx; the second
(and more important) addresses the issue of the *dialectic* that may be
established between the "logic" of Ilparakuyo notions of history and
culture and their apprehension of the *transparency* of socio-political
relations in this social formation, both past and present (Rigby 1985),
on the one hand, and what I have called a "specific form of Marxist phenomenology," on the other. Let me deal with these levels in
that order.

I have already noted that, in some contexts, the critique of

Hountondji's view of African philosophy is taken as a critique of Marxism, translated to Africa. But in many cases, other African philosophers do not necessarily agree. Even Gyekye, for example, while being severely critical of Hountondji and the latter's attack on culturalism, sees the possible, if qualified, relevance of what he calls "nineteenth century European philosophers." This is how he puts it (1987:36):

> The philosophical enterprise is connected ultimately with the search for the wisdom needed to form the basis for a satisfactory way of life. . . . African societies in the past half century have certainly been grappling with a variety of problems, most of which are the results of colonialism, imperialism and industrialism. Solving such problems and reconstructing African societies in the postcolonial era will certainly require professional investigation into fundamental ideas and general principles.

So far, so good; but this is where Gyekye takes evasive action (1987:39):

> It is the task of modern African philosophers not only to deal with the consequences of colonialism in African society and culture, but also to face squarely the challenges of industrialization and modernization. In doing so, they might take their cue from the philosophical activities of nineteenth-century European philosophers like Marx, Hegel, and Saint-Simon, and their responses to the consequences of the French Revolution. I am not referring to the specific doctrines and solutions such philosophers put forward, but to the way they responded to the circumstances of their societies. They philosophized with the contemporary situation in mind; they gave conceptual interpretation to contemporary experience.

This passage could easily be interpreted as implying that "traditional" African ethnophilosophies cannot handle the problems of contemporary Africa (a position with which Hountondji would probably concur) and that the concepts of "modernization" and "industrialization" are unproblematic in themselves. I hope these interpretations are not true, for they would seriously undermine the point of Gyekye's book. But nowhere in it are we told what these "fundamental and general principles" are; nor is the form and content of "industrialization" and "modernization" in African countries delineated anywhere. Since they are inseparable from *class formation* and growing exploitation, we are left in the air; *this* is what so upsets Hountondji, and myself.

It is also evident, however, that when Gyekye comes to look for these "fundamental ideas and general principles" in traditional

Akan philosophy (the major subject of his book), he has to abandon any attempt at a "Pan-African philosophy" for an "Akan conceptual scheme," the specific culture of the Akan peoples. So too, B. Hallen and J. O. Sodipo (1986) focus upon *Yoruba* concepts when they are looking for epistemological ideas, not upon Africa as a whole. It should be noted here that this methodology, used successfully by Gyekye and Hallen and Sodipo for certain limited but rigorous questions, is very different from that of more generalizing studies, such as Tempels's *Bantu Philosophy* or the work of Kagame (what Mudimbe calls the "Tempels and Kagame's school"), and the even larger claims for a "Pan-African" set of philosophical ideas as represented in John Mbiti's writings (Mudimbe 1988:154–161 *et passim;* cf. Rigby 1985:74–75).

Mudimbe deals comprehensively and systematically with the relations between Marxism, African philosophy, and movements for African liberation, both past and present. He carefully explores the historical links of leading African (and other Third World) intellectuals with Marxist intellectuals in Europe and their ideas, particularly in France, devoting a whole section to the question of "J-P Sartre as an African Philosopher?" (Mudimbe 1988:83–87 *et passim*). This is because of the role Sartre played in the promotion of works by African thinkers that expounded the philosophy of Negritude. He succinctly sums up this period as follows (Mudimbe 1988:83):

> Up to the 1920s, the entire framework of African social studies was consistent with the rationale of an epistemological field and its socio-political expression of conquest. Even then, social realities, such as art, languages, or oral literature, which might have constituted an introduction to otherness, were repressed in support of sameness. . . . Within this context, negritude, a student movement that emerged in the 1930s in Paris, is a literary coterie despite its political implications. Besides, these young men—Aimé Césaire, Léon Damas, Léopold Senghor—mostly used poetry to express and speak about their differences as blacks. . . . It is Sartre who in 1948 with his essay, *Black Orpheus,* an introduction to Senghor's *Anthology of New Negro and Malagasy Poetry,* transformed negritude into a major political event and a philosophical criticism of colonialism. . . . The growing influence of Marxism from the 1930s onwards opened a new era and made way for the possibility of new types of discourse, which from the colonial perspective was both absurd and abhorrent. The most original include the negritude movement, the fifth Pan-African Conference and the creation of *Présence Africaine.* Eventually, these signs of an African will for power led to political and intellectual confrontations. . . . In the 1950s, one also witnessed a radical criticism of anthropology and its inherent preconceptions of non-western cultures. Since then a stimu-

lating debate about the African significance of social sciences and the humanities has taken place.

Despite Sartre's "high-handed" appropriation, then, of Negritude for his own theoretical purposes (Mudimbe 1988:84–85), the link with Marxism became crucially important at this time of struggle. Dealing with the period of the end of formal colonialism and the newly found political independence of African nations, Mudimbe continues (1988:85):

> First, *Black Orpheus* was in large measure responsible for the blossoming in Francophone Africa of the Negritude literature of the 1950s. . . . A *littérature engagée*, a highly political literature, put forward Sartre's basic positions concerning African spiritual and political autonomy. This new generation of writers born between 1910 and 1920 includes Cheikh Anta Diop, Bernard Dadié, René Depestre, Frantz Fanon, Keita Fodéba, Camara Laye, Ferdinand Oyono, among others. Second, black intellectuals, particularly Francophone, read Sartre, discussed his anticolonialist positions and, generally, upheld them. Fanon disagrees with Sartre yet offers a good example of his impact. In his *Peau noire, masques blancs*, Fanon accuses Sartre of treason, for Fanon does not believe that "Negritude is dedicated to its own destruction." Some years later, in his *Les Damnés de la terre*, the West Indian theorist firmly applies Sartre's dialectical principle and bluntly states: "there will not be a Black culture: the Black problem is a political one."

I now turn to Léopold Senghor, another major figure whose influence on African politics, culture, and literature remains rightfully enormous: Mudimbe is quite emphatic on this (1988:93):

> Senghor tends to define African socialism as just a stage in a complex process beginning with negritude and oriented towards a universal civilization. He emphasizes three major moments: negritude, Marxism, and universal civilization. . . . Marxism is, for Senghor, a method. In order to use it adequately, the Senegalese thinker dissociates Marxism as humanism from Marxism as a theory of knowledge. The first offers a convincing explanation of the notion of alienation in its theory of capital and value and exposes the scandal of human beings under capitalism becoming mere means of production and strangers vis-à-vis the product of their work. . . . For this reason, Senghor readily accepts Marxism's conclusions insofar as they indicate a recognition of the natural rights of humans, who are and must remain free agents and creators of culture. For Senghor, Marxism as a theory of knowledge nevertheless constitutes a problem.

Senghor's problem with a Marxist theory of knowledge is really three-fold. The first is that Senghor sees Marx abandoning the true nature of a dialectical theory of knowledge, and as reverting instead "to the old concept of mechanistic materialism" and seeming to "deny the active role of the subject in knowledge" (Senghor 1964:43). While this is a misreading of Marx, it is nevertheless, unfortunately, true of a considerable number of "positivist Marxists," especially when theory is to be translated into practice. In arriving at this interpretation, Senghor is in agreement with Sartre.

The second part of Senghor's problem is the way in which Marxism-Leninism in Europe became distorted by the practices of Stalinism, resulting in often insurmountable problems for European communist parties and their international ties. We now know, of course, that Senghor was not alone in his feelings at the time; but we cannot pursue this here. In terms of Hountondji's interrogation of "culturalism," with Senghor we again lose sight of class struggle and political mobilization; they become buried once again in ideology, of a different kind from "ethnophilosophy," but much more explicitly this time. As Mudimbe accurately points out (1988:93–94), for Senghor, "it is one thing to use [Marxism's] schemas for analyzing and understanding the complexity of social formations, and another to accept the concept of class struggle and express the need to deny religion."

This brings us immediately to the third part of Senghor's problem with Marxism as epistemology: the matter of religion. This is of major concern to any discussion of African philosophy, since so much theorizing about it has been done by African theologians and in the context of theology (Mudimbe 1983:133, 1988:*passim*). Senghor reacts against the reductionist, economistic, and mechanistic strands of a certain period in European communism, and laments that "Marxism has lost its soul." It was apparent to him that the Marxist theories current at the time had forgotten Marx's denial of the need for an ideology of atheism in a socialist society, and Engels's attempts to situate early Christianity historically (Engels 1964). In the passage on "socialist man" already referred to from the 1844 *Economic and Philosophical Manuscripts*, Marx continues (1975:357):

> Since the *essentiality* [*Wesenhaftigkeit*] of man and of nature, man as the existence of nature for man, has become practically and sensuously perceptible, the question of an *alien* being, a being above nature and man—a question which implies an admission of the universality of nature and of man—has become impossible in practice. *Atheism*, which is a denial of this unreality, no longer has any meaning, for atheism is a *negation of God*, through which negation it asserts the *existence of man*. Its starting point is the *theoretically and practically sensuous consciousness* of man and of nature *as essential beings*.

This passage is extremely important for the second level of my initial two questions on African philosophy and Marxism. But before I proceed, I must, in concluding this topic, stress that Senghor does not abandon the Marxist problematic for his project; instead, he adopts an eclectic position by turning to the work of Pierre Teilhard de Chardin, which, Senghor maintains, offers a revitalized dialectical method.[5] This transition by Senghor from Marx and Sartre to Teilhard is perhaps best expressed by Irele (1981:28–29):

> Senghor's critique of Marxism does not imply a total negation, for he recognizes that it provides a dynamic vision of man in his relationship to nature, and as a consequence, a liberating view of social relationships in which the primary concern is the fulfilment of human virtualities. He believes however that Marxism is a theory that needs to be completed in the light of new developments since it was propounded, especially in the sciences, and modified to fit the African situation.

Having begun this debate on the formal links between African philosophy and Marxism with Hountondji and his critics, we come full circle to end this section with his emphatic plea, which, to be fair to him, I must quote *in extenso* (Hountondji 1983:183):

> We must promote positively a *Marxist theoretical tradition* in our countries—a continuing scientific debate around the work of Marx and his followers. For let us not forget this: Marxism itself is a *tradition*, a plural debate based on the theoretical foundations laid by Marx. There have been plenty of disagreements in this tradition, but the progress of Marxist thought has been possible thanks to public debates between Lenin and Rosa Luxemburg or between Lenin and his fellow countrymen Plekhanov, Bukharin, Bazarov, Trotsky, etc.;[6] and thanks to the theoretical individuality of thinkers like Gramsci or Mao, to cite only the greatest among hundreds.

To which we may add, from these "hundreds," such Third World names as Samir Amin, Amilcar Cabral, Walter Rodney, Archie Mafeje, Ngugi wa Thiong'o, Clive Thomas, and many, many more.

◆ **III**   I have, in the first part of this chapter, tried to establish some of the more formal links that exist between African philosophical theorizing and Marxism. Focusing now upon the second level of this "problematic of convergence," I wish to explore in somewhat more detail the relationship between Ilparakuyo and Maasai theorizing, both as an abstract schema of terms and as a "practical ideology," and certain elements of historical materialist theory, particularly those that address the production of social knowledge, language, and discourse and their expression in political *praxis*. But before I come to grips with this rather difficult enterprise, I must deal with some anthropological materials relating to Maasai and other pastoralist and agro-pastoralist societies, and their epistemological status. It is necessary to relate other discourses on the same social formations; they form a part of the construction (or deconstruction) of the discursive space occupied by the various genres dealing with these social formations, and a brief discussion of some of them (particularly those with which I cannot agree, but also some that are epistemologically self-conscious) illuminates the manner at which I arrived at the present one.

As I have already discussed at some length, the "authenticity" of anthropology has, for some time now, been the center of a theoretical crisis besetting the discipline as a whole (Diamond 1974; Rigby 1985:1–24). This is not to say that the false epistemological foundations of, say, functionalism (itself derived from theories of marginal utility in economics: cf. Patterson 1987) or structuralism (whose epistemology leads ultimately to a theory of neuro-physiology) are applied by Europeans and Americans exclusively to the study of "the other." On the contrary, as Mafeje has brilliantly pointed out (1976:311, 329, *et passim*), they were, in different ways, paradigmatic of advanced, capitalist (that is, bourgeois) society itself; it applied in "mirror-image" form both to the "other" and to the "self." Both problematics are epistemologically based upon positivist assumptions, as is the vain attempt to achieve an epistemological break through symbolic anthropology (cf. Geertz 1973 *et passim*).[7]

I use the concept of "epistemological break" in Althusser's sense, without subscribing either to his distinction between "ideology" and "science" or to his differentiation between the "young Marx" and the "mature Marx." In a letter to his translator, Ben Brewster, Althusser (1977:257) compares his use of the concept with those of Gaston Bachelard, Georges Canguilhem, and Michel Foucault. As Brewster points out for his translation of Althusser, the kind of break I am thinking of is "Marx's rejection of the Hegelian and Feuerbachian ideology . . . and the construction of the basic concepts of dialectical and historical materialism" (Althusser 1977:249; cf. Dupré 1983: *passim*).

What is extremely perplexing in contemporary anthropology, however, is that there is still research being published on various societies around the globe, and on Maasai pastoralists to boot, that is blissfully unaware of any crisis or epistemological problem in the first place. For example, in his study of Ilmatapato section of Kenya

Maasai, Spencer, whose work I have touched upon in several contexts, selects this section on the grounds that in 1975–1977, when he was doing his fieldwork, they were "remote and in the heart of Maasailand, but still accessible," and that they are more "traditional" and have "had less administration than any other tribal section," as well as "less contact with recent change, and virtually no tourism" (Spencer 1988:3).

Spencer does not mention that Namanga, the border town on the main road between Kenya and Tanzania, in the middle of Ilmatapato section, is where elderly ladies sell Maasai beadwork and jewelry to tourists, even going begging in bad years. But more importantly, except for Waller's historical work, Spencer makes absolutely no mention of the literally voluminous amount of recent writings on "development," history, and change that is now available on both Kenya and Tanzania Maasailand, and he even ignores the excellent studies by Galaty on the semiotics of Maasai rituals, their symbolic structures, and their significance for age-set organization (Galaty: 1977, 1982, 1983, *passim*), topics with which Spencer is ostensibly concerned. A great many of these studies were readily available before Spencer completed his manuscript in 1987. This prodigious amount of literature, based upon very diverse methodological and theoretical frameworks, has only one thing in common: that Maasai, particularly in Kenya, have undergone tremendous historical upheavals and transformations, through which they have struggled desperately to maintain and reproduce as much as possible of their unique culture and social organization by adhering to pastoral *praxis* and its "practical ideology" (Rigby 1985:4).

Furthermore, to the extent that he allows any "theory" to get in the way of his descriptions, Spencer recruits Max Gluckman's notion of the "rituals of rebellion," dating from the late 1950s and early 1960s, to illuminate Maasai society in the 1970s and (presumably) 1980s. While I have nothing against Gluckman's concept (cf. Rigby 1968), Spencer does not even refer to what Maurice Bloch calls "Gluckman's many followers" who, despite the fact that they refined this theoretical notion, could not in any case provide a cogent analysis of social change (Bloch 1977:280). As a "conclusion" to his book, Spencer provides us with a discussion of how he thinks the ideas of Freud and Plato may help us understand Maasai "rituals and rebellion and the trusteeship of culture."

Quite apart from the fact that Spencer lacks any theoretical sophistication, his ignorance of the work of other scholars, many of them Maasai, is unfortunate.[8] Finally, adding insult to injury, Spencer has the temerity to claim that Ilmatapato Maasai "share a pride in their past, but have no developed sense of their own history or of the changing opportunities of the contemporary scene" (cf. Rigby 1985:67–91 *et passim* and the present book, note 8 and Bibliography). I have returned to comment again upon this anachronistic work not in order to prosecute an *ad hominem* attack on Spencer, but to emphasize the positively dangerous repercussions that such irresponsible studies may have for the future of the peoples and cultures they purport to interpret.

Turning with relief to other literatures, we find among studies of pastoral or semi-pastoral peoples several "non-Marxist" attempts to overcome the distancing created by what Fabian (1983:21) accurately calls a "schizophrenic use of Time" and its resultant inauthenticity, so aptly exemplified by Spencer's book. These attempts take the form of a certain "reflexivity" in the consciousness of the investigator in approaching his material. An excellent example of this is Paul Riesman's book, *Freedom in Fulani Social Life.* Its subtitle is "An Introspective Ethnography," and Riesman introduces it as follows (1977:1–2):

> The goal which I have set myself in this book . . . is neither an ethnographic description, nor a description of social structure, nor a functional analysis, nor the discovery of social and economic determinations, though I make use of all these approaches in my work. It would be more accurate to say that this book is a resultant of the encounter of a man belonging to western civilization, and haunted by questions which life there raises for him, with a radically different civilization which he investigates with those questions constantly in mind. Two principle traits give this essay its shape and focus: first, a theme, the problem of freedom, which takes shape in the presentation as it took shape in the field; second, an attempt to give the reader an idea of how this encounter took shape. This is not just for atmosphere; it is an essential aspect of my methodology.

And certainly, Riesman's is a very illuminating and rewarding study.

This is not the place or the time to determine whether Riesman achieves entirely what he sets out to do; rather, it is to examine its epistemological implications. To some extent, Riesman is making explicit what has long been regarded as a standard for good fieldwork and ethnography, which should be seen, as Bloch reminds us for Bronislaw Malinowski, as a "long conversation taking place among the people with whom we live during fieldwork and in which we inevitably join" (Bloch 1977:278). He goes on (1977:290,n.1): "This type of view of the subject matter of social study is one which runs through the work of many writers in opposition to various 'structuralist' theories. It is present in linguistic philosophy and phenomenology and has through this channel influenced recent social scientists including Geertz."

This view of the nature of social reality is, not surprisingly, the one taken by some African social scientists who have written extensively about their own societies and cultures although, as we shall see, it is a methodology that does not in itself always guarantee the same quality of results. An excellent example of this is Francis Mading Deng, whose outstanding work on his own society, the agropastoral Dinka of Sudan, is widely available (e.g., Deng 1971, 1972*a*, 1972*b*, 1978, 1986, *passim*). If one compares closely the results of the "long conversations" of Clifford Geertz and Deng, however, a very major difference, crucial to what follows, arises.

Through his analysis of time in Balinese society, American anthropologist Geertz concludes that "Balinese social life lacks climax because it takes place in a motionless present, a vectorless now" (Geertz 1973:404; cf. Bloch 1977:284). Deng, a Sudanese jurist and anthropologist, on the other hand, constantly refers to the history of Dinka society and its historicity, encompassing pre-colonial, colonial, and post-colonial periods. Obviously, "conversations" can be very different in their consequences. Bloch correctly raises doubts about Geertz's version of Balinese time concepts and notions of history, noting that, since Bali had been under two colonialisms (Dutch and Japanese) before Geertz arrived on the scene, neither of which had been particularly pleasant for the Balinese, and that they were later involved in the crises of nationalism and the growth of revolutionary parties, somewhere along the line a "linear view of time" and historicity must have been incorporated into Balinese conceptualizations.

Deng shows brilliantly that Dinka not only question explicitly the grounds upon which the authenticity of oral history rests, but also comment upon the epistemological differences between oral and written sources, as well as the power that may derive from alternative forms of the appropriation of the latter. Deng begins by noting, for example (1978:29–30):

> A fundamental principle, which paradoxically gives Dinka . . . history a dynamic character that makes it adaptable to current realities while also rendering it vague, ambiguous, and uncertain, is that it is transmitted by word of mouth through successive generations. Authenticity of information is largely based on the fact that the receiving generation not only listens to the transmitting generation but also has the additional advantage of proximity and observation.

From this it is clear that Dinka do not unquestioningly receive every-thing they are told by their elders, and the elders frequently express doubts about what they themselves are transmitting. Dinka there-fore acknowledge that there is often a discrepancy between what is told and what ought to be told; I deal later with the implications of this for Ilparakuyo and Maasai.

There are two consequences that stem from Dinka notions of history: first, that "knowledge of their history is more pervasive and more broadly assimilated than is generally the case in literate soci-eties where the sources of knowledge are available through formal institutions"; and second, that despite this enhanced awareness on the part of the general population, "it does not mean that [a knowl-edge of history] is equally shared nor does it mean that all are equally knowledgeable" (1978:30–31).[9] Deng continues (1978:31): "As a re-sult of these dynamics, it does not always follow that the older per-sons are necessarily better informed than the younger. . . . Amid all this complexity and uncertainty, the Dinka quite often express a commitment to the truth and nothing but the truth."

Dinka also see a commitment to the truth, insofar as history is concerned, to be deeply affected by modern written history. But, significantly, they do not necessarily see history "as written down" as any more reliable. Chief Lino Aguer, for example, "paradoxically alleges that distinctions and complications have now resulted from the recent recording of tradition in a manner that welds oral litera-ture with other sources and presents the amalgam as an authentic Dinka version" (Deng 1978:33). Finally, Deng shows that, "while the Dinka now tend to rely on the accuracy of the written word, the traditionals also associate writing and the knowledge derived from it with a degree of secretiveness. . . . This rather suspicious view of the secret world of the educated appears to stem from the fact that whereas traditional knowledge is open and broadly shared, mod-ern knowledge, acquired from books as it is, is more exclusive and therefore seen as 'secret' " (1973:33, 34).

The writing down of Dinka knowledge, whether of the past or the present, Deng goes on to show, is viewed as creating not only "secretiveness" but also a source of power, a power that results from a form of appropriation. As Deng puts it, "The traditional Dinka do not expect anyone to be a neutral observer. A researcher may be viewed as a person of influence by virtue of status in society or of academic involvement" (1973:34). Foucault in Dinkaland.

What follows from a discussion of what I have called "histori-cal consciousness" for Ilparakuyo and Maasai (Rigby 1985:67–91 *et passim*), or lack of it, is that it applies equally to the specificity of the social formation being discussed, as well as its interpreter, the anthropologist, historian, novelist, or whatever. And it appears from these examples, and from numerous others, that reflexivity and a search for a historical consciousness is most likely to be found in the work of people interpreting their own societies, social scientists who adopt a Marxist perspective, anthropologists who are generally more epistemologically sophisticated, especially in linguistics; or, finally, some combination of these three viewpoints. Why is this so? For African societies, can an exploration of African philosophy offer an answer? Or is there something fundamental about the relation between historical consciousness and an epistemological break from the stifling grip of a Western bourgeois intellectualism? [10]

While I cannot adduce numerical evidence for this assertion, I can refer briefly to a few examples other than my somewhat detailed comments on Deng's outstanding contribution and the Ilparakuyo Maasai materials in this book. Going back to Riesman, we find an acknowledgment of the importance for Jelgobe Fulani of certain historical events, particularly concerning religion, although he does state that "the history of Jelgoji remains to be written" (Riesman 1977:45, cf. 44, 96–101).

Turning to one of the very few studies of African social formations based upon a historical materialist problematic, Donald Donham (1985:29–70) emphasizes the pivotal importance of historical processes, going back 2,000 years or more, for an understanding of the Maale social formation of southwestern Ethiopia. The work of French and other Marxist anthropologists, such as Catherine Coquery-Vidrovitch, Claude Meillassoux, Pierre Bonte, Emmanuel Terray, André Bourgeot, and others, amply attests to serious concern with the need to understand historical processes; indeed, it is inseparable from the Marxist notion of "social formation."

✦ **IV**   There is, however, a difference between the conscious apprehension of history as indispensible to an understanding of *any* social formation and the use of specific *historicities* as an epistemological necessity in establishing the relation between theory and *praxis* in the social sciences (cf. Mudimbe 1988:176–177). If history and the question of dealing with it on an epistemological level is as important as I claim it to be, we are faced with a number of problems. These problems are as common to the construction of an African philosophy (or "philosophies") as they are to the epistemology of

African history; as I noted earlier, one cannot deal with one and not the other. It behooves us, then, to explore briefly the appearance of an epistemologically sound and critical African history.

The first phase of the post-colonial movement of African history was to demonstrate the errors of colonialist historiography, in which, notoriously, there was assumed to be *no* history before the imperialists got there. In the immediate post-colonial period, African history had to re-focus its interest upon *Africans* themselves as serious actors in the process of "making our own history." This movement was exemplified by what came to be called the "Dar es Salaam school." It constituted a very important moment in the necessary *ideological* shift required at that time; and Terrence Ranger, one of its founding fathers at the University of Dar es Salaam, aptly called this shift "the need to recover African *initiative* in Tanzanian history" (Ranger 1969; cf. Ranger 1968). History in Africa became "nationalized" precisely at the time nationalist ideology was politically crucial. The major *methodological* shift was the rise to intellectual respectability of *oral history*.[11] There is no doubt that this "Afro-centered" period of historiography produced major studies whose results *and* certain methodological achievements are still useful for re-interpretation (Bernstein and Depelchin 1978:II:31–32), much as many significant studies in anthropology were produced under the theoretical aegis (or is it hegemony?) of functionalism.

Although historical studies in Africa were now focused on Africans, and oral sources became acceptable to most professional historians, an epistemological break remained elusive. Calling this movement "professional Africanist history," Arnold Temu and Bonaventure Swai (1981:61) correctly observe:

> Its limits are the inner organizational possibilities of the facts under investigation rather than their setting in space and history. Postcolonial Africanist historiography demands that African history should be explained in terms of its own facts. In this endeavour it is colonial history which has been regarded as being problematic rather than professional metropolitan history, which has been viewed as unproblematic and a model to be emulated consciously. In this belief it has been forgotten that colonial historiography and professional metropolitan history share the same empiricist method, and that imperial history branched off from metropolitan history in conformity with the empiricist parcellization of knowledge.

What is clearly implied here is that historical research as a whole, the entire discipline, requires an epistemological break; Temu and Swai aptly conclude their book with a chapter entitled "Towards an International Problematic for Africanist Studies."

For our present purposes, it is more important that Temu and Swai go beyond the need for a "shake-up" in history, by saying (1981: 160): "We have been arguing that an objective history of Africa must be written within an international problematic which takes cognizance of imperialism and the changing character of capital. This, however, should apply [equally] to other disciplines which are concerned with the recovery of African social reality."

If my argument on the close analogy or, more strongly, a direct parallel between the epistemological needs and contributions of African philosophy and African history is accepted, then neither philosophy nor history can merely be "Africanized"; they must go through an epistemic transformation. The way in which both may be achieved, I submit, is through a responsive and constructive historical materialism. This is precisely the argument of Temu and Swai, as well as Henry Bernstein and Jacques Depelchin, for the future of African history; it is my argument for African philosophy and the construction of a radical and subversive epistemology for the social sciences in Africa. The difficulties I have already enumerated for the problem of "levels of discourse" for specific African social formations on the one hand and Pan-African continuities and uniformities on the other also apply equally to both fields. It is significant that two recent attempts to present a history of Africa as a whole are based upon an historical materialist problematic (Freund 1984; Jaffe 1985).[12]

The central role of a theorized historicity in the revitalization of *all* African social sciences has been expressed by Mudimbe. Commenting upon Jean Copans's periodization of African studies (Copans 1976), Mudimbe asserts (1988:177):

> Marxism achieves a radically new approach. It does not westernize a virgin terrain, but confronts inattentiveness, the supporting walls which suppose them, and assembles under the roof of the analogue, relations, contradictions, imaginations. In effect the method results in an original type of visibility of differences in terms of theoretical traces of *taking the place of* and *representing*. . . . The great originality of French Marxists and their African counterparts in the 1960s resides in this. Beginning with Balandier's proposition on macro-perspectives in the field (1955*a*, 1955*b*) . . . a new discourse unites what had been kept separate and opens the way to a general theory of historical and economic derivation as exemplified in the work of Osende Afana, Suret-Canale, Meillassoux, Coquery-Vidrovitch. . . . The centrality of history is thus remarkable in what Marxism expounds as African Studies.

Despite the fact that Mudimbe cannot "whole heartedly" agree with Copans's analysis of the "succession of methodological paradigms," he nevertheless states (1988:177):

The concept of "African history" marked a radical transformation of anthropological narratives. A new type of discourse valorizes the diachronic dimension as part of knowledge about African cultures and encourages new representations of the "native," who previously was a mere object within European history. Its Marxist version offers the immediacy of objectivity through systems-signs of socioeconomic relations that permit both good pictures of local organizations of power and production and intercultural comparisons.

Now, I partially disagree with the position taken here by Mudimbe, since it admits of the synchronic-diachronic dichotomy. In this, the *epistemological* impact of Marxism is underrated for this particular discursive space; and the "synchronic" project of Lévi-Straussian structuralism is overrated. I say this for two reasons: despite the "structuralist" reading of Marx attributed to Althusser, the latter attempts to dissolve the synchronic-diachronic dichotomy as a false one (Althusser and Balibar 1970:96–109; Rigby 1985:78–79); and despite the lengthy critiques of Althusser that abound, his enormous impact upon anthropology, history, and Marxism has still to be measured (cf. Callinicos 1982), largely because most of the thinkers (including Hountondji) upon whom he has had this fundamental influence do not accept his project in its entirety (see Elliott 1987).

Finally, the inescapable necessity of beginning at the micro-level for the construction of an ethnophilosophy (particularly with regard to its epistemological implications rather than its ethical ones) does not directly contradict broader efforts to establish Pan-African continuities; but neither level can escape the necessity of taking "cognizance of imperialism and the changing character of capital" if the result is to be relevant to past, present, or future. As Mudimbe tells us, Smet has tried to show the complementarity of the two levels. This is how he puts it (1988:161): "Smet dissolves the methodological and ideological oppositions between ethnophilosophers and their critics in terms of a diachronic complementarity of schools."

Having realized that one can begin looking for epistemological ideas in African philosophy, the question arises: can we do so only at the restricted level of relativized ethnophilosophies, or can we move across the spectrum of African *Weltanschaaungen* to auto-critical reflection?

◆ V   I have already noted that, while earlier African theological philosophers had attempted to find philosophical continuities within larger groups or categories of African peoples and cultures (Tempels for the "Bantu-speaking" peoples; Mbiti for all of [Black] Africa; cf. Diop, a non-theologian, for all of Africa), more recent attempts to focus upon epistemological issues with more rigor tend to deal with "single" cultures, even if large populations are involved. In the latter case, the areas chosen for analysis are often defined on the basis of linguistic criteria. Keeping in mind the intellectual trap of "culturalism," which Hountondji has so vigorously attacked, let me refer to a couple of cases.

But to begin with, a reminder of some warnings. First, the categories of philosophical discourse in the West are the product of a specific history and its successive modes of production, culminating in capitalist imperialism; they are _not_ universal categories, even if some philosophers still maintain that they are. Second, we must avoid a reductionist view of epistemological categories—for example, the reduction of epistemology to "world-view" (cf. Mudimbe 1988:144). This is common in a good deal of anthropological theorizing. Third, we must also note, with Hountondji, that, however "small" a social formation, and however undifferentiated along class lines, not all the people who make up that social formation at any one point in time have identical ideas. The old myth of "primitive conformity" must be buried, even if, in some anthropological studies, the "total cosmology" of a people or culture is often derived almost entirely from one "ritual expert" or elder. Finally, while philosophical systems differ wildly from one another, there _are_ common problems with which, for obvious reasons, they must deal.

I return to Gyekye and his essay on Akan philosophical thought. His first concern is to debate with Robin Horton's reduction of philosophy to epistemology (Horton 1976 _et passim_). Horton had suggested that African traditional thought should not be equated with philosophy, since African traditional thought did not, as far as he was concerned, provide any theory of knowledge. After taking issue with the assumptions Horton has made in respect to Western philosophy, Gyekye states that "African traditional thought _did_ develop some epistemology, at least of a rudimentary kind" (Gyekye 1987:5). He continues:

> Concepts such as "truth", "mode of reasoning", "skepticism", "explanation", and so on appear in _Akan thought_, and the linguistic expressions, proverbs, and the general metaphysic of African peoples are replete with epistemological ideas and positions. . . . Paranormal cognition, for instance, is an important feature of African epistemology. (The fact that this mode of knowing does not occur, or occurs only marginally, in Western epistemology is irrelevant.)

I agree. But what I find most interesting in this debate is Gyekye's quotation, in support of his argument and materials, from K. A. Busia (1963:149): "The African has not offered learned and divergent disputations to the world in writing, but in his expression in conduct of awe, and reverence for nature, no less than in his use of natural resources, he demonstrates his own epistemology."

Gyekye then proceeds to suggest that, although there is not much evidence that "epistemological ideas or proposals were developed to any high degree in African traditional thought comparable to that achieved in, say, post-Socratic Greek thought or post-Renaissance Western thought," "the position is analogous to that of pre-Socratic Greek philosophical thought, which, of course, is known to have developed great metaphysical systems, but which appears to have paid inadequate attention to the analysis of epistemological concepts as such."

My point here, however, is not to assess whether or not Gyekye wins the argument on the grounds that he has chosen; I am amazed that he chooses these grounds to begin with, and that he finds it necessary to join battle here, in the first place. Gyekye lacks a theory of ideological forms. Why should Western bourgeois definitions of what is, or what is not, philosophy constrict the argument? It seems that in the task I outlined in the beginning, the task of overthrowing Western cultural imperialism, "professional philosophy" in Africa is far behind history, and even some forms of anthropology. When Gyekye does get around to specifying what the epistemological foundations of Akan knowledge are (1987:201–203), he deals mainly with the "paranormal" aspects of thought, "namely spirit mediumship, divination, and witchcraft."[13]

In their study of epistemological concepts in Yoruba traditional thought, Hallen and Sodipo (1986), despite considerable philosophical hedging over the very real problems of translation, focus upon examining in detail the notions of "to know" (*mo*) and "to believe" (*gbagbo*). After a careful use of oral evidence, and such eminent anthropological work as Rodney Needham's *Belief, Language, and Experience*, Hallen and Sodipo establish what Dorothy Emmett, in her foreword, calls "a Yoruba epistemology more sophisticated than is generally acknowledged in the anthropological literature. . . . The study of usages of these particular words show that the Yoruba *onisegun* [sages] are more sophisticated epistemologically, and more critically, and indeed empirically, minded than has been generally supposed" (Hallen and Sodipo 1986:2).

This exercise, while being valuable, reminds me somewhat of

those theologians, one of whose intellectual purposes is predominantly to demonstrate that African religions are valuable *because* they approximate in some way, in some set of beliefs, to Christianity. While I praise the meticulous methodology of Hallen and Sodipo's achievement, the whole endeavour is based on W. V. O. Quine's "indeterminacy of translation" thesis. There is absolutely no social or historical contextualizing, no reference to the nature of the Yoruba social formation at *any* time, past, present, or future. They end their discussion, as did Gyekye, by considering the paranormal theories of witchcraft, both Yoruba and Western.

But to return, at last, to Busia's claim that "the African . . . in his expression in conduct of awe, and in reverence for nature, no less than in his use of natural resources, . . . demonstrates his own epistemology." This, perhaps, could not be a more concise formulation of the Marxist notion of epistemology. Moving from the most abstract to the most concrete, as Marx recommended in "The Method of Political Economy" (1973:100–101), and as I have attempted to follow in this book, I review briefly Marx's concept of epistemology. In his chapter on the dialectics of object and subject, Ira Gollobin (1986:404–405) notes concisely:

> The history of a very general knowledge is a history of dialectics, logic, and epistemology, three spheres of knowledge long deemed competitive rather than complementary. *Only with Marx's and Engels' discovery of materialist dialectic*—the revolutionary transformation of idealist dialectics and of metaphysical materialism—did comprehension become possible of the three spheres' *inner connections*, or their *ceaseless confluence* in the integral development of knowledge.

For Marx, and historical materialism generally, an epistemology cannot be found theoretically; epistemology for Marx is the relation between theory and practice in all human activity which, by definition, is conscious. We cannot talk about the theory of knowledge as distinct from dialectics and logic, since all are conjoined in "the practice of mankind and of human history" (Lenin 1961:280). And "the bottom line," as it is fashionable to say these days, is that: "If we recall Marx's concept of knowledge—a conception, x, is knowledge if, and only if, x is used to alter the world in accordance with human needs—we can see that it is a matter of extreme epistemological import. . . . In non-Marxian parlance, but according to Marxian principle, the Good is, when realized, the True" (McMurtry 1978:239).

We again return to Hountondji's notion of a "practical ideology" as the basis for an epistemology that is at once African, in that it is identified with African history, experience, and culture, and Marx-ist, since it would not have been recognized as epistemology without Marx. But let Hountondji speak for himself (1983:178):

> When one observes the daily life of our cities and countryside and tries to investigate certain practices, rituals, and behaviors, one cannot help feeling that they are really institutionalized manifestations of a col-lective code of conduct, patterns of thought which, viewed as a whole, can constitute what might be called a *practical ideology*. Moreover . . . quite apart from this practical ideology there exists a considerable body of oral literature, esoteric or exoteric, the importance of which we are only beginning to suspect. We must have the patience to study it, ana-lyze it, investigate its logic, its function, and its limits. . . . My view is that every society in the world possesses practico-theoretical codes or "practical ideologies" on the one hand and, on the other, written or oral texts, transmitted from generation to generation.

If this is *not* "ethnophilosophy" for Hountondji, and he says it isn't, then so what? He should try going back to Marx rather than going beyond Althusser.

◆ **VI**   Certainly, as I have indicated above, the "dog-matic" Marxism of the Second International and Stalinism was (and is) totally inappropriate for any contemporary applications, whether in the Third World or in "advanced" capitalism. As Perry Ander-son beautifully demonstrates (1984:15–16) these dogmatisms led, in Europe, to a virtually unbridgeable chasm between the *praxis* of the communist parties on the one hand and the philosophical dis-course of Marxism, "itself centered on questions of method—that is, more epistemological than substantive in character" (Anderson 1984:16). The epistemological significance of this philosophical dis-course (in the theorizing, for example, of Theodore Adorno, Althus-ser, Gramsci, Korsch, Lukács, Herbert Marcuse, Ernst Bloch, Lucio Colletti, and, eventually, Sartre) was in creating a historical materi-alist theory of cultural processes, language, and history, a theoretical development of "brilliance and fertility . . . as if in glittering com-pensation for their neglect of the structures and infrastructures of politics and economics" (Anderson 1984:17).

The transformation of this philosophical tradition and the re-birth of Marxist political *praxis*, mainly since the 1960s, has two strands: first, within the capitalist West from the late 1960s (in France, Spain, Portugal, etc.) and, second, in the Third World. De-spite the influence of such scholars as Althusser and Sartre upon the latter, the European strand of Marxism is at least partially shut out by the continuity of Third World Marxisms of scholars and revolutionaries from the 1920s to the 1940s (e.g., C. L. R. James, Mao, Ho Chi Minh, Cabral, and the later Nkrumah) up to the contemporary work of scholars such as Samir Amin, Hountondji, Walter Rodney, Clive Thomas, Archie Mafeje, and others, together with other Black intellectuals of the African diaspora such as Oliver Cox and Manning Marable. The strength of Marxist cultural critique in Africa can be seen from the writings of such major figures as Ngugi wa Thiong'o, Sembene Ousmane, Omafume Onoge, Peter Nazareth, and numerous others (see, e.g., Ngara 1985; Gugelberger 1985).

This brings me right back to a consideration of language and the understanding of the "practical ideology" of Ilparakuyo and Maasai and the historical transformations of their social formations. I could, of course, do a study of Maasai concepts similar to those by Gyekye and Hallen and Sodipo for Akan and Yoruba culture and language respectively; I have done so at various points in this book. But if I were challenged again upon the issue of a *conceptual* epistemology for Maasai, I would first, of course, reiterate that one cannot arrive at an epistemology purely on theoretical or conceptual grounds. Then, since it is so important, I would return to a discussion of linguistic forms, some of which would be the following.

In the language of Ilparakuyo and other pastoral Maasai, which can be called *enkutuk oo 'lMaasai* (lit. "the mouth of the Maasai people"), there is a proliferation of verbs to denote various "shades" of some activity. Simply "to do" is *aas* in its transitive form, or *aasisho*, "to work," intransitive. "To work *at*" something is *aasishore*. Nouns derived from this verb are *enkiaas* (sing.), *inkiaasin*, (pl.): "productive work/s." *Aiko* also means "to do," and to do something in the sense of "prepare" is *aitobir*, and "to do something satisfactorily" is *aitobiraki*. Among the derivative forms of auxiliary verbs are *ang'as*, "to do first," "to begin"; *aitoki*, or *agil*, "to do again," or "to repeat something you do"; "to do something soon" is *asioki*; and "to do something early, or early the next day," is *ayooki*. These are auxilliary verbs that are followed by the simple infinitive or subjunctive: for example, the infinitive of the verb "to milk" is *alep*. Thus, *asioki alep*, "I will milk immediately," *matasioki aalep*, "Let us/That we may soon, or quickly, milk"; and so on (Tucker and Mpaayei 1955:96–97; Mol 1978:14, 56).

These variations upon the verb "to do," "to act," "to practice" would seem to indicate that the Maasai language is focused upon practices; and this notion is strengthened by Archie Tucker and Mpaayei's expert opinion (1955:51). They assert, "The verb system in Maasai is very elaborate, and contains the real spirit of the language."

This in itself is not, of course, any indication of the "deeper significance" of what may be called "grammatical meaning" in *Olmaa*. Linguists normally separate semantic from "grammatical structures";
but Roman Jakobson broke this axiom. For my argument in this book
it is sufficiently important to record Jakobson's position, and I digress
briefly.

In an interview published in 1968, Jakobson states categori-
cally: "Grammatical meanings, as many linguists have established,
and as poetry demonstrates from the beginning, have great importance for our daily life, our emotional life, our poetic life, even for
our scientific creations."

Ilparakuyo and Maasai make distinctions among a number of
other concepts, some of which have tentatively interesting features.
For example, the verb "to believe" is *airuk*, which behaves in the normal fashion for a verb in Class II (those with verb stems beginning
with "*i-*"). But it also means "to obey," "to respond," or "to answer
when addressed." It could be said that *airuk* refers to "receiving
something without question." It is almost a "reflex" response, in
which no *thought* is involved. Thinking itself is firmly tied to the
notion of *words* or *verbalization*: the same verb *ajo* means "to think"
and "to say." There is another verb, *adamu*, which is "to think," and
amus, which means "to have an idea" or "to guess."[14]

"To know" is quite another matter. The basic verb is *ayiolo*.
Most Maasai verbs remain the same for the present habitual and the
future; *ayiolo*, however, more commonly takes the suffix *-u* for the
future and the subjunctive, which makes it somewhat unusual but
not morphologically distinctive. There is a diverbative noun from
ayiolo, which means "knowledge" in the strict sense, *eyiolounoto*,
and which is different from the notion of "wisdom," *eng'eno*, as in
eng'eno oo 'lMaasai, "the wisdom of the Maasai." Both have plural
forms: *iyiolounot* and *ing'enoritin*. Then again, there is another verb
ais, which may on occasion mean to "pretend to knowledge" (Mol
1978:92). Among other verbs that regularly have irregular future
forms is *ara*, "to be"; "I will be" is *aaku*. Another diverbative form
is *enkitayiolore*, specifically "knowledge."

"Experience" is represented by a compound form, *oleng'eno*, lit.
"it of wisdom" or "it of mind," which may also mean "cleverness,"
but in a very specific sense. Experience is considered *qualitatively*
different for the depth of knowledge different people may acquire.
Thus there is a metaphorical form denoting someone who knows
her or his surroundings, but may not have any depth of knowledge:
enkong'u naipung'o, lit. "the eye which has been out, been places."
Finally, the verb "to learn" is *ang'enu*, from the same root as *eng'eno*,

and thus means "to gain wisdom," in the future, or conditionally. "To be an expert," on the other hand, can be expressed adjectivally as -*arriya* (sing., pl. -*arriyiak*); the noun "expertise" is derived from the same root, *enkarriyiano*.

Despite these elaborations, which demonstrate the richness of Ilparakuyo Maasai conceptual categories dealing with knowledge, belief, and experience, I am, as I have insisted, much more concerned with the *context* of *utterances* than with the linguistic and philosophical status of *terms*. In Chapters 4, 5, and 6, I have attempted an analysis of the dialogical form of discourse, as proposed by Bakhtin/ Voloshinov, to illuminate the manner in which Ilparakuyo and other Maasai deal with the drastic threats to their existence posed by, for example, government "development" policies.

In Chapter 6, I pursued Diamond's discussion of the relation between prose and poetry, in which he says (1980:320): "The origin of language—its metaphorical, connotative, associative, and yet concrete character, are in poetry. Myths are imaginative, not abstract, universals, the poetic personification of history." This, as I have stated, represents the very opposite of a structuralist approach to language, such as that derived from Ferdinand de Saussure by Claude Levi-Strauss, and that Voloshinov calls "abstract objectivism" (Voloshinov 1986:57–63 *et passim*). Diamond's conception lies squarely in the revolutionary problematic (prefigured by Saussure but dissolved by modern structuralism and deconstructionism) for the Marxist understanding developed by Bakhtin/Voloshinov/Medvedev.[15] Holquist (1981:xviii) is quite succinct: "If you expect a Jacobsonian systematicalness in Bakhtin, you are bound to be frustrated." In a characteristic passage in *The Dialogic Imagination*, Bakhtin says (1981:291):

> At any given moment, languages of various epochs and periods of socio-ideological life cohabit with one another. Even languages of the day exist: one could say that today's and yesterday's socio-ideological and political "day" do not, in a certain sense, share the same language; every day represents another socio-semantic "state of affairs," another accentual system, with its own slogans, its own ways of assigning blame or praise. Poetry depersonalizes "days" in language, while prose . . . often deliberately gives them embodied representation and dialogically opposes them to one another in unresolvable dialogue.[16]

But more than this. Voloshinov, referring to Medvedev's work on the "poetic qualities acquired by language," states that these qualities are also not inherent merely in the form of the utterance, but in the context in which the utterance is made. Voloshinov concludes (1986:183): "Therefore, the proper point of departure for investigation into the specificity of literature is not poetic language (a fiction in any case) but poetic context, poetic construction—literary works of art themselves."

◆ **VII**   I began this book with a reference to a number of "genres" through which Ilparakuyo and Maasai are "represented." One of these is the literature on "development," the other an inauthentic anthropology; in neither case is the discursive space created in any way congruent with the Ilparakuyo social formation and its forms of discourse. The content of capitalist development is presented to Ilparakuyo and Maasai, *inter alia*, in the form of: being forced to "settle down" ("sedentarization"); being forced to "cultivate"; commoditizing their herds; commoditizing their land (particularly in Kenya); or losing their resource base to non–Ilparakuyo/Maasai cultivators (in Kenya, often large-scale wheat farmers; in Tanzania, peasant farmers or game reserves).

I have tried to deal with how Ilparakuyo and Maasai conceptualize these processes, allowing for mobilization to halt or, at least, to slow some of them down (Rigby 1985). But peoples who follow land-use patterns totally different from Ilparakuyo and Maasai have always figured in the way in which they create their own identity (Galaty 1977, 1982, *et passim*). I therefore conclude with a valedictory text that comments on this identity-formation process, an analysis that owes a lot to Galaty. But first, a brief reminder on how such a text may be considered a "dialogical utterance," or stream of utterances.

Voloshinov makes it very clear that, although "verbal interaction is the basic reality of language," the nature of the "dialogic" is much broader than this:

> Dialogue in the narrow sense of the word, is, of course, only one of the forms—a very important form to be sure—of verbal interaction. But dialogue can also be understood in a broader sense, meaning not only direct, face-to-face, vocalized verbal communication of any type whatsoever. A book, i.e., a *verbal performance in print*, is also an element of verbal communication. . . . Thus the printed verbal performance engages, as it were, in ideological colloquy of larger scale: it responds to something, objects to something, anticipates possible responses, seeks support, and so on.

Thus Bakhtin can interpret "Rabelais and His World" not only as a product of the "dialogic imagination," but also as a struggle between "folk culture" and the "official middle ages" (Bakhtin 1984:437 *et passim*).[17]

Here is the Ilparakuyo Maasai text,[18] and its interpretation in the social process of its role in the formation of the "practical ideology" of pastoralist *praxis*; and how better to end than at "the beginning"?

> *Enkiterunoto oo 'lMaasai o 'lMeek*: "The beginning of Maasai and the Cultivators."
>
> When Leeyo (the first Maasai man) became a great elder, he called his children and said, "My children, I am now an elder of many days, and I want to instruct you."
>
> He then asked his eldest son, "What is it that you want from all my treasures?" And the eldest son replied, "I want everything in this country." And the old man said, "Since you want everything, take a few head of cattle, a few small goats and sheep, and some food of the earth [agricultural produce], since there are a large number of things." And the eldest son replied, "Very well."
>
> Then Leeyo called his youngest son and said, "And what is it that you want?" And he said, "Father, I wish that I should be given that fly-whisk in your hand." And his father said, "My child, because you have chosen only this fly-whisk, may God give you prosperity [i.e., many wives, children, dependants, and cattle], so that you will have control among your brothers."
>
> And so the one who wanted everything became a cultivator, and he who took the fly-whisk became the father of all Maasai.

Although Ilparakuyo and Maasai pastoralists conceive of themselves as "pure pastoralists" as opposed to cultivators (both Maasai-speaking—classified as Ilkurrman, "those of the fields"—and non-Maasai) and "hunters" (Iltorrobo), their continued historical and economic interdependence with these "others" is expressed both mythologically and in the constantly changing day-to-day exchange of pastoralist products for non-pastoral ones. This reciprocity depends upon the maintenance of distinct identities. But Maasai identity also rests upon the interplay between nature and culture, in which cattle (and other livestock) play a mediatory role, both as the major means of production, appropriated directly at the household as well as at the larger community level, and as symbolic "communicators" between physical and social domains (cf. Rigby 1985:48–66).

For Ilparakuyo and Maasai, then, and in keeping with the analysis of verbal forms in the Maasai language, people and "things" are not merely identified by what they are (nature, in an ontological sense) but also by what they do (culture as social labor). Thus Ilparakuyo and Maasai identity relates on the one hand to descent and kinship, as in *enkaji nabo* ("one house," "descendants of one mother"), *osarge obo* ("one blood") combined with age-set organization, *olaji obo* ("one great house"), and on the other to *esiasi* ("work" as social production) and *olkerreti* ("skin ring" signifying "talent"); in short, in terms of substance as well as *praxis*.

Appendix

Table 1:
Livestock Units per Capita: Stratified Samples from Ilparakuyo and Ilkaputiei

Category	Ilparakuyo		Ilkaputiei	
	% of domestic groups	LSUs per capita	% of domestic groups	LSUs per capita
Rich	26.1	14.86	29.2	28.20
Middle	21.7	8.39	42.3	10.44
Poor	52.2	3.17	28.5	4.83
Total	100.0		100.0	

Note: Figures for Ilparakuyo are from 1977 (N = 23); those for Ilkaputiei are from 1980 (N = 202).

Source: The sources for these figures, for which I am most grateful, are: (1) for Ilparakuyo in 1977, Mustafa, Matwi, and Ruben 1980; (2) for earlier Ilparakuyo data, Ndagala 1974 (cf. Ndagala 1986); (3) for Ilkaputiei group ranches at Olkarkar, Merueshi, and Mbirikani, ILCA 1981 (cf. Bekure et al. 1982). One Livestock Unit (LSU) is based upon the arbitrary equation: 1 cow = 2 small stock (sheep and goats). This is a crude figure; other studies use very different equations. For example, Evangelou's (1984:105) figures for livestock distribution in Elang'ata Wuas group ranch in Kenya's Kajiado District (based in turn on Bille and Anderson 1980) equate 1 LSU = 1 bovine = 10 small stock.

Table 2:
Livestock Units per Capita in Four Pastoral Maasai Areas

	Community section			
	Ilparakuyo (1977)	Ilkaputiei (1980)	Ngorongoro (1960–1978)	Komolonik (1980)
LSUs per capita	8.81	14.44	14.84	4.58

Table 3:
Total Livestock Growth, Bagamoyo District, 1935–37

Type of stock	*1935*	*1936*	*1937*
Cattle	2,375	3,194	4,516
Sheep	2,355	3,794	3,944
Goats	8,664	8,364	8,190

Source: Ndagala 1974, 1986.

Table 4:
Ilparakuyo Cattle, Bagamoyo District, between 1954 and 1957

	Adult			*Under 2 years*		*Total*	
Year	Bulls	Steers	Cows	Bulls	Heifers	No.	% of
1954	2,919	1,158	16,487	2,902	3,787	27,251	85
1957	1,399	858	14,838	2,066	4,489	23,650	85.1

Source: Ndagala 1974, 1986.

Table 5:
Changes in Livestock Units (LSUs) per Capita, Ngorongoro Maasai, 1960–1978

Year	LSUs per capita	% of small stock in herd
1960	16.55	38
1966	14.75	42
1970	15.75	39
1974	15.95	56
1978	11.20	63

Source: Arhem 1985.

Table 6:
Herd Size in One Ilparakuyo Homestead, 1975–1987

Year	No. of "houses"	Total pop. of homestead	LSUs per domestic group	LSUs per capita
1975	4	19	520	27.37
1978	5	23	380	16.52
1980	6	25	485	19.40
1987 (total)	8	—	105	—
A	3	8	63	7.88
B	5	19	42	2.21

Note: A = 1975–1980; B = 1980–1987.

Notes

♦ Chapter 1

1. Goldschmidt is absolutely correct in suggesting that pastoral social formations frequently adapt to changed local, ecological, historical, and economic conditions by taking up agriculture; the archaeological record confirms this. But the opposite is also true: that agricultural populations select a pastoralist, even nomadic, alternative in certain conditions (see Chapter 3; Robertshaw and Collett 1983*a*, 1983*b*).

2. I have commented elsewhere on the problems encountered when development anthropologists seek to avoid epistemological (and political) responsibility by submerging themselves in interdisciplinary teams (Rigby 1985:2).

3. One of the anthropologists on the team told me in 1983 (personal communication) that professional activity had been seriously disrupted by the amount of time taken up in settling quarrels and disputes between other members of the team and the local Maasai population.

4. Samir Amin has shown convincingly that the capitalist mode of production represents not only a decisive historical "break" with all earlier forms but also an *inversion* of the hierarchy of articulation among the economic, politico-juridical, and ideological instances characteristic of precapitalist modes of production (Amin 1989:1–2; see also below).

5. That the elements of ideology represented in what I have termed "pastoral *praxis*" among Ilparakuyo and Maasai do not necessarily form a coherent, easily legible ideology is discussed very briefly in *Persistent Pastoralists* (Rigby 1985:3–4; cf. Hountondji 1983; Augé 1982).

6. As with Sartre, Bakhtin's work has been subjected to both radical (or "left") readings and "liberal" ones (Stam 1988:144, n.2). In his "dialogi-

cal representation" of "Who Speaks for Bakhtin?" Gary Saul Morson (whose reading is classified as "liberal" by Stam) has "Moi" telling "Elle," "Well, there *is* one Frenchman I think of in connection with Bakhtin—Jean-Paul Sartre. . . . Sartre objects to a mechanical, 'vulgar formalism.' Both *-isms* attempt to derive everything particular from overarching general laws" (Morson 1986:9–10). Sartre calls the rigidities of Soviet thought at the time a "lazy Marxism."

◆ Chapter 2

1. "Primitive accumulation" is both a necessary epoch in the historical development of the capitalist mode of production and a continuing form of expropriation by international capital in its exploitation of underdeveloped social formations.

2. An excellent discussion of colonial and post-colonial literature in Kenya, including references to Maasai, can be found in David Maughan-Brown (1985).

3. The accuracy and illuminating nature of this text is no doubt attributable both to John Eames's sensitivity to issues of importance to Maasai and to Naomi Kipury's consultative oversight, even if her name is wrongly spelled! (Amin *et al.* 1987:10). Amin, Duncan Willets, and Eames do not seem to find it necessary, as the Hindes did seventy-one years before, to explain why they chose their title.

4. The complex issues involved in wildlife preservation and management and the rights of local communities are sympathetically dealt with, for Zambia, by Stuart Marks (1984; cf. Parkipuny 1983 for Maasai comparisons).

◆ Chapter 3

1. Robert Carneiro (1970:733–734) offers a parallel classification of state formation theories as "coercive" or "voluntaristic," a dichotomy I take up in another context below.

2. Fried turns, significantly, to Bertrand de Jouvenel's definition of authority ("the faculty of gaining another man's assent") as the best. The analysis of power and authority espoused by de Jouvenel (1945, 1957) is indistinguishable from the bourgeois mainstream association of voluntaristic social order, moral good, and political action.

3. The "temptation" has been elaborated and ingeniously theorized by G. A. Cohen (1978).

4. In a most peculiar and somewhat convoluted argument, during the course of an otherwise cogent critique of David Goodman and Michael Redclift's book on "peasant transitions" (1982), Brass (1984:110) accuses them of "unproblematically lumping together" under the rubric of "French Marxist anthropology" various authors who reject historical materialism in favor of idealist models, among whom are, according to Brass, Jean Baudrillard and Clastres. While he is quite correct in singling out Baudrillard as "idealist," I cannot help but wonder at this assertion since, as Brass himself notes, Good-

man and Redclift do not mention *either* of these authors in their book, and cannot therefore be asserting that they are Marxists. A far more penetrating critique (of which great numbers abound) of structuralist influences on French Marxist anthropology is provided by Allen Abramson (1979).

5. While retaining the terms "internal" and "external," Balandier (1970:36) sees the processes described by them as inseparably bound together in the generation of political power. He notes that "although power obeys *internal* determinisms that reveal it is a necessity to which every society is subject, it seems none the less to result from an *external* necessity."

6. Gervase Mathew (1975:155) notes, however, that this location for Rhapta has not yet "been given a modern identity."

7. So far, a chronology based upon Maasai and Ilparakuyo age-sets takes us back approximately two hundred years (Fosbrooke 1956a; Jacobs 1968; Rigby 1985). John Lamphear uses a similar technique to provide the Nilotic semi-pastoralist Jie of eastern Uganda with a chronology of almost three hundred years (Lamphear 1976:34–37 *et passim*).

8. The first British ship to Zanzibar did not arrive until 1591.

9. Nineteenth-century evidence strongly supports this interpretation, as well as indicating continual Maasai/Ilparakuyo contact with the coast. During Christopher Rigby's consulate in Zanzibar (1858–1861), Sultan Majid refused to permit missionary Rebmann's return to Rabai, near Mombasa, because it had been "invaded by the warlike Masai, who periodically came down and plundered all the more peaceable tribes towards the coast. The Sultan would not permit his return [after a visit to Zanzibar] while the country was disturbed, as protection would have been impossible" (Russell 1935:221). Significantly, C. E. B. Russell (Rigby's daughter) adds, "When [Rebmann] went back to his mission-station eighteen months later, he was surprised to find that the invaders had scrupulously respected it. Rigby suggested to the Royal Geographical Society that this demonstrated how easy it would be to make friends with the Masai and explore the county. It was in fact opened up shortly after by Joseph Thomson" (Russell 1935:221–222; cf. Krapf 1860; Thomson 1885; Jacobs 1979; Rigby 1985).

10. The work of Catherine Coquery-Vidrovitch (1978) and Balandier (1955b) makes the same point for other parts of Central and West Africa. For example, Coquery-Vidrovitch (1978:270) notes that "one of the characteristics of African societies is that they have never lived in isolation."

11. Bonte's penetrating analysis of Maasai religion (1975:393–394 *et passim*) points in the direction suggested here, but it does not explore either the historical circumstances of these transformations or the significance of the multiple contradictions generated by these historical circumstances. He does, however, see the prophetic institution as a "new institution which does not replace the other institutions but which stands alongside and above them," concluding that any transformation in the relations of production "presupposes a prior transformation in the religious organization itself" (Bonte 1975:391). Why and how the religious transformation is prior is not historically established, although it is theoretically elaborated.

12. The enormous importance of ritual firemaking and the histori-

cal and political significance of "firemakers" among other Nilotic people is stressed by J. Lamphear (1976:121–122). Significantly, this function is retained by secular elders and within age-set contexts among Maasai, and is not transferred to the descent-controlled ritual influence of the prophets.

13. The role of warriors' "mothers" in, for example, *eunoto* implies further contradiction in weakening father-son ties by emphasizing matrifiliation in non-prophetic lineages, while leaving untouched the ideology of patrilineal descent at all levels (see Chapter 7), including the patrilineal inheritance of the power of prophecy among Inkidong'i Ilaiser.

◆ Chapter 4

1. Any such crude economistic position would also make nonsense of such works as Engels's "On the History of Early Christianity" (Marx and Engels 1964:316–347).

2. In other works, Althusser and Balibar (1970) would also appear to contradict these contentions, and Feuchtwang similarly abandons them when he notes (1975:68) that "an ideology is a structure which has a social and historical existence."

3. This "highly specialized" labor was usually herding in exchange for grazing rights in lands that were previously theirs, or for livestock (as with Lord Delamere, who had taken over vast areas of Kenya Maasailand), or participation in military expeditions in which livestock was the "payment" (a point to which I return, and see Chapter 2; cf. Tignor 1976; Waller 1976). Tignor's sociology is straightforwardly Weberian, through the mediation of Talcott Parsons (cf. Tignor 1972). For reasons already outlined, this curtails his ability to pursue his insights to their conclusion.

4. This was the first time rinderpest had ever appeared in epidemic form, decimating livestock in East Africa; it was introduced (like the human diseases of bilharzia and syphilis) by foreigners and their animals (cf. Kjekshus 1977).

5. In his work on the impact of formal education upon social change in Kenya Maasailand, Sarone ole Sena uses a similar but more complex periodization: the nineteenth century, early colonial period, 1895–1914; the first state schools, 1915–1930; establishment of "out-schools," 1931–1945; preparing for independence, 1946–1962; independence, integration, and development, 1963–1983 (Sena 1986). I briefly take up again the nature of the impact of formal education on the age-set system and hence upon the reproduction of the Maasai social formation in Kenya, a topic admirably explored and elucidated by ole Sena.

6. The Ilaimer and Iltalala in Kenya were themselves *ilmurran* between 1866–1886 and 1886–1905 respectively (see Jacobs 1968:16; ole Sena 1986:65); they were equivalent to the Ilmerisho (Ilaimer) and Ilkishomu (Iltalala) among Ilkisonko section in Tanzania (Fosbrooke 1968:194–195), and to Ilkenyeiyie/Ilsujita and Ilpariho/Isiyiapai among Ilparakuyo section, also in Tanzania (Rigby 1985:84).

7. In Tanzania, virtually all freehold title to land has been abolished in

accordance with socialist development policy. Maasailand and other pastoral or semi-pastoral areas came under the special provisions of the Range Development and Management Act, no. 51/1964. From 1963 until the present, the Tanzania government has "accepted the argument that the maximum advantages can only be enjoyed in such a way that the range land is owned and managed communally" (James 1971:229; Nyerere 1967; Rigby 1969b; Ndagala 1982).

8. I have described in some detail elsewhere (Rigby 1985:158–161 *et passim*) how *ilmurran* among Ilparakuyo and other Tanzanian Maasai pastoral sections take on new "functions" that mediate the relations of unequal exchange, commoditization, and political inequality between local pastoral communities and the national political economy and government, the latter often misrepresented by its local structures.

9. The case for the "necessity" or "inevitability" of the capitalist model for at least the initial stages of economic development in the underdeveloped world was made by the late Bill Warren (1980), and is taken up in a very different way by Goran Hyden (1983).

✦ Chapter 5

1. Jon Elster (1985:56) makes a similar point in a somewhat back-to-front (or even upside-down) manner, when he states that "there is no sense in which Marx's theory of history accords a privilege to the material as opposed to the mental. He invokes 'spiritual' productive forces such as science and language on a par with technology, and affirms their importance for the process of social change."

2. Making a somewhat different statement that retains the Saussurean opposition between *langue* and *parole*, John O'Neill (1972:94) suggests that "we may . . . distinguish between the institution of language as the objective structure studied by linguists and *speech*, which is the use-value language acquires when turned towards expression and the institution of new meanings." It is important to note also that the Marxist approach to language as embodied in the work of Gramsci, Voloshinov, and Williams, and even Althusser, rejects the theoretical distinction between *langue* and *parole*, or even synchrony and diachrony, proposed by Saussure and his structuralist followers, and which is associated with, or more precisely, derived from, a Durkheimian sociology (Williams 1977:27–28; Salamini 1981:188; Rigby 1985:78).

3. Compare the excellent study by Ruth Finnegan (1973:135–144) of the similarities and differences between literature in "literate" and "oral" cultures (also, Goody 1968).

4. By this I mean, for example, Paul Riesman's study, *Freedom in Fulani Social Life* (1977), and my own analysis of Ilparakuyo concepts (Rigby 1985).

5. Compare *erisio* above. Much of the following discussion is derived from my own research among Ilparakuyo Maasai and the interpretations of my brother, Toreto ole Koisenge, as well as those of Melkiori Matwi, Katao

ole Koisenge, and other Ilparakuyo and Imparakuyo. Further valuable insights are derived from the extensive work of Naomi Kipury, John Galaty, Sarone ole Sena, and Frans Mol (see Bibliography).

6. Maasai usage locates strength, or the capacity to be good and have a sense of respect, in the "stomach" (*enkoshoke*). For example, to encourage someone to take up a dangerous task is *aitogol enkoshoke*, "to harden the stomach" (cf. Kipury 1983*a*). There is also a proverb that states, *enkoshoke naata osotua*, lit. "the stomach has the umbilical chord [*osotua*]." The figurative meaning of this saying, as Kipury points out (1983*a*:152), is that "food is essential for the maintenance of life and, therefore, if one provides this essential commodity, he will have established a relationship with the receiver. In this regard, it is an essential step towards friendship and closeness." By extension, *osotua* also implies unity, peace, close friendship, and love (*enyorrata*).

7. This is not the place to consider the events in eastern Europe, the U.S.S.R., and other parts of the "socialist world" that occurred throughout 1989 and 1990, save to dismiss the croaking chorus of Western claims for the final, glorious victory of global capitalism and the "end of history" for what it is—a return to the ephemeral "end of ideology" debates of the 1950s and 1960s.

8. Under the dispensation of President Bush's "new world order," the United Nations Development Program has devised a "Human Freedom Index" to determine where development aid should go. Yet the new aid policies of the capitalist world directed toward Africa, the Caribbean, and Latin America are designed specifically to consolidate the economically and politically privileged comprador and petit bourgeois classes in these countries.

◆ Chapter 6

1. Hobsbawm succinctly adds (1964:49), "No misunderstanding of Marx is more grotesque than the one which suggests that he expected a revolution exclusively in the advanced industrial countries of the West." Reference here may be made to Marx's "late writings" (see Shanin 1983).

2. For Sartre, this "inertness" is pejorative and characteristic of a structuralist interpretation, representing exclusively *past praxis* in his concept of the practico-inert.

3. As Anderson points out (1984:36), Sartre's *Critique* was "an attempt to understand not the truth of one person but—as Sartre put it—the 'truth of humanity as a whole' (even if, for him, there was a basic epistemological continuity between the two). It pointed towards a global history, whose declared terminus would be a totalizing comprehension of the meaning of the contemporary epoch." Despite the fact that this promise was never kept, Sartre consistently addressed the issues of colonialism and racism (e.g., the *Critique*, pp. 716–734 *et passim*) in global perspective. The weakness of his investigations, as already noted, lies more in the fact that he failed to develop a comparative and consistent political economy of social formations, as a necessary element in his anthropology of "humanity as a whole."

4. In the interviews that Sartre gave to *Lotta Continua* and *Le Nouveau Observateur* in 1977 and that were published just before his death, he claimed his position to be one of "radical neo-anarchism." At this time, Sartre had lost his physical powers, and Simon de Beauvoir said that the interviewers had been "manipulative," distorting Sartre's position on a number of issues (Anderson 1984:29,n.24).

5. In an extremely important paper, Omafume Onoge (1985:23) distinguishes two "tendencies" in the Negritude movement, "which, initially, were merely divergent, [but] are today quite opposed. They are the *revolutionary* affirmation associated with Césaire, and the *mystical* affirmation associated with Senghor."

6. This is a revised translation by myself of the text published originally in Hollis (1905:277–278). I have other versions that do not add or detract from the one used here. Although I collected numerous historical texts and songs from my Ilparakuyo age-mates, relatives, and friends, many contain references to some clandestine activities of the contemporary period, in which those involved are all too easily identified. This characteristic of these texts is in itself confirmation of my assertion that historical and transcendental consciousness are juxtaposed in them. But this is why I use older texts collected by others, such as Lemenye's transcriptions for Hollis or those that refer to sections of Maasai other than Ilparakuyo, as in Kipury's excellent book (1983*a*).

7. Berntsen (1979:138) notes of the principle of succession: "In general, it seems that the successor to the chief prophet was a son who was also a member of the warrior age-set [*sic*] at the time of his death."

8. J. Tompo ole Mpaayei is a leading Maasai Christian in Kenya who collaborated with Archie Tucker on an excellent Maasai grammar (Tucker and Mpaayei 1955). My translation here is a modified version of that given in Mpaayei (1954:24, 30–36). It is interesting to note that in the earlier Ilparakuyo text, the word for Europeans is *ilaisungun*, a term not commonly heard today. The word common in contemporary usage is *olmusunkui* (pl. *ilmusunku*), from Kiswahili *mzungu* (pl. *wazungu*). In the Mpaayei text, the term used is *olashumpai* (pl. *ilashumpa*), a word with, at best, a hazy etymology (Mol 1976:63) or, at worst, an unknown one. However, an Olparakuoni person who has become totally "westernized" and is thus "lost" to Maasai culture can be referred to as *olashumpai orok* (lit. "black European [or Arab]," pl. *ilashumpa orook*), as well as by various other terms (Sena 1986:95–96,112). None of these terms really relate to a Maasai "stranger" or "visitor," who is *olomoni* (pl. *ilomon*); the plural form also means "news."

9. Helge Kjekshus (1977:132–134) refers to Fischer's (1884:89) and Johnston's (1886:303) reports that, in the 1880s and 1890s, Maasai "were extremely apprehensive of foreigners visiting their lands because of an illness. . . . identified as smallpox," which, in epidemic proportions, attacked children and adults because of their lack of immunity to an externally introduced disease. Significantly, Kjekshus continues, "The Masai [*sic*] referred to it as the 'White Illness' and associated it with the coming of the Europeans" (Johnston 1886:303).

10. Although Ilparakuyo and Maasai have, of course, a full set of kinship and affinal terms of reference *and* address, closely related and cooperating kin, age-mates, and friends usually address each other by terms based upon the words for the livestock (both cattle and small stock) that they have exchanged with each other (see Chapter 7). A similar system of livestock terms used metaphorically is also manifested in certain rituals among the Wagogo of central Tanzania, who, although "Bantu-speakers," have absorbed an age-set system and some kinship terminology from Ilparakuyo (Rigby 1969*a*, 1971, *et passim*).

11. All prophets, as we have noted above, belong to one clan and sub-clan, Ilaiser Inkidong'i, as the gift of prophesy is inherited patrilineally. Ilparakuyo began to turn to their own great prophets in about 1800, presaging their rift with other Maasai sections around 1832. The prophetic descent groups among Ilparakuyo were also divided, in about 1855, between the sons of Mtango, called Kirigo and Kirkong. Mtango became *Oloiboni kitok* in about 1835 (Rigby 1985:7–11, 81–85, *et passim*; cf. Berntsen 1979). Among Ilparakuyo, the prophetic sub-clan is also called Ilwarakishu.

12. Another important category of songs for *ilmurran* is the historical epic song (*eoko*), or poetic recitation, in which are recounted stories of their bravery, achievements, and exciting escapades of the past (Rigby 1985:47; Kipury 1983*a*:225–227).

13. The saliva of elders carries a blessing and invokes both good and, on occasion, bad ritual statuses. Married women can also assert their outrage over bad male behavior in a ritual called *inkamulak oo 'nkituaak*, lit. "the married women's saliva" (see Kipury 1989).

14. In a footnote, the editors of this edition of the *German Ideology* state that Marx and Engels had originally written, "Men are the producers of their conceptions, ideas, etc., and precisely men conditioned by the mode of production of their material life."

15. Paddock grazing, and even stall feeding, are totally foreign to Maasai and are characteristic either of modern development policies or of the pastoral practices of neighboring, predominantly agricultural, mountain or highland-dwelling peoples, such as the Wachagga of Mt. Kilimanjaro (which Maasai call *Oldoinyo oibor*, or "the White Mountain").

16. *Kanga*, a Kiswahili term, denotes printed clothes bought in the stores as commodities to replace original leather garments.

◆ **Chapter 7**

1. Names of all the "actors" in this study have been changed. A brief history of Ilparakuyo movements into West Bagamoyo is given in Beidelman 1960; Ndagala 1974, 1986; Rigby 1985; Mustafa *et al.* 1980.

2. The relative unimportance of sorcery and witchcraft beliefs in Ilparakuyo and Maasai society is discussed in Rigby 1985:99–101. It is also important to note that the usual word given by Ilparakuyo for "sorcery" and translated as *uchawi* in Kiswahili is *esetan* (pl. *isetani*), which is not

an Olmaa root but derived from Kiswahili/Arabic *Shetani*, "evil spirit," "demon," "devil," "Satan."

3. An earlier summary and comparative figures for unstratified averages are given in Rigby 1985:134.

4. This result is partly due to the problem of matching the stratification parameters in the two samples; there are insufficient "raw data" available to correct for this error. The comparison is, nevertheless, still instructive.

5. Figures for northern Tanzania are derived from Ndagala 1978, 1982; for Ngorongoro, the source is Arhem 1985 *et passim*.

6. Small stock rather than cattle are also consumed in greater numbers for ritual meat-feasts (*ilpuli*; see Rigby 1985:41–66) and other ceremonial occasions in times of drought and bad years caused by other conditions.

7. The word *olparakuoni* (fem., *emparakuoni*; pls. *ilparakuo* and *imparakuo* respectively) means "one who is very well-off in cattle and livestock generally" (Rigby 1985:7).

8. The trend toward higher proportions of small stock in Kenya Maasai herds is general and continuing (Jacobs: personal communication); see also Arhem 1985:50–51. This is *opposite* to trends among Ilparakuyo, as we have seen.

9. The unfortunate necessity for this reliance upon agricultural produce was sadly remarked on in 1978 by Ilparakuyo, illustrated by a statement I recorded in my previous book (Rigby 1985:40–41): "The food we Ilparakuyo have to eat these days, *ugali* [maizemeal porridge] and beans, is not really food at all; this is because our cattle are dying so fast, we have to send most of the herd away to a safer camp, and there is little milk at the homestead (*ti ang'*)."

10. In my experience, when Ilparakuyo in West Bagamoyo need extra labor for *pastoralist* duties, they hire (or even adopt) Wagogo youths (from Dodoma Region) for wages and board. Many of these youths are eventually absorbed into the Ilparakuyo community. This is also true of Ilparakuyo-Wagogo relations in other Ilparakuyo communities, since the Wagogo are considered knowledgeable about cattle and pastoral *praxis* generally (see Rigby 1969a:112–113, 19, 103, 253–254 *et passim*).

11. As noted elsewhere, I do not subscribe to the notion of dual sectors in peasant economies: the "subsistence" versus "non-subsistence" (whether "modern," "market," or other).

12. Hedlund clearly establishes that exploitation among Ilkaputiei Maasai in Kenya derives from the ability of individual ranchers "to draw resources from two asymetrically linked modes of production," a situation possible *only* when an exploitative relationship exists "between the emerging underdeveloped and the precapitalist modes of production" (Hedlund 1979:32, 16; cf. Rigby 1985:20–22; Table 2, and discussion above).

13. My position here does not invalidate Bonte's argument on class formation among East African pastoralists, but merely puts a historical gloss upon it. He states (1981:41): "The formation of social classes is the result of

an extremely complex process. We can only outline certain aspects of this process here. The starting point will be the above outlined contradiction between the unequal accumulation of livestock among autonomous domestic groups [that cannot exist in reality] and the equal access of those groups to collective resources. This contradiction determines the laws of transformation of the productive system." Ndagala takes a somewhat similar position for Tanzania Maasai, although his "autonomous accumulators" are *individuals*, not domestic groups (Ndagala 1982:36–38; cf. Rigby 1985:17–19 *et passim*).

14. When I was in the community in 1987, it appeared that the movements of Ilparakuyo domestic groups and their herds out of Mindu Tulieni and Lugoba Ward were relatively unhindered; this was in contrast to previously stricter controls on the populations of *ujamaa* villages.

15. I had just walked about sixteen miles from the *enkang'* where I was living to the administrative center of the area, together with a non-Maasai companion; we arrived "out of the blue."

16. As we have already shown, the problem of the inheritance of land, an unheard-of and totally foreign issue for Maasai, has led to a wide range of individual, *ad hoc*, responses on the part of holders of titles to individual and group ranches. Some elders have divided their land up, giving some to every wife or married woman in the domestic group and their children; others have divided it up among all their sons equally, or equally among all their children, male and female; still others have deeded all their land to the eldest son of the first (senior) wife's house; and so on.

17. I do not here raise the classic issue of the distinction between witchcraft and sorcery (Evans-Pritchard 1937); the terms are left deliberately ambiguous (cf. Rowlands and Warnier 1988:131, n.1).

18. There is a specific case of an elder who has adopted this option; but I cannot elaborate here. Suffice to say that he has been a local government functionary for many years, is a convert to Christianity, and has sent several of his children to school.

◆ **Chapter 8**

1. It may very well be objected that the role of intellectuals and their productions, such as this book and the research and various works to which it refers, are so distant from the "actual *praxis*" of transformation to which they pertain in Africa as to be virtually insignificant. If the readers were of this opinion, I trust they have changed their minds by now, since I have hoped convincingly to demonstrate otherwise. For the moment, and despite its Hegelian overtones, I will concur with Michel Foucault in the following passage (1980:133), in which he says: "The essential political problem for the intellectual is not to criticize the ideological contents supposedly linked to science, or to ensure that his scientific practice is accompanied by a correct ideology, but that of ascertaining the possibility of constituting a new politics of truth. . . . It is not a matter of emancipating truth from every system of power (which is a chimera, for truth is already power) but of de-

taching the power of truth from the forms of hegemony, social, economic, and cultural, within which it operates at the present time." This position is consistent with one derived from Gramsci, and not at variance with a dialectical Marxist view of *praxis.*

2. By "Africa" I mean here both the most *general* conditions of African history: the history in which Africa has seen the transformations that occurred before imperialist penetration—that is, the depredations of the period immediately preceding colonial penetration and the colonial period itself—as well as the post-colonial recent past and the more specific and localized historicities, forms of thought and practice related to one or more African peoples. *None* of the latter can be conceived of as "closed systems," since they have never, at any period, been truly isolated from one another.

3. Even among "underdeveloped" countries, the process of class formation, as it is "over-determined" (Althusser 1977:252–253; Althusser and Balibar 1970:*passim*), varies a great deal from one country to another, although the conditions of class formation remain the same everywhere.

4. Mudimbe provides a superb account of the context and critique of Hountondji's position in African philosophy; here, I refer only to one or two aspects of the latter's work. It is also important to note that Mudimbe alludes to the influence upon Hountondji of Georges Canguilhem and Gaston Bachelard, through Althusser (cf. Althusser 1977; Althusser and Balibar 1970).

5. Senghor states (1964:134), "Engels tried to explain . . . [a] . . . unified science in *Dialectics of Nature.* But at that time (about 1890) the great scientific discoveries . . . had not yet been made. Teilhard de Chardin picked up Engels's project in *The Phenomenon of Man,* invoking not only natural sciences but also physics, chemistry, and even mathematics. Teilhard de Chardin has a twofold advantage: the great scientific discoveries had already been made; as a paleontologist, he was himself a specialist in natural sciences." The epistemology of the natural sciences had not had, at that time, the shake-up it was later to receive. It is also of interest to note that French Marxist Roger Garaudy underwent a "conversion" to the ideas of Teilhard de Chardin (Caute 1964).

6. It should be noted that many of these figures were banished or relegated to the status of "non-persons," certainly deprived of their theoretical standing and importance, during the Stalinist period in the Soviet Union. Many of them, however, have been (or were being) restored to the front ranks of Marxist theoreticians through Gorbachov's *Glasnost* and *perestroika* programs.

7. Fabian, commenting delightfully on anthropological relativism and symbolic anthropology, says (1983:45): "There is now an anthropology which is fascinated with 'symbolic' mirrors (signs, signifiers, symbols) lining the inside walls of 'cultures' and reflecting all interpretive discourse inside the confines of the chosen object. These reflections give to an anthropological observer the illusion of objectivity, coherence, and density (perhaps echoed in Geert's 'thick description'); in short, they account for much of the pride anthropology takes in its 'classical' ethnographies. One is tempted to continue [Ernst] Bloch's metaphorical reverie [in 1962] and to muse over the

fact that such mirrors, if placed at propitious angles, also have the miraculous power to make objects disappear—the analyst of strange cultures as magician or sideshow operator, a role that is not entirely foreign to many a practitioner of anthropology and one that is most easily assumed under the cover of cultural relativism." For another spirited attack upon the more bizarre forms of cultural relativism, see Maurice Bloch (1977).

8. On many of these issues, see Rigby 1985:67–91 *et passim*; Arhem 1985; Sena 1981, 1986; Parkipuny 1975, 1983; Kipury 1983*a*, 1983*b*, 1989; Galaty 1977, 1982, 1983; Sankan 1971, 1979; Mpaayei 1954; Mukhisa Kituyi 1990; Jacobs 1965*a*, 1965*b*, 1968, 1975, *et passim*; Fosbrooke 1956*a*, 1956*b*, *et passim*; and so on.

9. These variations in Dinka historical knowledge and consciousness are parallel to Hountondji's insistence that, although a particular African social formation may have a *dominant* ideology, it is not necessarily shared by all the members of that social formation.

10. I do not, of course, claim by this argument that the use of historical materials is confined to African and Marxist anthropologists. Clearly, the work of such major figures as Paul Bohannan, Jack Goody, E. E. Evans-Pritchard, Aidan Southall, M. G. Smith, and so on are also closely concerned with historical processes that are *necessary* to their analyses. An excellent example is Derrick Stenning's work on Wodaabe Fulani (1959). Also, there is the whole recent literature on "ethnohistories," such as Lee Cassanelli's on Somali society (1982).

11. The gaining of this *widespread* respectability by oral sources of historical data could be said to have begun with the publication in 1961 of Jan Vansina's book *De la tradition orale: essai de méthode historique*, translated by H. M. Wright as *Oral Tradition* and published by Routledge and Kegan Paul in 1965.

12. An earlier Marxist attempt to encompass all of Africa (south of the Sahara) on the basis of a historical materialist problematic in history is E. Sik's *The History of Black Africa*, 2 vols., Budapest (1966).

13. As is common in many such studies, "Akan thought" is frequently generalized to "African thought" without evidence for this extension being presented. This is particularly a constant feature of Mbiti's *African Religions and Philosophy* (1970).

14. Other verbs can take these suffixes, but they do not regularly do so. There are also local variations for a number of these verbs.

15. This, of course, is not the place to introduce the intractable debate on the "true identities" of these three pioneering figures in the development of a historical materialist approach to language; but, from my reading of them, certainly, at least Bakhtin and Voloshinov are the same person.

16. I agree entirely with Allon White (1984:123) that, "since literary structuralism and deconstruction are ultimately linked to the same debate, I believe Bakhtin's theory simultaneously encompassed and pushed beyond them too. By 'pushed beyond' I mean that Bakhtin's work prefigured both structuralist and deconstructionist views of the language of literature, but

crucially placed them both in a sociolinguistic framework which thereby makes them responsive to an historical and thoroughly social comprehension of literature."

17. I must emphasize again here that I do not subscribe to the Saussurean structuralist notion as developed by, for example, Jacques Derrida (1972; cf. Callinicos 1982), which implies that "there is nothing outside the text."

18. This folk-tale is also recorded by Hollis (1905:171–173). I have other versions; this translation is my own combination of them.

Bibliography

Abélès, Marc. 1981. "'Sacred Kingship' and Formation of the State." In H. J. M. Claessen and P. Skalnik (eds.), *The Study of the State*. The Hague: Mouton.

Abramson, Allen. 1979. "Unhistorical Historical Materialism: British Social Anthropology and French Marxism Reconciled." *Critique of Anthropology* 13/14:165–178.

Alavi, Hamza. 1972. "The State in Post-Colonial Societies: Pakistan and Bangladesh." *New Left Review* 74:59–81.

Althusser, Louis. 1971. "Ideology and Ideological State Apparatuses: Notes towards an Investigation." In *Lenin and Philosophy and Other Essays*. London: New Left Books.

——— . 1977. *For Marx*. London: New Left Books.

Althusser, Louis, and Etienne Balibar. 1970. *Reading Capital*. London: New Left Books.

Amin, Mohamed, Duncan Willetts, and John Eames. 1987. *The Last of the Maasai*. London: Bodley Head.

Amin, Samir. 1989. *Eurocentrism*. New York: Monthly Review Press.

Anderson, Perry. 1984. *In the Tracks of Historical Materialism*. Chicago: University of Chicago Press.

Arens, William, and Ivan Karp (eds.). 1989. *The Creativity of Power: Cosmology and Action in African Societies*. Washington, D.C./London: Smithsonian Institution Press.

Arhem, Kaj. 1985. *Pastoral Man in the Garden of Eden: The Maasai of the Ngorongoro Conservation Area, Tanzania*. Uppsala, Sweden: University of Uppsala, Department of Anthropology, and Scandinavian Institute of African Studies.

Asad, Talal. 1979. "Equality in Nomadic Systems? Notes towards the Disso-

lution of an Anthropological Category." In Équipe écologie et anthropologie des sociétés pastorales (eds.), *Pastoral Production and Society*.
Cambridge, Eng.: Cambridge University Press.

Augé, Marc. 1982. *The Anthropological Circle: Symbol, Function, History*.
New York: Cambridge University Press.

Asante, Molefi. 1980. *Afrocentricity: The Theory of Social Change*. Buffalo,
N.Y.: Amulefi.

Bailey, Anne, and Josep R. Llobera (eds.). 1981. *The Asiatic Mode of Production: Science and Politics*. London: Routledge and Kegan Paul.

Bakhtin, Mikhail. 1981. *The Dialogic Imagination*. Translated by Caryl
Emerson and Michael Holquist. Austin: University of Texas Press.

———. 1984. *Rabelais and His World*. Translated by Helene Iswolsky.
Bloomington: Indiana University Press.

Balandier, Georges. 1955a. *Sociologie des Brazzavilles Noires*. Paris:
A. Colin.

———. 1955b. *Sociologie actuelle de l'Afrique noire*. Paris: Presses Univer-
sitaires de France.

———. 1970. *Political Anthropology*. New York: Random House.

Balogun, F. Odun. 1987/88. "Ngugi's *Devil on the Cross*: The Novel as
Hagiography of a Marxist." *Ufahamu* 16:76–92.

Barongo, Yolamu (ed.). 1983. *Political Science in Africa: A Critical Review*.
London: Zed Books.

Barth, Frederick. 1973. "General Perspectives on Nomad-Sedentary Relations in the Middle East." In C. Nelson (ed.), *The Desert and the Sown*.
Berkeley: University of California Press.

Baumann, O. 1894. *Durch Massailand zur Nilquelle*. Berlin: Reimer.

Baxter, P. T. W. 1972. "Absence Makes the Heart Grow Fonder." In M. Gluckman (ed.), *The Allocation of Responsibility*. Manchester, Eng.: Manchester University Press.

Baxter, P. T. W., and Uri Almagor (eds.). 1978. *Age, Generation, and Time:
Some Features of East African Age Organizations*. New York: St.
Martin's.

Beidelman, Thomas O. 1960. "The Baraguyu." *Tanganyika Notes and Records* 55:245–278.

———. 1962a. "A Demographic Map of the Baraguyu of Tanganyika."
Tanganyika Notes and Records 58/59:8–10.

———. 1962b. "A History of Ukaguru." *Tanganyika Notes and Records* 58/
59:11–39.

———. 1980. "Women and Men in Two East African Societies." In Ivan Karp
and Charles Bird (eds.), *Explorations in African Systems of Thought*.
Bloomington: Indiana University Press.

Bekure, Solomon. 1982. "Phasing of ILCA's Research on the Maasai Livestock Production Systems in Kajiado District, Kenya—A Briefing." In
ILCA, *East African Range Livestock Systems*. Nairobi: ILCA.

Bernal, Martin. 1987. *Black Athena: The Afroasiatic Roots of Classical*

Civilization, vol. 1. New Brunswick, N.J.: Rutgers University Press.

Bernardi, Bernardo. 1985. *Age Class Systems: Social Institutions and Politics Based on Age*. Cambridge, Eng.: Cambridge University Press.

Bernstein, Henry. 1977. "Notes on Capital and Peasantry." *Review of African Political Economy* 10:60–73.

Bernstein, Henry, and Jacques Depelchin. 1978. "The Object of African History: A Materialist Perspective." *History in Africa* Part I, 5:1–19 and Part II, 6:17–43.

Berntsen, John L. 1979. "Maasai Age-Sets and Prophetic Leadership." *Africa* 49:134–146.

Bhalla, Ajok. 1986. "Plains of Darkness: The Gothic Novel and the Pastoral Myth." *Journal of Peasant Studies* 14:1–26.

Bille, J.-C. and F. M. Anderson. 1980. "Observations from Elangata Wuas Ranch in Kajiado District." Working Document no. 20. Nairobi: ILCA.

Bloch, Maurice. 1977. "The Past and the Present in the Present." *Man* (NS) 12:278–292.

Bonte, Pierre. 1975. "Cattle for God: An Attempt at a Marxist Analysis of the Religion of East African Herdsmen." *Social Compass* 22:381–396.

———. 1978. "Non-Stratified Social Formations among Pastoral Nomads." In J. Friedman and M. Rolands (eds.), *The Evolution of Social Systems*. London: Duckworth.

———. 1979. "Pastoral Production, Territorial Organization, and Kinship in Segmentary Lineage Societies." In P. C. Burnham and R. F. Allen (eds.), *Social and Ecological Systems*. Association of Social Anthropologists no. 18. New York: Academic Press.

———. 1981. "Marxist Theory and Anthropological Analysis: The Study of Nomadic Pastoralist Societies." In Joel Kahn and J. P. Llobera (eds.), *The Anthropology of Pre-capitalist Societies*. London: Macmillan.

Bourdieu, Pierre. 1977. *Outline of a Theory of Practice*. Cambridge, Eng.: Cambridge University Press.

Bourgeot, André. 1981. "Nomadic Pastoral Society and the Market: The Penetration of the Sahel by Commercial Relations." In J. G. Galaty, and P. C. Salzman (eds.), *Change and Development in Nomadic and Pastoral Societies*. Leiden: E. J. Brill.

Brass, Tom. 1984. "Review Article" on David Goodman and Michael Redclift, *From Peasant to Proletarian*. In *Journal of Peasant Studies* 11: 108–117.

Brewster, Ben. 1967. "Glossary" and translation of Louis Althusser, *For Marx*. London: New Left Books.

Burton, M. L., and L. Kirk. 1979. "Differences in Maasai Cognition of Personality and Social Identity." *American Anthropologist* 81:841–875.

Busia, K. A. 1963. "The African World-View." in Jacob Drachler (ed.), *African Heritage*. New York: Crowell, Collier and Macmillan.

Callinicos, Alex. 1982. *Is There a Future for Marxism?* London: Macmillan.

———. 1983. *Marxism and Philosophy*. Oxford, Eng.: Oxford University Press.

Carneiro, Robert L. 1970. "A Theory of the Origin of the State." *Science* 169:733–738.

Cassanelli, Lee. 1982. *The Shaping of Somali Society: Reconstructing the History of a Pastoral People.* Philadelphia: University of Pennsylvania Press.

Catalano, Joseph S. 1986. *A Commentary on Jean-Paul Sartre's Critique of Dialectical Reason,* vol. 1. Chicago: University of Chicago Press.

Caute, David. 1964. *Communism and the French Intellectuals.* London: Andre Deutsch.

Certeau, Michel de. 1984. *The Practice of Everyday Life.* Berkeley: University of California Press.

Cheche Kenya. 1982. *Independent Kenya.* London: Zed Books.

Chittick, H. Neville. 1975. "The Peopling of the East African Coast." In H. N. Chittick and R. I. Rotberg (eds.), *East Africa and the Orient: Cultural Synthesis in Pre-Colonial Times.* New York: Africana.

Claessen, H. J. M., and Peter Skalnik (eds.). 1978. *The Early State.* The Hague: Mouton.

———. 1981. *The Study of the State.* The Hague: Mouton.

Clark, Katerina, and Michael Holquist. 1984. *Mikhail Bakhtin.* Cambridge, Mass.: Harvard University Press.

Clastres, Pierre. 1977. *Society Against the State.* New York: Urizen Books.

Cohen, G. A. 1978. *Karl Marx's Theory of History: A Defence.* Princeton, N.J.: Princeton University Press.

Colletti, Lucio. 1975. "Introduction" to Karl Marx. In *Early Writings,* translated by Rodney Livingstone and Gregor Benton. Harmondsworth, Eng.: Penguin/New Left Books.

Collins, Hugh. 1984. *Marxism and Law.* Oxford, Eng.: Oxford University Press.

Copans, Jean. 1976. "African Studies: A Periodization." In Peter Gutkind and Peter Waterman (eds.), *African Studies: A Radical Reader.* New York: Monthly Review.

Coquery-Vidrovitch, Catherine. 1978. "Research on an African Mode of Production." In D. Seddon and J. Copans (eds.), *Relations of Production.* London: Frank Cass.

Coulson, Andrew (ed.). 1979. *African Socialism in Practice: The Tanzanian Experience.* London: Spokesman.

Davidson, Alastair. 1984. "Gramsci, the Peasantry, and Popular Culture." *Journal of Peasant Studies* 11:139–154.

Deng, Francis Mading. 1971. *Tradition and Modernization: A Challenge for Law among the Dinka of Sudan.* New Haven, Conn.: Yale University Press.

———. 1972a. *The Dinka of the Sudan.* New York: Holt, Rinehart and Winston.

———. 1972b. *The Dinka through Their Songs.* Oxford, Eng.: Clarendon.

———. 1978. *Africans of Two Worlds.* New Haven, Conn.: Yale University Press.

————. 1986. *The Man Called Deng Majok*. New Haven, Conn.: Yale University Press.

Derrida, Jacques. 1972. *Positions*. Paris: Minuit.

Diamond, Stanley. 1955. "Dahomey: A Proto State in West Africa." Ph.D. dissertation, Columbia University, New York.

————. 1960. "Anaguta Cosmography: The Linguistics and Behavioral Implications." *Anthropological Linguistics* 2:31–38.

————. 1974. *In Search of the Primitive*. New Brunswick, N.J.: Transaction Books.

————. 1980. "Theory, Practice, and Poetry in Vico." In Stanley Diamond (ed.), *Theory and Practice: Essays Presented to Gene Weltfish*. The Hague: Mouton.

Diop, Cheikh Anta. 1974. *The African Origins of Civilization*. Westport, Conn.: Lawrence Hill.

Doherty, Deborah A. 1979*a*. "A Preliminary Report on Group Ranching in Narok District." Nairobi: Institute for Development Studies Working Paper no. 350 (mimeograph).

————. 1979*b*. "Factors Inhibiting Economic Development on Rotian Olmakongo Group Ranch." Nairobi: Institute for Development Studies Working Paper no. 356 (mimeograph).

Donham, Donald. 1985. *Work and Power in Maale, Ethiopia*. Ann Arbor, Mich.: UMI Research Press.

Dupire, Marguerite. 1962. *Peuls Nomades*. Paris: Institute d'Ethnologie.

————. 1970. *Organization sociales des Peul*. Paris: Plon.

Dupré, Georges, and Pierre-Philippe Rey. 1978. "Reflections on the Relevance of a Theory of the History of Exchange." In D. Seddon, and J. Copans (eds.), *Relations of Production*. London: Frank Cass.

Dupré, Louis. 1983. *Marx's Social Critique of Culture*. New Haven: Yale University Press.

Duyvendak, J. J. L. 1949. *China's Discovery of Africa*. London: Probsthain.

Dyson-Hudson, Neville. 1962. "Factors Inhibiting Change in an African Pastoral Society: The Karimojong of Northeast Uganda." *Transactions of the New York Academy of Science* 24:771–801.

————. 1982. "Changing Production Strategies in African Range Livestock Systems." In ILCA, *East African Range Livestock Systems*. Nairobi: ILCA.

Dyson-Hudson, Neville and Rada. 1980. "Nomadic Pastoralists." *Annual Review of Anthropology* 9:15–61.

Eagleton, Terry. 1985. "Capitalism, Modernism, and Post-Modernism." *New Left Review* 152:60–73.

Ehret, Christopher. 1971. *Southern Nilotic History: Linguistic Approaches to the Study of the Past*. Evanston, Ill.: Northwestern University Press.

Elliott, Gregory. 1987. *Althusser: The Detour of Theory*. New York: Verso.

Elster, Jon. 1985. *Making Sense of Marx*. Cambridge, Eng.: Cambridge University Press; and Paris: Editions de la Maison des Sciences de l'homme.

Engels, Frederick. 1964. "On the History of Early Christianity." In Karl Marx and Frederick Engels, *On Religion*. Moscow: Foreign Languages.

———. 1970. "The Origin of the Family, Private Property, and the State." In Karl Marx, and Frederick Engels, *Selected Works*, vol. 3. Moscow: Progress Publishers.

Evangelou, Phylo. 1984. *Livestock Development in Kenya Maasailand.* Boulder, Colo.: Westview.

Evans-Pritchard, E. E. 1937. *Witchcraft, Oracles and Magic among the Azande.* Oxford, Eng.: Clarendon.

Fabian, Johannes. 1983. *Time and the Other: How Anthropology Makes Its Object.* New York: Columbia University Press.

Feuchtwang, Stephan. 1975. "Investigating Religion." In Maurice Bloch, (ed.), *Marxist Analyses and Social Anthropology*. Association of Social Anthropologists no. 2, London: Malaby.

Fields, Karen E. 1982. "Political Contingencies of Witchcraft in Colonial Central Africa: Culture and State in Marxist Theory." *Canadian Journal of African Studies* 16:567–593.

Finnegan, Ruth. 1973. "Literacy Versus Non-literacy: The Great Divide?" In Robin Horton and Ruth Finnegan (eds.), *Modes of Thought*. London: Faber and Faber.

Fischer, G. A. 1884. "Bericht über die im Auftrage des Geographischen Gesellschaft in Hamburg unternommene Reise in das Massai-land." *Mittheilungen des Geographischen Gesellschaft in Hamburg* (1884–1885):36–99, 189–237, 258–279.

Fosbrooke, Henry A. 1948. "An Administrative Survey of the Masai Social System." *Tanganyika Notes and Records* 26:1–50.

———. 1956*a*. "The Masai Age-Group System as a Guide to Tribal Chronology." *African Studies* 15:188–206.

———. 1956*b*. "Introduction and Annotations." In Justin Lemenye, "The Life of Justin: an African Autobiography." *Tanganyika Notes and Records* 41:31–57 and 42:19–33.

Foster, Alan Dean. 1986. *Into the Out Of*. New York: Warner Books.

Foster-Carter, Aidan. 1987. "Knowing What They Mean: or Why Is There No Phenomenology in the Sociology of Development." in J. Clammer (ed.), *Beyond the New Economic Anthropology*. New York: St. Martins.

Foucault, Michel. 1980. Colin Gordon (ed.), *Power/Knowledge: Selected Interviews and Other Writings*. New York: Pantheon Books.

Franke, Richard W. and Barbara H. Chasin. 1980. *Seeds of Famine: Ecological Destruction and the Development Dilemma in the West African Sahel*. Montclair, N.J.: Allanheld/Osmun.

Freeman-Grenville, G. S. P. 1962. *The East African Coast: Select Documents from the First to the Earlier Nineteenth Century*. Oxford, Eng.: Clarendon.

Freund, Bill. 1984. *The Making of Contemporary Africa: The Development of African Society since 1900*. Bloomington: Indiana University Press.

Fried, Morton F. 1967. *The Evolution of Political Society*. New York: Random House.

Gailey, Christine W. 1985a. "The Kindness of Strangers: Transformations of Kinship in Precapitalist Class and State Formation." *Culture* 5: 3–16.

———. 1985b. "The State of the State in Anthropology." *Dialectical Anthropology* 9: 65–90.

———. 1987a. "Culture Wars: Resistance to State Formation," in Thomas C. Patterson and C. W. Gailey (eds.), *Power Relations and State Formation*. Washington, D.C.: American Anthropological Association.

———. 1987b. *Kinship to Kingship: Gender Hierarchy and State Formation in the Tongan Islands*. Austin: University of Texas Press.

Galaty, John G. 1977. "The Pastoral Image: The Dialectic of Maasai Identity." Ph.D. dissertation. University of Chicago.

———. 1980. "The Maasai Group Ranch: Politics and Development in an African Pastoral Society." In P.C. Salzman (ed.), *When Nomads Settle*. New York: Praeger.

———. 1981. "Introduction: Nomadic Pastoralists and Social Change—Processes and Perspectives." In John G. Galaty and P. C. Salzman (eds.), *Change and Development in Pastoral Societies*. Leiden, Holland: E.J. Brill.

———. 1982. "Being 'Maasai'; Being 'People of Cattle': Ethnic Shifters in East Africa." *American Ethnologist* 9: 1–20.

———. 1983. "Ceremony and Society: The Poetics of Maasai Ritual." *Man* (NS) 18: 361–382.

———. 1989. "Seniority and Cyclicity in Maasai Age Organization." Montreal: McGill University/East African Pastoral Systems Project Discussion Paper no. 6.

Geertz, Clifford. 1973. *The Interpretation of Cultures*. New York: Basic Books.

Geras, Norman. 1983. *Marx and Human Nature*. London: New Left Books.

Geschiere, Peter. 1988. "Sorcery and the State: Popular Modes of Action among the Maka of Southeast Cameroon." *Critique of Anthropology*, 8: 35–63.

Godelier, Maurice. 1975. "Modes of Production, Kinship, and Demographic Structures." In M. Bloch (ed.), *Marxist Analyses and Social Anthropology*. London: Malaby.

———. 1978. "The Concept of the Asiatic Mode of Production and Marxist Models of Social Evolution." In D. Seddon and J. Copans (eds.), *Relations of Production*. London: Frank Cass.

Goldschmidt, Walter. 1965. "Theory and Strategy in the Study of Cultural Adaptation." *American Anthropologist* 67: 402–408.

———. 1971. "Independence as an Element in Pastoral Social Systems." *Anthropological Quarterly* 3:132–142.

———. 1981. "The Failure of Pastoral Economic Development Programs in Africa." In John G. Galaty, D. Aronson, and P. C. Salzman (eds.), *The Future of Pastoral Peoples*. Ottawa: International Development Research Centre.

Gollobin, Ira. 1986. *Dialectical Materialism: Its Laws, Categories, and Practice*. New York: Petras.

Goodman, David, and Michael Redclift. 1982. *From Peasant to Proletarian: Capitalist Development and Agrarian Transitions.* New York: St. Martin's.

Goody, Jack (ed.). 1968. *Literacy in Traditional Societies.* Cambridge, Eng.: Cambridge University Press.

Gramsci, Antonio. 1971. *Selections from the Prison Notebooks.* London: Lawrence and Wishart.

Gugelberger, Georg M. (ed.). 1985. *Marxism and African Literature.* Trenton, N.J.: Africa World Press.

Gulliver, P. H. 1953. "The Age-Set Organization of the Jie Tribe." *Journal of the Royal Anthropological Institute* 83: 147–168.

————. 1969. "The Conservative Commitment in Northern Tanzania: The Arusha and Masai." In P. H. Gulliver, (ed.), *Tradition and Transition in East Africa.* London: Routledge and Kegan Paul.

Gyekye, Kwame. 1987. *An Essay on African Philosophical Thought: The Akan Conceptual Scheme.* Cambridge: Cambridge University Press.

Haas, Jonathan. 1982. *The Evolution of the Prehistoric State.* New York: Columbia University Press.

Hallen, B., and J. O. Sodipo. 1986. *Knowledge, Belief, and Witchcraft: Analytic Experiments in African Philosophy.* London: Ethnographica.

Hanson, F. A. 1977. *The Meaning of Culture.* London: Routledge and Kegan Paul.

Hart, Keith, and Louise Sperling. 1988. "Cattle as Capital." *Ethnos* 3–4: 324–338.

Harvey, Mark. 1972. "Sociological Theory: The Production of a Bourgeois Ideology." In T. Pateman (ed.), *Counter Course: A Handbook for Course Criticism.* Harmondsworth, Eng.: Penguin.

Hedlund, Hans. 1979. "Contradictions in the Peripheralization of a Pastoral Society: The Maasai." *Review of African Political Economy* 15/16: 15–34.

Hinde, Sidney, and Hildegarde Hinde. 1901. *The Last of the Masai.* London: William Heinemann.

Hindess, Barry, and Paul Q. Hirst. 1975. *Pre-capitalist Modes of Production.* London: Routledge and Kegan Paul.

Hirst, Paul Q. 1967. *Social Evolution and Sociological Categories.* London: George Allen and Unwin.

Hoben, Alan. 1976. "Social Soundness of the Maasai Livestock and Range Management Project." Washington, D.C.: Agency for International Development.

————. 1979. "Lessons from a Critical Examination of Livestock Projects in Africa." Washington, D.C.: Agency for International Development, Program Evaluation Paper no. 26.

Hobley, Charles. 1929. *Kenya: From Chartered Company to Crown Colony.* London: H. F. and G. Witherby; 2nd ed., London: Frank Cass (1970).

Hobsbawm, Eric J. 1964. "Introduction." In Karl Marx *Pre-capitalist Economic Formations.* New York: International.

Holland, Killian. 1987. "On the Horns of a Dilemma: The Future of the Maasai." Montreal: McGill University Centre for Developing Area Studies, Discussion Paper no. 51.

Holquist, Michael. 1981. "Introduction." In M. M. Bakhtin, *The Dialogic Imagination*. Austin: University of Texas Press.

Hollis, A. C. 1905. *The Masai: Their Language and Folklore*. Oxford, Eng.: Clarendon. Reprinted 1970, Westport, Conn.: Negro Universities Press.

———. 1910. "A Note on the Masai System of Relationship and Other Matters." *Journal of the Royal Anthropological Institute* 30: 473–482.

Horton, Robin. 1976. "Traditional Thought and the Emerging African Philosophy Department: A Comment on the Current Debate." *Second Order* 6: 64–80.

Hountondji, Paulin. 1983. *African Philosophy: Myth and Reality*. Bloomington: Indiana University Press / London: Hutchinson University Library for Africa.

Huxley, Elspeth. 1935. *White Man's Country*. 2 vols. London: Chatto and Windus.

———. 1987. "Foreword." In Mohamed Amin, D. Willetts, and J. Eames, *The Last of the Maasai*. London: Bodley Head.

Hyden, Goran. 1980. *Beyond Ujamaa in Tanzania: Underdevelopment and an Uncaptured Peasantry*. London/Nairobi: Heinemann.

———. 1983. *No Shortcuts to Progress: African Development Management in Perspective*. London/Nairobi: Heinemann.

International Livestock Centre for Africa (ILCA). 1981. "Introduction" to *East African Range Livestock Systems Study/Kenya*. Nairobi: ILCA.

Irele, Abiola. 1981. *The African Experience in Literature and Ideology*. London/Ibadan: Heinemann.

———. 1983. "Introduction." In Paulin Hountondji, *African Philosophy: Myth and Reality*. Bloomington: Indiana University Press.

Jacobs, Alan H. 1965a. "The Traditional Political Organization of the Pastoral Masai." D. Phil. dissertation, Nuffield College, Oxford University.

———. 1965b. "African Pastoralists: Some General Remarks." *Anthropological Quarterly* 38: 144–154.

———. 1968. "A Chronology of the Pastoral Maasai." In B. A. Ogot (ed.), *Hadith 1*. Nairobi: East African Publishing House.

———. 1975. "Maasai Pastoralism in Historical Perspective," in T. Monod (ed.), *Pastoralism in Tropical Africa*. London: Oxford University Press for International African Institute.

———. 1978. "Development in Tanzania Maasailand: The Perspective over 20 Years, 1957–1977." Report prepared for USAID Mission in Tanzania. Washington, D.C.: U.S. Agency for International Development.

———. 1979. "Maasai Inter-Tribal Relations: Belligerent Herdsmen or Peaceable Pastoralists?" In K. Fukui and D. Turton (eds.), *Warfare among East African Cattle Herders*. Osaka: Senri Ethnological Studies no. 3.

———. 1981. "Firemaking, Sexuality and Political Authority among Pastoral Maasai of East Africa." Paper presented at 24th African Studies Association meeting, Bloomington, Ind., October 21–25.

Jaffe, Hosea. 1985. *A History of Africa*. London: Zed Books.

Jakobson, Roman. 1968. "Interviews." *La quinzaine littérature* 51: 38–56.

James, R. W. 1971. *Land Tenure and Policy in Tanzania*. Dar es Salaam: East African Literature Bureau.

Jameson, Fredric. 1981. *The Political Unconscious: Narrative as a Socially Symbolic Act*. Ithaca, N.Y.: Cornell University Press.

———. 1984. "Postmodernism as the Cultural Logic of Capitalism." *New Left Review* 146: 53–93.

———. 1988. "Postmodernism and Consumer Society." In E. A. Kaplan (ed.), *Postmodernism and Its Discontents*. New York: Verso.

Johnston, H. H. 1886. *The Kilima-Njaro Expedition*. London: Kegan Paul.

Jouvenel, Bertrand de. 1945. *Power: The Natural History of Its Growth*. Geneva: Cheval Aile.

———. 1957. *Sovereignty*. Cambridge, Eng.: Cambridge University Press.

Kahn, Joel P., and Josep R. Llobera (eds.). 1981. *The Anthropology of Pre-Capitalist Societies*. London: Macmillan.

Kapferer, Bruce. 1988. *Legends of People: Myths of State*. Washington, D.C.: Smithsonian Institution Press.

Karp, Ivan. 1987. "Laughter at Marriage: Subversion in Performance." In D. Parkin and D. Nyamwaya (eds.), *Transformations of African Marriage*. Manchester, Eng.: Manchester University Press for International African Institute.

King, Kenneth. 1971a. "A Biography of Molonket Olokirinya ole Sempele." In K. King and Ahmed Salim (eds.), *Kenya Historical Biographies*. Nairobi: East African Publishing House.

———. 1971b. *Pan-Africanism and Education*. Oxford, Eng.: Clarendon.

———. 1971c. "The Kenyan Maasai and the Protest Phenomenon, 1900–1960." *Journal of African History* 12: 177–137.

Kinyatti, Maina Wa (ed.). 1980. *Thunder From the Mountains: Mau Mau Patriotic Songs*. London: Zed Books.

Kipury, Naomi. 1983a. *Oral Literature of the Maasai*. Nairobi/London: Heinemann.

———. 1983b. "From Pastoralists to Security Guards: Rural-Urban Pastoral Migrants in East Africa." Department of Anthropology, Temple University, Philadelphia.

———. 1989. "Maasai Women in Transition: Class and Gender in the Transformation of Maasai Society." Ph.D. dissertation, Temple University, Philadelphia.

Kirk, L., and M. L. Burton. 1977. "Meaning and Context: a Study of Contextual Shifts in Meaning of Maasai Personality Descriptions." *American Anthropologist* 79: 734–761.

Kitching, Gavin. 1980. *Class and Economic Change in Kenya*. New Haven, Conn.: Yale University Press.

———. 1988. *Karl Marx and the Philosophy of Praxis*. London: Routledge.

Kituyi, Mukhisa. 1990. *Becoming Kenyans: Socio-Economic Transformation of the Pastoral Maasai*. Nairobi: Acts.

Kjekshus, Helge. 1977. *Ecology Control and Economic Development in East*

African History: The Case of Tanganyika. London: Heinemann.

Klima, George J. 1964. "Jural Relations Between the Sexes Among the Barabaig." *Africa* 34: 9–20.

———. 1970. *The Barabaig: East African Cattle Herdsmen*. New York: Holt, Rinehart and Winston.

Knowles, J. N., and D. P. Collett. 1989. "Nature as Myth, Symbol and Action: Toward a Historical Understanding of Development and Conservation in Kenyan Maasailand." *Africa* 59: 433–460.

Krapf, J. L. 1860. *Travels, Researches, and Missionary Labours During Eighteen Years Residence in East Africa*, 2d. ed. 1968, London: Frank Cass.

Kulet, Henry R. ole. 1971. *Is It Possible?* Nairobi: Longman.

———. 1972. *To Become a Man*. Nairobi: Longman.

Kuper, Leo. 1970. "Non-Violence Revisited." In R. I. Rotberg and A. A. Mazrui (eds.), *Protest and Power in Black Africa*. New York: Oxford University Press.

Lakoff, Robin. 1973. "Language and Women's Place." *Language and Society* 2: 45–80.

Lamphear, John. 1976. *The Traditional History of the Jie of Uganda*. London: Oxford University Press.

Lang'at, S. C. ole. 1969. "Some Aspects of Kipsigis History Before 1914." In B. G. McIntosh (ed.), *Ngano*. Nairobi Historical Studies 1: East African Publishing House.

Lanternari, V. 1963. *The Religions of the Oppressed*. Toronto: Mentor.

Lawren, W. L. 1968. "Masai and Kikuyu: An Historical Analysis of Culture Transmission." *Journal of African History* 9: 571–583.

LeClair, Edward E., and Harold K. Schneider (eds.). 1968. *Economic Anthropology: Readings in Theory and Analysis*. New York: Holt, Rinehart and Winston.

Lecourt, Dominique. 1975. *Marxism and Epistemology: Bachelard, Canguilhem, and Foucault*. London: New Left Books.

Lefébure, Claude. 1979. "Introduction: The Specificity of Nomadic Pastoral Societies." In Équipe écologie et anthropologie des sociétés Pastorales (ed.), *Pastoral Production and Society*. Cambridge, Eng.: Cambridge University Press.

Lemenye, Justin [Sameni ole Kipasis]. 1956. "The Life of Justin: An African Autobiography," translated and annotated by H. A. Fosbrooke. In *Tanganyika Notes and Records* 41: 31–57 and 6: 19–30.

Lenin, V. I. 1961. *Philosophical Notebooks*. London: Lawrence and Wishart.

———. 1972. *Materialism and Empirio-Criticism*. Moscow: Progress.

Lewis, I. M. 1955. *Peoples of the Horn of Africa*. London: Oxford University Press for International African Institute.

Leys, Colin. 1975. *Underdevelopment in Kenya*. London/Nairobi: Heinemann.

Leys, Norman. 1926 [1924]. *Kenya*. London: Hogarth.

Lindstrom, J. 1977. "Cattle in Pastoral and Agro-Pastoral Societies." Department of Anthropology, University of Gothenberg, Sweden.

Llewelyn-Davies, Melissa. 1978. "Two Contexts of Solidarity among Pastoral

Maasai Women." In P. Kaplan and J. M. Bujra (eds.), *Women United, Women Divided*. London: Tavistock.

———. 1981. "Women, Warriors and Patriarchs." In S. Ortner and H. Whitehead (eds.), *Sexual Meanings*. Cambridge, Eng.: Cambridge University Press.

Low, D. A. 1965. "British East Africa: The Establishment of British Rule, 1895–1912." In Vincent Harlow and E. M. Chilver (eds.), *History of East Africa*, vol. 2. Oxford, Eng.: Clarendon.

Lukács, Georg. 1971. *History and Class Consciousness: Studies in Marxist Dialectics*. Cambridge, Mass.: MIT Press.

McMahon, Joseph H. 1971. *Humans Being: The World of Jean-Paul Sartre*. Chicago: University of Chicago Press.

McMurtry, John. 1978. *The Structure of Marx's World View*. Princeton, N.J.: Princeton University Press.

Mafeje, Archie. 1976. "The Problem of Anthropology in Historical Perspective: An Inquiry into the Growth of the Social Sciences." *Canadian Journal of African Studies* 10: 307–333.

———. 1977. "Neocolonialism, State Capitalism, or Revolution." In Peter Gutkind and Peter Waterman (eds.), *African Studies: a Radical Reader*. New York: Monthly Review.

———. 1988. "African Philosophical Projections and Prospects for the Indigenisation of Political and Intellectual Discourse." Paper presented at 31st Annual Meeting of African Studies Association, Chicago, Ill., October 28–31.

Mandel, Ernest. 1962. *Marxist Economic Theory*. London: Merlin.

Mandel, Ernest, and George Novack. 1970. *The Marxist Theory of Alienation*. New York: Pathfinder.

Marcus, George, and Michael Fischer. 1986. *Anthropology as Cultural Critique: An Experimental Moment in the Human Sciences*. Chicago: University of Chicago Press.

Marks, Stuart A. 1984. *The Imperial Lion: Human Dimensions of Wildlife Management in Central Africa*. Boulder, Colo.: Westview.

Marshall, Fiona, and Peter Robertshaw. 1982. "Preliminary Report on Archaeological Research in the Loita-Mara Region, S.W. Kenya." *Azania* 17: 173–180.

Marx, Karl. 1962. *The Communist Manifesto*. In Karl Marx and Frederick Engels, *Selected Works*, vol. 1. Moscow: Progress.

———. 1967. *Capital*. 3 vols. New York: International.

———. 1973. *Grundrisse*. Harmondsworth, Eng.: Penguin/New Left Books.

———. 1975. *Early Writings*. Harmondsworth, Eng.: Penguin/New Left Books.

Marx, Karl, and Frederick Engels. 1964. *On Religion*. New York: Schoken.

———. 1970. *Selected Works*. 3 vols. Moscow: Progress.

———. 1976. *The German Ideology*. In Collected Works, vol. 5. Moscow: Progress.

Mathew, Gervase. 1975. "The Dating and the Significance of the *Periplus* of the Erythrean Sea." In H. N. Chittick and R. I. Rotberg (eds.), *East Africa and the Orient*. New York: Africana.

Maughan-Brown, David. 1985. *Land, Freedom, and Fiction: History and Ideology in Kenya*. London: Zed Books.

Mbiti, John. 1970. *African Religions and Philosophy*. Nairobi/London: Heinemann.

Meillassoux, Claude. 1978. "The 'Economy' in Agricultural Self-sustaining Societies: A Preliminary Analysis." In D. Seddon and J. Copans (eds.), *Relations of Production*. London: Frank Cass.

———. 1981. *Maidens, Meal and Money: Capitalism and the Domestic Community*. Cambridge, Eng.: Cambridge University Press.

Mesaki, Simeon. 1988. "Uchawi and Ujamaa: Witchcraft, Sorcery and Magic in Socialist Tanzania." Paper presented at 31st Annual Meeting of African Studies Association, Chicago, Ill., October 28–31.

Meszaros, Istvan. 1970. *Marx's Theory of Alienation*. London: Merlin.

Mol, Frans. 1978. *Maa: A Dictionary of the Maasai Language and Folklore*. Nairobi: Marketing and Publishing.

Morson, Gary Saul. 1986. "Who Speaks for Bakhtin?" In G. S. Morson (ed.), *Bakhtin: Essays and Dialogues on his Work*. Chicago: University of Chicago Press.

Moskvichov, L. N. 1974. *The End of Ideology Theory: Illusions and Reality*. Moscow: Progress.

Mpaayei, J. Tompo ole. 1954. *Inkuti Pukunot oo 'lMaasai*. London: Oxford University Press.

Mudimbe, V. Y. 1983. "African Philosophy as Ideological Practice: The Case of French-Speaking Africa." *African Studies Review* 26: 113–154.

———. 1985. "African Gnosis: Philosophy and the Order of Knowledge: An Introduction." *African Studies Review* 28: 149–233.

———. 1988. *The Invention of Africa: Gnosis, Philosophy, and the Order of Knowledge*. Bloomington: Indiana University Press.

Mungeam, G. H. 1967. "Introduction to the Second Edition." In G. W. Hobley, *Kenya: From Chartered Company to Crown Colony*. London: Frank Cass (1970).

———. 1970. "Masai and Kikuyu Responses to the Establishment of British Administration in the East African Protectorate." *Journal of African History* 11: 127–143.

Mustafa, Kemal, Melkiori Matwi, and Jonas Reuben. 1980. "A Preliminary Survey of Pastoralist Development in Mindi Tulieni Village." In Philip Donner (ed.), *Jipemoyo, no. 3*. Uppsala, Sweden: Scandinavian Institute of African Studies, for Ministry of National Culture and Youth, Dar es Salaam, Tanzania.

Nazareth, Peter. 1985. "The Second Homecoming: Multiple Ngugis in *Petals of Blood*." In Georg Gugelberger (ed.), *Marxism and African Literature*. Trenton, N.J.: Africa World Press.

Ndagala, Daniel. 1974. "Social and Economic Change among the Pastoral Wakwavi and Its Impact on Rural Development." M. A. thesis, University of Dar es Salaam.

———. 1978. "Ujamaa and Pastoral Communities in Tanzania: A Case Study of the Maasai." Ph. D. dissertation, University of Dar es Salaam.

———. 1982. " 'Operation Imparnati': The Sedentarization of the Pastoral Maasai in Tanzania." *Nomadic Peoples* 10: 28–39.

———. 1986. "The Ilparakuyo Livestock Keepers of Bagamoyo: Persistent Fighters but Ultimate Losers." Uppsala: African Studies Program and Department of Anthropology Working Papers in African Studies no. 32.

Ndeti, Kivuto. 1972. *Elements of Akamba Life*. Nairobi: East African Publishing House.

Newcomer, P. J. 1972. "The Nuer Are Dinka: An Essay on Origins and Environmental Determinism." *Man* (NS) 7: 5–11.

Ngara, Emmanuel. 1985. *Art and Ideology in The African Novel: A Study of the Influence of Marxism on African Writing*. Trenton, N.J.: Africa World Press.

Ngugi Wa Thiong'o (James Ngugi). 1977. *Petals of Blood*. Nairobi/London: Heinemann.

———. 1981*a*. *Writers in Politics*. Nairobi/London: Heinemann.

———. 1981*b*. *Detained: a Writer's Prison Diary*. Nairobi/London: Heinemann.

———. 1982. *Devil on the Cross*. Nairobi/London: Heinemann.

———. 1983. *Barrel of a Pen: Resistance to Oppression in Neo-Colonial Kenya*. Trenton, N.J.: Africa World Press.

———. 1986. *Decolonizing the Mind*. Nairobi/London: Heinemann.

Nyerere, Julius K. 1967. "Socialism and Rural Development." In J. K. Nyerere, *Ujamaa: Essays in Socialism*. Dar es Salaam: Oxford University Press.

Nzongola-Ntalaja. 1987. *Revolution and Counter Revolution in Africa: Essays in Contemporary Politics*. London: Zed Books.

Oboler, Regina S. 1985. *Women, Power, and Economic Change*. Stanford, Calif.: Stanford University Press.

Ogot, Bethwell A. 1967. *History of the Southern Luo*, vol. 1. Nairobi: East African Publishing House.

Ogot, Bethwell A. (ed.). 1968. *Hadithi 1: Proceedings of the Annual Conference of the Historical Association of Kenya, 1967*. Nairobi: East African Publishing House.

Oliver, Roland. 1963. "Discernible Developments in the Interior, c. 1500–1840." In R. Oliver and G. Mathew (eds.), *History of East Africa*, vol. 1. Oxford: Clarendon.

Ollman, Bertell. 1971. *Alienation: Marx's Concept of Man in Capitalist Society*. Cambridge, Eng.: Cambridge University Press.

O'Neill, John. 1972. *Sociology as a Skin Trade*. New York: Harper and Row.

Onimode, Bernard. 1988. *A Political Economy of the African Crisis*. London: Zed Books.

Onoge, Omafume F. 1985. "The Crisis of Consciousness in Modern African Literature." In G. M. Gugelberger (ed.), *Marxism and African Literature*. Trenton, N.J.: Africa World Press.

Owomoyela, Oyekan. 1987. "Africa and the Imperative of Philosophy: A Skeptical Consideration." *African Studies Review* 30: 79–99.

Owusu, Maxwell. 1978. "The Ethnography of Africa: The Usefulness of the Useless." *American Anthropologist* 80: 310–334.

Paci, Enzo. 1972. *The Function of the Sciences and the Meaning of Man.* Evanston, Ill.: Northwestern University Press.

Parkin, David (ed.). 1982. *Semantic Anthropology.* New York: Academic.

———. 1984. "Political Language." In *Annual Review of Anthropology* 13: 345–365.

Parkipuny, L. M. ole. 1975. *Maasai Predicament and Beyond.* M. A. thesis, Institute of Development Studies, University of Dar es Salaam (mimeo).

———. 1979. "Some Crucial Elements of the Maasai Predicament." In Andrew Coulson (ed.), *African Socialism in Practice: The Tanzanian Experience.* London: Spokesman.

———. 1983. "Maasai Struggle for Home Rights in the Land of the Ngorongoro Crater." Paper presented at 11th International Congress of Anthropological and Ethnological Sciences, Vancouver, B.C., August 20–25.

Parsons, Talcott. 1963. "On the Concept of Political Power." *Proceedings of the American Philosophical Society* 107: 3.

Passerin D'Entrèves, Alexander. 1967. *The Notion of the State: An Introduction to Political Theory.* Oxford, Eng.: Clarendon.

Patterson, Thomas C. 1983. "Archaeological Systems and the Origin of the State: A Critique." Paper presented at Annual Meetings of Canadian Ethnological Society, Hamilton, Ontario, May.

———. 1987. "Development, Ecology, and Marginal Utility." *Dialectical Anthropology* 12: 15–31.

P'Bitek, Okot. 1970. *African Religions and Western Scholarship.* Nairobi: East African Literature Bureau.

Poulantzas, Nicos. 1973. *Political Power and Social Classes.* London: New Left Books.

Rabinow, Paul. 1986. "Representations are Social Facts: Modernity and Post-Modernity in Anthropology." In J. Clifford and G. E. Marcus (eds.), *Writing Culture: The Poetics and Politics of Ethnography.* Berkeley: University of California Press.

Ranger, Terrence (ed.). 1968. *Emerging Themes in African History.* Nairobi: East African Publishing House.

———. 1969. "The Recovery of Local Initiatives in African History." University of Dar es Salaam (mimeo).

Read, David, and Pamela Chapman. 1982. *Waters of the Sanjan.* Nairobi: Read.

Rey, Pierre-Philippe. 1979. "Class Contradictions in Lineage Societies." *Critique of Anthropology* 13/14: 41–60.

Riesman, Paul. 1977. *Freedom in Fulani Social Life: An Introspective Ethnography.* Chicago: Chicago University Press.

Rigby, Peter. 1968. "Some Gogo Rituals of Purification: An Essay on Social and Moral Categories." In Edmund Leach (ed.), *Dialectic in Practical Religion*. Cambridge Papers in Social Anthropology no. 5., Cambridge, Eng.: Cambridge University Press.

———. 1969*a*. *Cattle and Kinship among the Gogo: A Semi-Pastoral Society of Central Tanzania*. Ithaca, N.Y.: Cornell University Press.

———. 1969*b*. "Pastoralism and Prejudice: Ideology and Rural Development in East Africa." In R. J. Apthorpe and P. Rigby (eds.), *Society and Social Change in Eastern Africa*. Nkanga Editions no. 4. Kampala, Uganda: Makerere Institute for Social Research.

———. 1971. "The Symbolic Role of Cattle in Gogo Ritual." In Thomas Beidelman (ed.), *The Translation of Culture: Essays to E. E. Evans-Pritchard*. London: Tavistock.

———. 1985. *Persistent Pastoralists: Nomadic Societies in Transition*. London: Zed Books.

Robertshaw, Peter, and David Collett. 1983*a*. "A New Framework for the Study of Early Pastoral Communities in East Africa." *Journal of African History* 24: 289–301.

———. 1983*b*. "The Identification of Pastoral Peoples in the Archaeological Record." *World Archaeology* 15: 67–78.

Rodney, Walter. 1972. *How Europe Underdeveloped Africa*. Dar es Salaam: Tanzania Publishing House; London: Bogle-L'Ouverture. Rev. ed., 1987. Washington, D.C.: Howard University Press.

Rorty, Richard. 1979. *Philosophy and the Mirror of Nature*. Princeton, N.J.: Princeton University Press.

Rosberg, C. G., and J. Nottingham. 1966. *The Myth of "Mau Mau."* New York: Praeger.

Rotberg, R. I., and Ali A. Mazrui (eds.). 1970. *Protest and Power in Black Africa*. Oxford, Eng.: Oxford University Press.

Rowlands, Michael, and Jean-Pierre Warnier. 1988. "Sorcery, Power and the Modern State in Cameroon." *Man* (NS) 23: 118–132.

Russell, C. E. B. (ed.). 1935. *General Rigby, Zanzibar, and the Slave Trade*. London: George Allen and Unwin.

Sahlins, Marshall. 1961. "The Segmentary Lineage: An Organization of Predatory Expansion." *American Anthropologist* 63: 322–435.

Saitoti, Tepilit ole. 1986. *The Worlds of a Maasai Warrior*. New York: Random House. Paperback with an Introduction by J. G. Galaty. Berkeley: University of California Press (1988).

Salamini, Leonardo. 1981. *The Sociology of Political Praxis: An Introduction to Gramsci's Theory*. London: Routledge and Kegan Paul.

Salzman, P. C. (ed.). 1980. *When Nomads Settle*. New York: Praeger.

Sankan, S. S. ole. 1971. *The Maasai*. Nairobi: East African Literature Bureau.

———. 1979. *Intepen e Maasai*. Nairobi: East African Literature Bureau.

Sapir, Edward. 1961. "Culture, Genuine and Spurious." In D. Mandelbaum (ed.), *Edward Sapir: Culture, Language and Personality*. Berkeley: University of California Press.

Sartre, Jean-Paul. 1963. *Les Mots*. Paris: Gallimard.

————. 1976*a*. *Black Orpheus*. Paris: Présence Africaine.

————. 1976*b*. *Critique of Dialectical Reason*. London: Verso.

Saul, John. 1979. *The State and Revolution in Eastern Africa*. New York: Monthly Review.

Saul, John (ed.). 1985. *A Difficult Road: The Transition to Socialism in Mozambique*. New York: Monthly Review.

Schneider, Harold K. 1974. *Economic Man: The Anthropology of Economics*. Salem, Wis.: Sheffield.

————. 1979. *Livestock and Equality in East Africa*. Bloomington: Indiana University Press.

Scott, James C. 1985. *Weapons of the Weak: Everyday Forms of Peasant Resistance*. New Haven, Conn.: Yale University Press.

Seddon, David, and Jean Copans (eds.). 1978. *Relations of Production: Marxist Approaches to Economic Anthropology*. London: Frank Cass.

Sena, Sarone ole. 1981. "Schemes and Schools: Two Agents of Change among the Maasai of Kenya." Paper presented at joint seminar of Temple University African Studies Committee and Department of Anthropology, April 15.

————. 1986. "Pastoralists and Education: School Participation and Social Change among the Maasai." Ph. D. dissertation, McGill University, Montreal, Que.

Senghor, Leopold. 1964. *On African Socialism*. London: Pall Mall.

Service, Elman R. 1978. "Classical and Modern Theories of the Origins of Government." In R. Cohen and E. R. Service (eds.), *The Origins of the State*. Philadelphia: Institute for the Study of Human Issues.

Sève, Lucien. 1978. *Man in Marxist Theory*. Atlantic Highlands, N.J.: Humanities.

Shanin, Teodor. 1983. *Late Marx and the Russian Road: Marx and the Peripheries of Capitalism*. New York: Monthly Review.

Shivji, Issa G. 1975. *Class Struggles in Tanzania*. Dar es Salaam: Tanzania.

Sider, Gerald M. 1976. "Lumbee Indian Cultural Nationalism and Ethnogenesis." *Dialectical Anthropology* 1: 161–172.

Sik, Endre. 1966. *The History of Black Africa*. 2 vols. Budapest: Akademiai Kiado.

Sindiga, Isaac. 1984. "Land and Population Problems in Kajiado and Narok, Kenya." *African Studies Review* 27: 23–39.

Sorrenson, M. P. K. 1968. *Origins of European Settlement in Kenya*. Nairobi: Oxford University Press.

Spencer, Paul. 1965. *The Samburu: A Study of Gerontocracy in a Nomadic Tribe*. London: Routledge and Kegan Paul.

————. 1984. "Pastoralists and the Ghost of Capitalism." *Production pastorale et société* 15: 61–76.

————. 1988. *The Maasai of Matapato: A Study of Rituals of Rebellion*. Bloomington: Indiana University Press for International African Institute.

Spender, D. R. 1980. *Man Made Language*. London: Routledge and Kegan Paul.

Stam, Robert. 1988. "Mikhail Bakhtin and Left Cultural Critique." In E. A. Kaplan (ed.), *Postmodernism and its Discontents*. New York: Verso.

Stenning, Derrick. 1959. *Savannah Nomads*. London: Oxford University Press for International African Institute.

Stewart, Susan. 1986. "Shouts on the Street: Bakhtin's Anti-Linguistics." In G. S. Morson (ed.), *Bakhtin: Essays and Dialogues on his Work*. Chicago: University of Chicago Press.

Strandes, Justus. 1961. *The Portuguese Period in East Africa*. Translated by J. F. Wallwork. Nairobi: East African Literature Bureau.

Swai, Bonaventure. 1985. "Precolonial States and European Merchant Capital in East Africa." In Ahmed I. Salim (ed.), *State Formation in Eastern Africa*. New York: St. Martins.

Talle, Aud. 1987. "Women as Heads of Houses: The Organization of Production and the Role of Women among the Pastoral Maasai of Kenya." *Ethnos* 1/2: 50–80.

Temu, Arnold, and Bonaventure Swai. 1981. *Historians and Africanist History*. London: Zed Press.

Therborn, Goran. 1980. *The Ideology of Power and the Power of Ideology*. New York: Verso.

Thomas, Clive. 1984. *The Rise of the Authoritarian State in Peripheral Societies*. New York: Monthly Review.

Thomson, Joseph. 1885. *Through Masai Land*. London: Sampson, Low, Marston, Searle, and Rivington. 3rd ed. London: Frank Cass (1968).

Tignor, R. L. 1972. "The Masai Warriors: Pattern Maintenance and Violence in Colonial Kenya." *Journal of African History* 13: 271–290.

———. 1976. *The Colonial Transformation of Kenya: The Kamba, Kikuyu, and Maasai from 1900–1939*. Princeton, N.J.: Princeton University Press.

Toulmin-Rothe, Paul. 1981. "Introducing the Masai to the 20th Century." (Nairobi) *Sunday Standard*, June 12.

Tucker, Archie, and J. Tompo ole Mpaayei. 1955. *A Maasai Grammar*. London: Longman Green.

Vansina, Jan. 1961. *De la tradition orale: essai de méthode historique*. Annales du Musée Royal de l'Afrique Centrale, Sciences humaine, no. 36. Translated by H. M. Wright as *Oral Tradition: A Historical Methodology*. London: Routledge and Kegan Paul (1965).

Voloshinov, V. N. 1986. *Marxism and the Philosophy of Language*. Cambridge, Mass.: Harvard University Press.

Vossen, Rainer. 1977. "Notes on the Territorial History of the Maa-speaking Peoples: Some Preliminary Remarks." University of Nairobi Department of History Staff Seminar Paper no. 8 (mimeo).

Vygotsky, L. S. 1962. *Thought and Language*. Cambridge, Mass.: MIT Press.

Waller, Richard. 1976. "The Maasai and the British, 1895–1905: The Origins of an Alliance." *Journal of African History* 17: 529–553.

Warren, Bill. 1980. *Imperialism: Pioneer of Capitalism*. London: Verso.

Watene, Kenneth. 1974. *Sunset on the Manyatta*. Nairobi: East African Publishing House.

Wheatley, Paul. 1975. "Analecta Sino-Africana Recensa." In H. N. Chittick and R. I. Rotberg (eds.), *East Africa and the Orient*. New York: Africana.

White, Allon. 1984. "Bakhtin, Sociolinguistics, and Deconstruction." In Frank Gloversmith (ed.), *The Theory of Reading*. Sussex, Eng.: Harvester/Barnes and Noble.

White, Leslie. 1959. *The Evolution of Culture*. New York: McGraw Hill.

Williams, Raymond. 1977. *Marxism and Literature*. Oxford, Eng.: Oxford University Press.

Wilson, Bryan R. (ed.). 1970. *Rationality*. New York: Harper and Row.

Wolf, Eric. 1982. *Europe and the People Without History*. Berkeley: University of California Press.

Woolfson, Charles. 1977. "Culture, Language, and Personality." *Marxism Today* 21: 229–240.

Worsley, Peter. 1957. *The Trumpet Shall Sound*. London: MacGibbon and Kee.

———. 1984. *The Three Worlds: Culture and World Development*. London: Weidenfeld and Nicholson.

Index

Since a number of Maasai words appear frequently in this book, and have crucial significance for the understanding of many issues, I have listed them in this index with basic translations in parentheses after each Maasai listing. The following serves therefore as both index and glossary.

These words appear in the text most often with their gender/number prefixes. They are listed as such and not, as would be linguistically more correct, with the first letter of their word roots. Thus, *emanyata* ("warrior camp") appears under "E" (feminine singular) and "I" (feminine plural) and not under "M."